AFTER THE **JUMP**

COLUMNS ON THE BEST 20 YEARS IN MEMPHIS SPORTS

GEOFF CALKINS

For information contact the Nautilus Publishing Company, 426 South Lamar Blvd., Suite 16, Oxford, MS 38655

ISBN: 978-1-936-946-04-4

The Nautilus Publishing Company
426 South Lamar Blvd., Suite 16
Oxford, Mississippi 38655
Tel: 662-513-0159
www.nautiluspublishing.com

First Edition

Cover design by John David Dowdle
Photography by Chip Chockley

Library of Congress Cataloging-in-Publication Data has been applied for.

To my mother and father, Virginia and Evan Calkins,
who taught me the joy of listening to other people's stories,
which is really where journalism begins.

CONTENTS

III
UNIVERSITY OF MEMPHIS BASKETBALL

IV
MORE PEOPLE

V
UNIVERSITY OF MEMPHIS FOOTBALL

VI
MOMENTS

VII
FAVORITES

VIII
THE MEMPHIS GRIZZLIES (2010-2015)

INTRODUCTION

Mom would haul the big, manual typewriter into Buffalo Children's Hospital, and she'd set it up next to my bed, and I would dictate stories, and that's how my life as a writer began. I was in third grade. I had been diagnosed with acute lymphoblastic leukemia, back when that was something kids didn't survive. But my father, Evan Calkins, a physician, connected with a medical colleague who knew of a new treatment regimen that just might work. And my mother, Virginia Calkins, also a physician, kept me occupied by lugging that typewriter to the hospital so she could record my stories.

They weren't very good stories, of course. But she arranged to send them back to my third grade classmates, who then wrote their own stories and sent them to me. This went on for weeks. Somewhere in there, I began to think of myself as a writer. I especially liked writing about sports. By the time I was in fifth grade — the leukemia in remission, thanks to the new regimen — I knew I wanted to be that guy whose photo ran above his stories in the sports section. I wanted to be a sports columnist.

Eventually, though, I decided that wasn't serious enough. You know how that goes, right? Childhood dreams are set aside as just childhood dreams. Time to do something important and meaningful. For me, that something was a legal career. I went off to study at Harvard Law School. I accepted a clerkship with the Hon. James Buckley (brother of William F. Buckley) on the U.S. Court of Appeals for the D.C. Circuit. I took a job at one of the biggest law firms in D.C. I had money, prestige and a swanky apartment directly across from the National Zoo. I went running with Justice Antonin Scalia. I was utterly miserable.

So at age 31, I decided to take a leap. I jumped back into journalism. I took a job covering high school sports for $225 a week at *The Anniston Star* in Anniston, AL, then took a bigger job covering the (then) Florida Marlins for *The Ft. Lauderdale Sun-Sentinel*, and then finally got the gig I had wanted since fifth grade. I would be the guy whose photo ran above his stories in the sports section. In Memphis, Tennessee.

It has been even more fun than I had imagined. I have covered seven Olympics, nine Masters golf tournaments and 12 Super Bowls. I have covered a city I have grown to love. Indeed, that has been the best part of the job, writing about Memphis, Memphians, and the way that sports have transformed the spirit of the place.

If you spend any time in Memphis, you will hear it has a self-image problem. That's not right. It used to have a self-image problem. When I first arrived in Memphis, people would ask, in all seriousness, "Why would you ever move here?" Now Memphians feel bad for their friends who have to leave.

Sports have played a significant part in that transformation. It began with AutoZone Park. Memphians couldn't quite believe that something so beautiful had been built in their city. It felt like someplace else. Then John Calipari arrived and led the Tigers to three straight Elite Eights and an NCAA Championship game. Memphis successfully hosted the Tyson-Lewis championship fight. And then came the Memphis Grizzlies, who changed everything, who gave the city the ability to see itself as a place of resilience and character, of opportunity and optimism.

These days, it's hard to remember how unpopular the Grizzlies were at the beginning. Most Memphians opposed the FedExForum deal. The first piece in this collection is a column I wrote on the eve of the Shelby County Commission vote on FedExForum, urging approval of the project. When commissioner Tom Moss cast his vote in favor, he explained, "My epiphany really was this morning, when I read Geoff Calkins's column in *The Commercial Appeal*." That was one of the most gratifying moments of my career in Memphis. Sometimes, words work.

Even then, the Grizzlies staggered along for many years. Skeptics kept saying the franchise would up and leave. Then Zach Randolph, Tony Allen, Marc Gasol and Mike Conley showed up, and even the skeptics became fans. Grit and grind became a civic mantra. Randolph explained that we don't bluff. The team printed tens of thousands of growl towels that said, "Believe, Memphis," and sure enough, people did. They believed. In Memphis. And not just in the basketball team. They began to believe that this scrappy, under-appreciated, big-hearted river town would find a way to harness the energy and creativity of its citizens to meet its many needs. That belief isn't the answer to everything, of course. That belief can't be naive. But without it, how is anything else possible? It's a beginning, not an end.

This book of columns is an attempt to capture that auspicious trajectory. It is a snapshot and a history, both. The title — After the Jump — refers not just to my own jump from the law to journalism, but to the palpable jump in civic pride. These really have been the best two decades in Memphis sports, not just because of what has happened, but because of the way sports have caused Memphians to reimagine what is possible.

The columns in this collection were chosen with this theme in mind. I left out most of the hirings, the firings, the squabbles and the controversies. I chose the good stuff over the bad. I focused on Memphis people and Memphis events. I could have filled an entire book with columns about Tiger Woods, Usain Bolt, Phil Mickelson and Michael Phelps. Instead, I filled the book with columns about Phil Cannon, George Lapides, DeAngelo Williams and Hubie Brown.

In many cases, I found myself picking the columns my mother would like. She subscribes to the paper by mail. It's as if I'm still dreaming up stories and sending them off, although now I do the typing myself.

It's been nearly 50 years since Mom hauled that manual typewriter into Buffalo Children's Hospital. It's funny how the universe works. Memphis is the home of St. Jude Children's Research Hospital, one of the foremost children's cancer hospitals in the world. I know in my head that's just a coincidence. I also know I'm in exactly the right place.

I

THE MEMPHIS GRIZZLIES (2001-2009)

HOPE OR FEAR? THAT'S THE CHOICE
BEFORE COUNTY COMMISSION
JUNE 12, 2001

So I was watching Heidi Shafer on Channel 5's Sunday night special on the NBA debate, when I realized what was at stake in today's County Commission vote. No, not just the future of the NBA in Memphis. Something larger.

Shafer was talking about the new arena. And she said that her resistance to the deal could be summarized in two words: Sidney Shlenker.

And in that name were the guts of the essential anti-NBA argument.

We've screwed up before.

We'll screw up again.

We should never try anything grand.

The NBA will fail in Memphis.

We don't support anything, anyway.

This is Memphis, after all.

Capital city of the botched job.

We produced Mud Island.

We produced The Pyramid.

And, yeah, in case you forgot, we produced Sidney Shlenker.

It's shorthand for fear, a neat summing up of all the community's insecurities and failures.

And that's why the choice today isn't just between the NBA and no NBA.

It's between optimism and pessimism, between a view that all things are possible in Memphis and a view that nothing is possible because this is Memphis.

Oh, I wish it were not so. I wish that the people who oppose the NBA did so because they think Memphis is a great place, anyway.

I certainly think it's a great place, brimming with promise. Indeed, if I have any real complaint about the town — OK, besides the soup called summer — it's that this view is not shared by enough of my neighbors.

Take a series of e-mails I've received recently. From an NBA opponent named Bill Nourse. He's smart, eloquent, passionate and civil. Given the tone of the last few weeks, I especially appreciate the civil.

But here are excerpts from recent e-mails he sent me.

"My last remaining life goal is not to die in Memphis," he wrote.

And also: "I don't usually give advice, but if I did, it'd be to get out while you're still young."

It was depressing to read. Not because it was unusual, but because it was typical.

When we moved here, six years ago, we were just thrilled at the prospect. You can't imagine how pleased we were to be trading up from South Florida.

So we were stunned to arrive and have people — dozens of people — ask, "Why would you move to Memphis?"

The place has a self-image problem. But then, you knew that already. If there's any city Memphians hate more than Nashville, it's this one.

We think we're uniquely poor. Uniquely inept. Uniquely capable of screwing up, big-time.

Blessedly, there are those in this community who don't think like this. People like Dean and Kristi Jernigan.

You remember the ballpark debate, don't you? Memphians just knew it would fail. Nobody would go downtown. Nobody would sit in the hot sun and watch baseball. This is Memphis, after all. Memphis doesn't support anything.

The Jernigans didn't listen. They built the thing anyway. And the ballpark didn't fail, it's been a triumph.

And there are others like them, others who aren't ruled by doubt. People like Pitt Hyde, as he plans a new biotech research center. People like Andy Cates, as he develops Soulsville. People like John Calipari, as he builds a national champion.

And then there are people like Shafer, brandishing the name Sidney Shlenker, to remind us of past failures.

So, yeah, if I were on the County Commission, I'd vote yes today. Not just to the NBA. To the idea that this is a new Memphis, limited only by those who can't recognize it.

NBA YES! GRIZZLIES' ARRIVAL
ENDS YEARS OF FRUSTRATION
JUNE 29, 2001

They lined the halls of The Peabody. It was just a press conference, in a smallish room on the third floor, but supporters and citizens and employees and friends lined the halls from the elevators to the room and beyond.

And sometime after 2 p.m., an All-American basketball player from Duke and a willowy basketball player from Spain and two mayors and a handful of others walked through the joyous gauntlet to the podium.

"This is," said Shelby County Mayor Jim Rout, "a very special day in the history of our community ... "

And so it was done. Or close enough that there will be a free, public celebration at Peabody Place beginning at 3 Saturday afternoon.

By a unanimous vote Thursday, the NBA's relocation committee approved the Grizzlies move from Vancouver to Memphis.

The NBA's Board of Governors still has to give its assent early next week, but that's considered a formality.

They will not be the Vancouver Grizzlies. They will not be the vagabond Grizzlies. They will be the Memphis Grizzlies, the first major-league team to ever make this community its home.

"This is the culmination of a lot of work," said Memphis Mayor Willie Herenton, "and it's the culmination of a lot of sweat."

Herenton and Rout didn't say this automatically makes Memphis a major-league city, by the way. Not many serious people do.

A community is measured by many things. The depth of its charity. The kindness of its citizens. The quality of its schools and its universities and its libraries and its parks.

But for a town that has struggled with its self-image — and that has found confirmation of its failings in its quixotic pursuit of major-league sports — it was a historic, even cathartic day.

"There's just a different mood in the city," said Frederick W. Smith, chairman and founder of FedEx. "It gives the city a point of pride."

This newspaper has kept a chronology of the city's efforts to land a major-league team. The chronology fills 11 legal-size pages.

The first entry, from 1965: "Shortly after the dedication of the new Liberty Bowl Stadium, Mike Lynn, who went on to become executive vice president and general manger of the NFL's Minnesota Vikings, starts a push aimed at gaining Memphis membership in the NFL."

That was 36 years ago. The start of a fruitless series of exhibition games and season-ticket drives and beauty contests and, well, you know the whole sorry drill.

As recently as 1996, when the Memphis Chicks announced they were leaving for Jackson, Tenn., it was hard to imagine the town at a lower sports ebb.

But then Dean and Kristi Jernigan spearheaded the construction of AutoZone Park. And then the fans started to pour downtown. And then R.C. Johnson renewed the University of Memphis basketball program with the dramatic hiring of John Calipari. And then a collection of local business people — you now know them as the pursuit team — started to think, "Hey, why not?"

"Staley Cates called me more than a year ago," said the leader of the Memphis group, J.R. 'Pitt' Hyde III. "At the time, I don't know how much confidence I had that it would work out."

It did work out, of course, and you didn't have to be at The Peabody Thursday to know that.

"You can just tell, just by stepping off the plane, that this city is electric," said Shane Battier, the All-American from Duke.

"First of all," said Pau Gasol, the willowy forward from Spain, "I agree with Shane."

"You'll go far in this business," said Battier, laughing out loud.

Nobody is suggesting that every day will be as merry and triumphant as this one.

The arena site could yet be a controversy. The team may lose a lot of games. If the Redbirds' experience at Tim McCarver Stadium is any indication, the Grizzlies may struggle at the gate at least until they move into their new building.

But after nearly four decades of frustration, you'll excuse everyone if they worry about this another day.

"I'm just thrilled to be in Memphis," said Battier.

It's hard not to like the ring of that.

CITY FINALLY OFF BENCH, TAKING ITS SHOT VS. BIG BOYS
NOVEMBER 1, 2001

The cartoon featured a lone football player. He was sitting on the bench. He wore an 89 on his back. He was asking a one-word, forlorn question: "Now?"

That was in 1989. The cartoon ran in this newspaper, a perfect summary of the city's already interminable campaign to attract a major-league team.

And so here we are, 12 years later, and we have the answer at last.

Go on in, kid.

You've waited long enough.

You've endured bad leagues (the CFL) and bad teams (the Pharaohs) and bad spelling (the Maniax) and bad names (the Tams).

You've even changed sports, from football to hoops.

So, yes, it's your turn. And welcome to the show.

"Man, I'm looking forward to it," said Memphis Mayor Willie Herenton. "It's a great day."

At 7 p.m. tonight, an NBA team with Memphis on the front of its uniforms will play its inaugural game at The Pyramid.

Justin Timberlake will sing the national anthem.

Isaac Hayes will sign God Bless America.

David Stern will be here to help tip it off.

And if you're still having a hard time believing it, we understand.

Everyone talks about this city's long effort to get a major-league team. Here's how long it was: Memphis had already given up.

A year ago, it was finished, over, done. Nobody was talking about the big leagues anymore. After the hideous experience with the Titans/Oilers, nobody even dared dream those dreams.

And yet, here we are. Trying to figure out which one is Antonis Fotsis. Welcoming 300 Pau Gasol groupies who've flown in from Barcelona for the game. Brushing up on the new defensive three-second rule.

Flip on ESPN tonight and watch the scoreboard updates. That's the Memphis Grizzlies, scrolling past.

Pick up any paper today and look at the NBA standings. That's the Memphis Grizzlies, in the Midwest (ahead of Utah!).

Shane Battier lives downtown. Jason Williams is playing golf at Southwind.

Lorenzen Wright is showing up at local elementary schools, encouraging your kids to read.

C'mon, admit it. It's all pretty cool.

Does it mean that Memphis is now a major league city?

Maybe it's better to look at it the other way around.

Memphis didn't become major league because the Grizzlies moved here; the Grizzlies came here because Memphis has become major league.

FedEx had a lot to do with this. So did Staley Cates and Pitt Hyde and the two mayors and Dean Jernigan and, really, all the people who go to work every day thinking about what's possible in this town, instead of what's not.

"It reinforces what we've been saying about Memphis," says Marc Jordan, the head of the Memphis Area Chamber of Commerce. "We already knew it, but Memphis is a big-league city."

And now it has a big-league basketball team. To go along with its big-league river and its big-league ribs. And if there are plenty of questions yet to be answered about this enterprise, maybe this is one day we should focus on the one that's been asked around here for nearly forty years.

Now?

Yeah, kid.

Now.

A NIGHT TO REMEMBER, AN ENDING TO FORGET

In the interest of history, here are your important firsts:

First basket: Cliff Robinson.

First rebound: Michael Dickerson.

First traveling call: Dickerson.

First national anthem singer whose introduction caused actual squealing: Justin Timberlake.

First evidence that Michael Heisley has a self-deprecating sense of humor: "Where else in the league do the owner and the mascot have the same build?"

Oh, and first winner of a regular season NBA game at The Pyramid: Alas, not your Memphis Grizzlies.

The Grizzlies took the wraps off the regular season against the Detroit Pistons Thursday night. It had everything but a happy ending.

First final score: Detroit 90, Memphis 80.

First reaction from Shane Battier: "Nobody said it would all be roses."

Well, no, but would a single, wee, little rose have been too much for starters?

On a night when 19,405 packed the place?

On a night when even the security guards wore tuxedos?

The fans started lining up for this one at 5 a.m., waiting for the $5 tickets to go on sale at noon.

By 12:14, they were all gone.

Leon Walker saw an opportunity.

"I'll sell one of mine," he said.

"How much?" someone asked.

"Twenty dollars," said Walker.

(Um, first scalper?)

But, hey, you can almost understand his point. This was a grand, bouncy happening.

NBA commissioner David Stern raved about Memphis at his press conference before the game. Isaac Hayes delivered a truly cool God Bless

America. There were clowns on stilts and T-shirts parachuting down from the rafters. Really, there was something for everyone.

Take Larry Wortham and his daughter, Amber. They were sitting in the $5 seats. He came for the hoops. She came to see Timberlake.

"If it were up to her," said Larry, "we'd leave after the national anthem."

As it turned out, that might have made some sense. If we didn't have too much self-respect, we'd say the locals just weren't 'N SYNC on this night.

They didn't make enough foul shots (20 of 29). They had too many turnovers (25). They played badly, built a 12-point lead they didn't quite deserve in the third quarter, and still managed to lose the thing.

"We can't do that," said head coach Sidney Lowe. "When you have a lead like that, you can't go down and just throw the ball around."

The clincher came with a minute and change left in the game. Jerry Stackhouse dropped in a three-pointer to give Detroit an insurmountable six-point lead.

The fans filed out. The players regrouped in the locker room.

"The good thing about the NBA," said Lorenzen Wright, "is that we'll play again tomorrow night."

First shot at redemption, anyone?

WEST, FAMILY CHANGED BY WAR
MARCH 30, 2003

Thirteen-year-old Jerry West went to go fetch the mail for his mother, Cecile.

This was 1951 in Cheylan, West Virginia. Going to fetch the mail back then didn't mean walking to the end of the driveway. It meant walking to the post office in Cabin Creek.

Jerry, a good son, volunteered for the job. When he arrived at the post office, he ran into a neighbor.

All these years later, West still flinches at the memory.

"He told me my brother had been killed in Korea," West says. "I said, 'That's not true!' and took off running. I ran about a mile to where we lived.

"It was awful. I can't describe how awful it was."

West is on a scouting trip today, trying to identify players who could be future Grizzlies.

But he will watch the coverage of the war in Iraq, too. And he will hear about the casualties. And he will mourn for the dead and for the families they leave behind, whose lives will be forever changed.

West understands this because his life was forever changed — in ways he can't entirely explain or enumerate — on June 6, 1951, when his older brother David was killed by an artillery shell.

"It hit near him and someone else," West says. "He was 21. He was just about the perfect brother."

That's a word that comes up a lot when the subject is David West.

Perfect.

He was the third of the six West children, and by all accounts the kindest, most generous of them all.

He wasn't as athletic as his little brother Jerry. He wasn't as effusive as his big brother Charles.

He led Bible studies. He invited friends to stay over if they needed a place to sleep.

He made the best pitchers of lemonade. He shared whatever he had.

"He got a job at the local grocery," says Hannah Lilly, David's younger sister, the fourth of the West children. "You know what he did with the money?

"He got his teeth fixed, then he got my teeth fixed, then he started in on Jerry's, too."

Ahhh, Jerry. David and Jerry were close.

There was an eight-year age difference between the two, but it never seemed to matter much.

Jerry considered David his mentor and pal. David took as much pride in Jerry's accomplishments as he did in his own.

"I remember there was one guy, who was kind of a braggart, you know?" says Charles West, the second oldest of the West clan. "David told him, 'I got a little brother that can play basketball better than you.'"

After high school, David enlisted in the army. It seemed like the right thing to do.

Charles had served in World War II. David was weary of his grocery job. There weren't a lot of other options in rural West Virginia back then.

So David left for Korea, where he was the same selfless and thoughtful kid he had been at home.

He won a Bronze Star for courage under enemy fire. He sent a letter to Charles, reminding him to tell Hannah about the birds and the bees.

At one point, David contracted hepatitis and the West family thought they'd get him back.

"We read about the son of a general who had hepatitis and was coming home," Hannah says. "But when David recovered, he went back in there."

On June 6, 1951, David was setting up camp along a creek bank. He had a friend in Korea who always tried to stay close to him, figuring if God would protect anyone, David was the one.

This day, the friend had to park a truck on the other side of the creek.

"He told us an artillery round came in right then," Charles says. "David had severe wounds to his leg and his back.

"He was still alive when they took him out of there. The friend said the last time he saw him, David was reading his Bible."

Back in Cheylan, it was as if a second artillery shell had landed, this one in the West household.

Jerry sprinted blindly home from the post office. Hannah was working at a summer job when she got the news.

"I saw two neighbors coming and I never dreamed it was for me," she says. "The telegram had arrived.

"When I got home, my mother was outside, crying and crying and wailing around the house, almost out of her mind."

The funeral was six months later. It took that long for David's body to come home.

The Christmas tree was already up. Jerry got a new sport coat for the funeral.

The family bought a house with the government check.

And that was that. Everyone returned to life as usual.

Except they didn't, of course, because life as usual didn't exist anymore.

"I'm just not sure people understand the devastation it causes families," Jerry says. "I know what it did to ours."

Jerry says he was a different kid, for one thing.

Quieter, more introspective. He played long, solitary games of basketball.

"There was a pipeline, along the river bank," Hannah says. "Jerry would see how far he could walk without falling off."

Their mother struggled, too. She was an unyielding woman, as strong as she needed to be. But David had looked out for her, in his way. The loss of that sweetness shook her life.

"I was too dumb to realize it," Charles says, "but my sisters said she kind of had a nervous breakdown after that."

The Wests didn't talk about David, much. They still don't today.

But the striking thing is that, nearly 52 years later, the sense of loss is still palpable, even raw.

The eldest sister, Patricia, declined to talk about her brother because she gets "too weepy."

Hannah won't allow a gun in her house.

Jerry says he "hates violence."

And the war in Iraq exacerbates all this, freshens it, and sets off emotional reactions — not at all consistent, even within the family — to the breaking news of the day.

Jerry finds himself getting angry at the war protesters.

Charles thinks it's time this country gives up its role as policeman to the world.

As for Hannah, she heard some soldiers were shipping out near her home the other day and decided to go wave them off.

"I'm for the troops," she says. "I wanted to show my support."

Hannah watched the soldiers head out of town. She waved until they were gone. And as she waved, she noticed something else, too.

"Tears were rolling down my cheeks," she says, "because of David.

"They're all so very young."

TEACHER BROWN – AT 70, FORMER HIGH SCHOOL COACH TAKES 'EM TO CLASS
APRIL 16, 2004

The clowns behind the bench had defeated the old man, and they took pleasure in rubbing it in.

It is not easy to defeat Hubie Brown, at basketball or at trash-talk.

He's a Jersey guy, see? Jersey guys can rip. On the road, Brown can be as vicious as he needs to be in defense of his team.

This game, in Atlanta, in an empty gym, he had routed the dozen or so Atlanta fans behind the bench who had spent most of the game baiting him.

"When I was coaching here, there were things to cheer about," Brown told them. "We wouldn't be wasting time doing this. Just look up at the banners. You'll see."

They looked up at the banners. Banners the Hawks won when Brown coached the team.

Hmmmpf.

The geezer had a point, you know?

But then the Hawks took the lead. Atlanta's Travis Hanson stepped to the line with a chance to seal the win. The dozen or so fans started a sing-song chant.

"You just lost to the Haaaawks, you just lost to the Haaaawks."

At which point, Hanson missed one of two shots. Shane Battier threw the ball to James Posey, who heaved in a 34-footer to send it into double overtime.

Griz win! Griz win!

"The fans didn't say anything after that," said Brendan Brown, Hubie's son and a Grizzlies assistant. "I mean, they saw it. What could they possibly say?"

Which goes double for this season, actually.

What can anyone possibly say?

Besides "I'll have what he's having?"

Hubie Brown, 70, has transformed a basketball team. He took the utterly inept Grizzlies and turned them into the playoff-bound Grizzlies.

In the process, he may have saved a franchise, too.

This city bet $250 million that an NBA team could succeed here. That bet is looking better because of Brown, because of the unselfish team he created and the unprecedented wins he wrought.

He didn't do it by adding a new superstar, either. He did it by teaching the guys on the roster how to get better.

Imagine that, eh? In the NBA, where stars run the show, where street cred and bling were supposed to have squeezed out actual teaching long ago.

But here comes this old guy with a slight stoop and gray hair and a raspy voice and these quaint ideas about winning and defense and sharing the ball and, damn if it didn't actually work!

The Grizzlies are going to the playoffs. The FedExForum has a shot. The NBA has a model of success that involves something other than capitulation to a superstar's whim.

All because of Brown.

All because of this Yoda with a whistle, this Socrates of hoops.

"How do you explain it?" said Jerry West, the Grizzlies president of basketball operations. "He's a teacher and he always has been.

"This team needed a teacher. This team needed Hubie Brown.

"He was the right man at the right time for the right job."

Hubie, in his own words, Part 1: "At Fair Lawn High School a basketball player hadn't gotten a college scholarship in 22 years. Why? Because it was the No. 1 wrestling school in the state. And the No. 1 track team. And the No. 1 swimming team. They were loaded with winter sports. So basketball was a low priority. Well, the first year I'm the coach we start three sophomores. Does this sound familiar at all? At the end of our third year, we were competing for the championship. All five starters — the three kids who started as sophomores and the two who came in behind them — got Division 1 scholarships."

Growing up, he did not want to be a teacher. He wanted to be a baseball player.

Of course, most kids in Elizabeth, N.J., wanted to be baseball players. Brown was born in 1933. You wanted to be a Yankee or a Dodger. That's just how it was.

Brown was the only child of Anna and Charlie Brown. That's right, Charlie Brown, and save the jokes, please. Have some imagination. Have some respect. Three decades after his father died, Brown cannot speak of him without a catch in his voice.

"My father's the greatest man I ever met in my life," Brown said. "Everybody knew him. He knew everybody. When he died, my mother was shocked. There was a line at the funeral parlor. I can see it right now. I call it the long gray line."

Charlie Brown worked in the Jersey shipyards for 19 years. When World War II ended, he was — the way his son describes it — "put out on the street."

"So he got a job at Singer Sewing Machine, where we lived," Brown said. "And it was a good job. And then they reopened the shipyards. And he and 3,000 foremen went back and within a month they were back on the street and they couldn't get a job.

"I watched him — we didn't have any money, OK? Seven months, he couldn't get a job. It was different times then. So he became the janitor of my high school for four years and he never missed a game."

This is the undergirding truth of Brown's life, it defines him to this day.

He is blue collar. He is unyielding. He doesn't care about the size of your house or the size of your deal. He cares whether you show up. Every day. And work hard. Every day.

Brown carried this ethic from Jersey to Niagara University, then to two high school jobs, then to William & Mary, Duke and the Milwaukee Bucks.

In 1974, a year after his father died, Brown was hired to coach the Kentucky Colonels in the ABA. His first game was in Freedom Hall. Brown asked for an extra seat behind the bench.

He left it empty, for his dad.

Hubie, in his own words, Part 2: "Bernard King, we traded for him the day before we opened up in '83. Now, if you know him at all, this guy's a killer. I have my meeting with Bernard. I said, 'We're happy to have you here. Now, the way we play, I'm going to play you 32 minutes and then play Ernie Grunfeld 16.' He goes, 'No, I play 36 minutes.' I said, 'Not here, here you're going to play 32 minutes.' He said, 'No, I play 36 minutes. Or maybe 38.' I said 'No, here you're going to play 32 minutes. But here's the difference. I'm going to get you the same amount of shots as in 36 minutes.' And he looks at me and he said, 'Can I believe you?' I said, 'Yep, you can believe me.' He said, 'What happens at playoff time?' I said, 'You play 38 minutes and Ernie plays 10.' He goes, 'OK' and he shakes my hand."

Eric Hasseltine, who does radio and TV work for the Grizzlies, recently asked Brown the standard question about how he manages to relate to today's players. Maybe Brown had heard it once too much this year. In the gentlest possible way, he snapped.

"First, I'm insulted by the question," he said. "I don't think I've ever had a problem, ever, from high school to college to the NBA. I just do what we've always done, from the work ethic to the discipline to everything. We haven't changed."

This is hard to believe, of course. Haven't changed? In these ever-changing times?

And then you read *Loose Balls*, the definitive book about the ABA.

Here's Hubie on his philosophy at Kentucky: "I felt the key to coaching in pro ball was to keep 10 guys happy instead of eight. For a player to be happy, he needs minutes. Most teams only used eight players a game, but if you use 10 guys, then you only have two guys on the end of the bench. But the key to winning is 10 guys. If you're going to play 10, then you have to use pressure defense. So I told the guys that we were going to use 10 players and that meant 10 guys would be contributing to a championship."

Hmmm.

Sound familiar, anyone?

Brown is doing in Memphis what he did in Kentucky, what he did in Atlanta, what he did in New York.

He won a title with the Colonels. He was wildly successful his first four years in Atlanta. Ted Turner even thought about asking him to manage the Braves. Brown's an old baseball guy, remember?

And then, after his fifth year, Brown was canned.

"It was devastating," he said. "I was 48, I was successful and I was out on the street. You would like to think that what we created in Atlanta would not have ended that way. You would like to believe that apple pie, vanilla ice cream, Chevrolet and the American flag always win. But they don't always win, see? It doesn't work that way."

The Knicks job quickly followed. After leading New York to the playoffs two years in a row, Brown had two dreadful, injury-riddled seasons and was fired at the start of the next.

Which is when a remarkable thing happened. Brown was born anew as a TV star.

It's hard to imagine, really. The guy has so much in his mind about basketball, it tends to spill out in paragraphs without end. But he knew the game, he could break it down better than anyone, and isn't that what a color man does?

So Brown was hired to be the lead NBA guy on Turner Broadcasting. He was flat-out great.

He was John Madden without the sound effects, Tim McCarver without the bluster.

In 2000, Brown was inducted into the Broadcasters Wing of the Hall of Fame.

As for his coaching career, it was over, finished, done.

"Did I think he would go back?" said Brendan Brown. "Never, never, never.

"I guess there was one time, eight or nine years ago when I thought it was realistic. But after that, he liked his life too much. I didn't see any way."

Hubie in his own words, Part 3: "My wife, Claire, and I were talking after the Atlanta game. We stayed up until 2 a.m. talking about a lot of stuff. I said, 'Isn't it funny, after all these years, on every coaching trip, Dean Smith would always come up to me and say, 'Hubie, you've got to come back one more time. It's not fair how it ended.' And I'd say, 'Dean, I've got the greatest job in my life.' But who knew Turner would get a new guy at the top? So when the phone call from the Grizzlies came, it came just at the right time. The perfect time. When you get into the Hall of Fame as a broadcaster, I think you're doing OK. But the new group said, 'What can a 69-year-old guy with gray hair, how can he relate to the new generation that is watching the NBA?' They call it demographics."*

There is some beautiful irony here, no?

Brown was bounced out of Turner because the suits didn't think he could relate to the street-wise kids who like the NBA. And now he's succeeding beyond anyone's dreams by relating to the street-wise kids who play in the NBA.

There were doubters, of course. There were the expected jokes.

Peter Vecsey, of *The New York Post*: "When I first heard Hubie Brown was coaching Memphis I figured it was the Tams."

Rick Morrissey, of *The Chicago Tribune*: "I give him a month before the lava starts to boil over."

It's been 17 months. That's not lava, those are wins.

The Grizzlies won 50 games. They'd never won more than 28 before.

In the season of LeBron and Carmelo, the Grizzlies have become the sweetest story in the NBA.

"It may be the best coaching job I've ever seen," West said. "I never worry about being out-coached. Never. He is the best thing that could have happened to this team."

Not to mention the broader NBA, which has been reminded of some important things: knowledge matters; substance has value; there's more to coaching than a snappy suit.

"He says to our guys that it's not the system, but it is the system," said Tony Barone, the Grizzlies assistant coach. "It's the system he's put in place based on these abstract thoughts of unselfishness, sharing the ball, playing the position and doing your job.

"All of this sounds hokey. All of this sounds like, 'Oh, gee, that sounds cool, that sounds like a high school coach.' But the reality of the situation is, that's what he's doing."

OK, but why does it work for Brown? And why hasn't it worked anywhere else?

"Because he is willing to try," Barone said. "Everyone says it but very few have tried it. Every team in the league is going to say we're playing together. Then you see what happens. One guy goes out and gets 38 shots."

Which is the other thing to notice here. Brown is unwavering, utterly true to the things he holds close.

Skeptics wondered whether Brown could relate to modern players. But the players understand that Brown is both genuine and fair.

He doesn't have favorites. He doesn't have a doghouse. If someone has a problem, he wants to know.

"The next time he's got a chance to talk, it's going down," said Lorenzen Wright. "No matter what happens, or who it is, it's getting taken care of the next day."

Jason Williams skipped out on the team for a day. Earl Watson popped off about playing time. Both players were given a chance to say their piece. Then they were back on board.

"If you don't hide from problems, there are no problems," said Brendan Brown. "It's kind of magical how it works."

Hubie in his own words, Part 4: "I have received letters from some of the biggest people in this city, very personal letters, telling me that we've had an impact here. I'm taken aback by that. Because, by the same token, this has been very satisfying for me. I'm a coffee and newspaper guy. And when I drink my coffee and read my newspapers in the morning, I feel good for what the players have done. And when they hit 50 — damn, that was a helluva day for me and my staff and the players and the city."

It is hard to fathom that it was not even two years ago that Brown took the call from West.

Remember the first press conference? Remember the practice? Remember the stunned looks?

"Basically, he told us it's either his way or the highway," said Stromile Swift, at the time. "I don't know how a lot of the players are going to accept him, so it's going to be interesting."

Brown lived in a hotel for six weeks. Now he has a place on Mud Island, a few doors down from his son.

He has turned 70 since he arrived. He has read a lot of books.

"You should see his library at home," said Brendan Brown. "You'll be amazed at the books. You go in and you're allowed to check them out. There's not a system, there are no cards involved. But you better bring them back."

Brown does not talk about his plans for next year. He'll re-evaluate when this year is done.

But he enjoys this place. He loves this team. As much as he's done for the Grizzlies, he understands what the Grizzlies have done for him.

A week ago, he gathered the team in a circle after practice. Nothing unusual about that. It's something Brown does every day, to give the players a chance to say whatever's on their minds.

This time, Brown had something to say. A one-sentence speech that had been in the making for 70 years.

"I want to thank you for giving me the opportunity to do what I was supposed to be doing, " he said.

He looked at Jason Williams and Pau Gasol and the whole gang.

He looked at this group of players who, together, had done something fine and rare.

They had been willing to listen. He had been eager to teach.

Fifty wins later, they're off to the playoffs.

Do lessons come clearer than that?

IT SEEMED LIKE A CAN'T-MISS NIGHT
APRIL 23, 2004

Mike Miller stood and crossed his arms on his chest and stared at the basket in disbelief.

Twenty-thousand fans stood and stared, too.

It didn't go?

The shot didn't go?

The shot that would have triggered the bedlam, that would have given the Grizzlies their first playoff win, it really didn't fall?

Hmmmmmpf.

Miller slowly moved toward the locker room.

The 20,000 fans slowly moved toward the doors.

San Antonio 95, Memphis 93.

"I thought that it was in," Miller said. "I was disappointed it didn't go in."

You and a whole city, Mike, still waiting to explode.

This was a fantastic birthday party with a really stale cake.

This was a 14-day trip to paradise with an upset stomach at the end.

This was the finest meal you ever tasted with a worm in the apple pie.

This was a night that Memphis will always remember.

And a finish that Memphis would just as soon forget.

"Incredible atmosphere," said Michael Heisley.

"It was just awesome," said former Tiger Hank McDowell.

"When a team gets 21 offensive rebounds," said Hubie Brown, "that's why you lose."

Awwww, Hubie. You're probably right.

But you know something?

Memphis will win a playoff game someday. It might happen Sunday. It might happen next year or the year after that.

But it's hard to imagine it will get any more emotional, any more tense, any more rewarding than this Thursday night in the soon-to-be abandoned building where a franchise grew up before our very eyes.

And this isn't about moral victories, either. The Grizzlies had 50 real victories this year. Moral victories, be stuffed.

But anyone in the building will tell you: This was a glorious, wrenching, ear-popping, mind-blowing, throat-rending, heartbreaking night.

It's impossible to pick a highlight. Impossible to sum it up in a sentence or a moment.

Was it Heisley nailing the national anthem, with 20,000 backup singers joining him on every note?

Was it the shouts of "Hubie, Hubie, Hubie," when Hubie Brown first walked on the floor?

Was it NBA commissioner David Stern handing Brown the Red Auerbach Trophy?

Was it Brown accepting it, then blowing kisses to his team?

Was it the electric first half, with both teams hitting everything they threw up?

Or was it the still hard-to-fathom fact that this night unfolded in the previously woe-is-us burg known as Memphis, Tennessee?

"This is crossing the bridge to the promised land for this franchise," Stern said. "It's the best in professional sports and I'm proud to be a part of it." He said that before the game, before the last five minutes, when nobody dared sit or breathe.

They were tied at 88, tied at 90. And — despite some questionable shots down the stretch — the Grizzlies had a final chance to win.

Pau Gasol went for the quick dunk with 4.6 seconds left. After a foul shot, the Grizzlies had 3.6 seconds and a chance.

What more has this team ever needed? James Posey against Atlanta. Shane Battier against Minnesota. A chance. That's always been enough.

This time it was Battier to Miller, who dribbled to straight away, just behind the arc.

"It looked like it was on line," said Tim Duncan. "That's the scary part."

And then it missed.

Go figure.

The Grizzlies' playoff slogan may need some tweaking, after all.

Say it, see it, believe it ...

Darn it.

Darn, darn, darn, darn.

HOW LUCKY WE WERE TO JOURNEY WITH DON POIER
JANUARY 22, 2005

It was one of the first exhibition games in Memphis, no TV, radio only. Jason Williams hit a 3-pointer down the stretch for the win.

"Only in the movies and in Memphis!" said Don Poier.

He hadn't come up with this in advance, hadn't written it down for the moment.

He saw the shot fall. He said the perfect thing.

Only in the movies and in Memphis.

Forget that Poier hadn't been in Memphis for more than a couple months.

Forget that he had no idea of the good times yet to come.

He made the call, and it became a sort of promise.

This would turn out well. This would have a happy ending. Just listen along, folks, and we'll get there together.

And we did, too.

With Poier as our narrator.

"Don Poier was the Grizzlies," said Andy Dolich, the team's president of business operations. "He was our ambassador to Memphis."

Poier, 53, was found dead in his Denver hotel room Friday morning. Pete Pranica and Sean Tuohy did the game against the Nuggets.

"There is an empty chair to our left and there is an empty place in our hearts for Don Poier," said Pranica, at the start of the broadcast.

It was eerie listening to it, eerie and forlorn and wrong, somehow.

Poier should have been there. He should still be there. Hunkering down with his microphone, and calling the action with that blend of truth, optimism and home-spun genius.

Defenders swarmed "like bees to bacon."

A player couldn't be stopped "with a Bible and a banjo."

An opponent "traveled in front of the Good Lord and everybody and they didn't call it!"

Not everyone could say this stuff, you know. It's corny, to read it.

But it worked because it was honest, and because we liked the guy who said it.

Everybody liked Poier. It's remarkable, really. The man had spent his entire life in the Pacific Northwest. His inflections were different. But in a city where you can still be "new in town" three decades after you get here, Poier fit in immediately.

Even he was worried about this. He once wrote about it for this paper.

"How would I be accepted?" he wrote. "I came with the credibility of being the original announcer, but would fans take to my style?"

Like bees to ...

Poier was a pro. He respected the game and respected his listeners.

"He didn't care what the team thought," said Steve Daniel, another original Grizzly, who recently left his job as director of basketball operations. "If we were bad, he was going to say that we were bad."

But it wouldn't ruin his day. Nothing could ruin his day, not even a 40-point loss to the Pacers.

"There wasn't a game when he didn't take the headsets off and say, 'There's only 30 of these jobs in the world. How lucky could I be?'" said Tuohy.

Poier was content. How rare is that?

He liked wine, and food, and having everyone over at the holidays.

He played golf. He loved the Lord.

He had a 36-foot Pace Arrow RV that he and his wife, Barb, drove around the country every summer.

They visited their kids. They saved on their phone bill.

"We teased him about how much he called her during the season," Tuohy said. "'I'm on the bus, Barb,' 'The bus is started, Barb,' 'The bus is moving, Barb.'"

Just like a play-by-play man, eh?

And now he's gone, silenced, and it's hard not to feel cheated, somehow.

The guy wanted to spend more time with his kids. He wanted to broadcast a Game Five of the playoffs.

"He wanted to broadcast every game for 40 years," said Mike Golub, the team's vice president of business operations. "He wanted to be the Memphis Grizzlies version of Chick Hearn."

So what to say now? How possibly to make sense of it?

Well, why not leave that to Poier, one last time?

The column he wrote for this paper was before last year's San Antonio series. The idea was to get some sense as to how it felt to have finally arrived in the playoffs.

Poier decided not to focus on the ending at all.

"It's all about the journey," he wrote.

CATCHING THAT CHRISTMAS GLOW
FROM DADDY'S HOUSE
NOVEMBER 25, 2005

Thirty-six years ago, in a simple house on Netherwood Avenue, Gailon Sheard made an important decision.

He would buy his daughter and granddaughter a real Christmas tree.

If this doesn't seem like an important decision to you, you don't know much about buying Christmas trees. All Christmas-tree decisions are important decisions. Otherwise, they wouldn't take so long to make.

You want a real one or a fake one? A tall one or a short one?

You want this one here? Or that one over there?

Sheard wanted a real one, and not just a real one, one with roots.

He hadn't always known they sold Christmas trees with roots. But his wife, Thelma, worked as a caterer.

"She worked in the rich white folks' houses," said Polly Walker, Sheard's daughter. "So we knew things other people didn't know."

Polly lived in the house on Netherwood. It was a bursting little house.

Her parents, Gailon and Thelma, slept in one bedroom. She slept in another with her husband, Cato Walker Jr., except when he was on the road, driving the bus for B.B. King.

She and Cato Jr. had three kids of their own, Lora, Thelma (yep, another one) and Cato III (yep, another one of those, too).

So, yes, the house was crowded. But happy most of the time.

"We made out fine," said Polly.

"We had a good time," said Lora, her daughter. "But in 1969, I got sick."

That's what inspired Gailon to get the tree. Lora was just 15. If his granddaughter was going to be lying around sick during Christmas, she should have a real tree to keep her spirits up.

So Gailon drove down to Stringer's and picked out the best tree he could find.

It was a White Pine, green and full and perfect for the season.

"It was pretty," Lora said.

"It was just regular Christmas-tree sized," Polly said. "Four or five feet."

They put it in the front window, so everyone could see the lights.

Not white lights, either.

"I like multicolored lights," Polly said.

And garlands. And ornaments. And an angel from the Goldsmith's downtown.

They put their presents under that tree. They sang it Christmas songs.

Then, when New Year's came, they planted it in the front yard.

And that was that.

They never watered it or anything.

Months passed.

Gailon died that August. It was his first and last real Christmas tree.

Everyone called it Daddy Gailon's tree after that.

Years passed.

Gailon's wife, Thelma, died.

The family kept going to Stringer's to buy Christmas trees.

Lora, Cato III and Thelma grew up, leaving Polly and her husband in the house.

Decades passed.

The children all had children.

Some of the children's children had children.

"I have nine great-grandchildren," said Polly, now 78.

In early July, Polly looked up at Daddy Gailon's tree and noticed a tilt.

"It was leaning over," she said. "Trees fall all the time in our neighborhood. I decided to take it down. I didn't want to build anyone a new house."

Polly told Lora. She was the inspiration for the tree, after all.

"We can't take it down," Lora said.

"We have to."

"Then we have to give it away."

Someone suggested the White House.

"Honey," Polly said, "the White House ain't that big."

Lora decided to call the Grizzlies.

Why?

"I wanted someone to have that tree," she said.

The Grizzlies said, sure, we'll get back to you.

A month passed. Lora called the Grizzlies again. This time, she was put in touch with a man named Howard Parker, the director of engineering at FedExForum.

"I got a big Christmas tree for you," Lora said.

"You do?" Parker said.

Last year, the Grizzlies paid $10,000 to import a tree from Canada.

It wasn't a particularly tall tree. Plus, it was smushed.

"They must have laid some other trees on top of it on the way down," Parker said.

Charlie Brown would have been proud.

So Parker headed out to Netherwood to examine Daddy Gailon's tree.

"What you want for it?" he said, finally.

"I want you to take it away," Polly said.

"NO!" said Cato III, Polly's son. "I want San Antonio tickets."

"I want Denver tickets!" said Thelma, Polly's daughter.

"How about both?" Parker said.

Thus the deal was struck.

A couple weeks ago, Parker showed up with a giant crane and a flatbed truck and ... hey, you call that a saw?

"What you bringing that toy saw here for?" Lora said.

Parker laughed, then started cutting.

A few minutes later, he left to get a bigger saw.

"That's better," Lora said.

Half an hour later, it was down.

Or up, because the crane swung the tree up and out and away. The experts said it was 65 feet high and 30 feet wide.

"Bet the Lakers aren't going to have a tree like that," Polly said.

So it was that on a chilly Tuesday night, the extended Walker family gathered in the plaza outside FedExForum for the formal unveiling of Daddy Gailon's tree.

There were pronouncements and proclamations. There were giveaways and dancing girls.

A switch was thrown. Six-thousand bulbs bathed the plaza in blue light.

"It's beautiful," said Polly.

"I love it," said Thelma.

After more than three decades, Daddy Gailon's only real Christmas tree was a Christmas tree once again.

"It just goes to show," said Lora.

Show what?

"What can happen if you care."

Lora was 15 then. She is 51 today.

"All I ever wanted," she said, "was for people to love my tree."

SO LONG, SHANE
JUNE 30, 2006

Shane Battier was just sitting down to dinner with the sponsors of his summer camp when his cell phone rang.

"Excuse me," he said. "I have to take this call."

Battier stepped outside, answered the phone, and learned that after five years, he was no longer a member of the Memphis Grizzlies.

He let this sink in for a long moment. He stepped back into the restaurant.

"I've just had some interesting news," he said. "I've been traded to Houston."

Pause.

"But I don't want it to ruin the dinner," he said, and is that perfect Battier or what?

The guy's life had just been flipped upside down. He had a new team and a new town.

But, hey, don't let it get in the way of your shrimp cocktail or anything.

Battier stayed and mingled for another two hours. Thursday morning, he was back at camp at 8:30 a.m., giving the kids the word of the day.

Perseverance.

"No matter what happens, you have to keep going and do your best," Battier said.

Good advice, no? For the kids and all of us.

So we say goodbye to Battier, and offer this page as tribute and thanks.

It is not a lamentation. The Grizzlies did what they had to do Wednesday night. Jerry West had a splendid draft, even if Austin Lacy did not.

Austin is 8 years old and a student at Battier's camp. When he heard Battier had been traded, he went upstairs to rub his lucky rabbit's foot.

"In hopes that he'd come back," said Kellie Miller, Austin's mother.

She gently explained that's not how the NBA works. Players get traded. Even players you really, really love.

The key is, you know, what Shane said.

Perseverance.

But it's sure going to be different, isn't it?

Shane Battier became a Memphis Grizzly on June 27, 2001. General Manager Billy Knight walked into the media room before the pick was even announced.

"You want to know who we're taking?" he said.

Sure!

"Shane Battier is the guy we picked," he said. "We knew as soon as Golden State said they were taking Jason Richardson."

Said Battier: "I can't wait to get to Memphis."

How could anyone not like the sound of that?

He couldn't wait to get to Memphis! He wanted to be one of us!

For a city that had struggled with its self-image, it was the best thing Battier could have said.

And for the next five years, he was one of us, a Memphian, and proud of it, too.

He lived downtown. He went to BarbecueFest and served on the board of the zoo.

Memphis had Battier longer than Duke had Battier.

Memphis had Battier longer than it had any Tiger great you can name.

He played through three coaches and two arenas. He got married as a Grizzly, opened and closed a restaurant, bought his first house.

So, absolutely, it's painful to see him go. But what a glorious run.

Battier's very first day of practice, the Grizzlies sent everyone on a 12-minute sprint.

"Shane," said coach Sidney Lowe, "he just took off and left everyone."

OK, Michael Dickerson caught Battier at the end. But he was learning, see.

Just like the city was learning about the entire professional enterprise.

Battier's NBA career matches Memphis's NBA career. You can tell our story through his words.

Oct. 2, 2001, after the first day of practice: "I was looking for my No. 2 pencils and my stapler."

Nov. 1, 2001, after the Grizzlies lost their first regular-season game: "Nobody said it would be all roses."

Dec. 21, 1001, after the Grizzlies' home win over the Los Angeles Lakers: "Not bad for a little ol' city like Memphis."

Nov. 31, 2004, after Hubie Brown resigned: "This, too, shall pass."

March 1, 2005, as the Grizzlies kept winning despite a horrendous string of injuries: "It's not our nature to draw love letters to the health fairy."

It wasn't either, not with Battier on the team. Everyone talks about Battier the splendid citizen. They forget he's a winner, too.

He helped set a new tone for the Grizzlies, every bit as much as West or Brown.

Just you watch. Houston will make the playoffs next year, and it won't all be because of Tracy McGrady and Yao Ming.

But that's not why Battier is beloved in Memphis. He's beloved because, well, here's a letter sent to the paper from a guy named Steve.

It's from way back in 2002. Steve, a Memphis football fan, said Battier happened by his tailgate.

"After the game, he came up to me and asked me where they needed to put the trash," Steve wrote. "Can you believe that with his millions of dollars he started picking up the trash and cleaning the area?"

Actually, yes. We can believe it because he did that kind of thing all the time.

He remembered names. He was always polite. If he went into the stands, it was only at the end of the year, to give a kid his shoes.

Battier isn't a mythic figure. He's just decent, and thoughtful, and he tries his best every day.

Isn't that what you want from your athletes? Isn't that what you want from your kids? And isn't it a pleasure to have had someone like that in the city, a player you could tell your sons and daughters to emulate without reservation?

As Battier's summer camp wound down Thursday, parents gathered to pick up their children. Some came early. It was just that kind of day.

Bill Walden, 41, watched his son Griffen race up and down the floor. Griffen is 8.

"I just wanted him to have some interaction with Shane," he said. "I wanted him to hear Shane talk about the things parents talk about all the time. Like hard work, integrity, things like that."

Walden shrugged. He said his son was "distraught" about the trade.

The kids are sure going to miss that Battier.

The grownups, too.

PICKING A WINNER – WALLACE
BLAZED HIS OWN PATH
JUNE 27, 2007

The new general manager of the Memphis Grizzlies, the man who will make the most important decisions for this franchise over the next few years, made his most controversial decision nearly three decades ago, when he dropped out of school.

Actually, he dropped out of school for a second time. Kids, do not try this at home.

Chris Wallace left the University of Kansas the first time in January, 1978. He took a job doing something called "dormitory maintenance."

"We cut grass and shoveled snow," Wallace said. "I picked up the trash in the dorms."

Eventually concluding he had no future in trash pickup, Wallace re-enrolled at Kansas.

"I lasted two more semesters," he said. "One day in class, I had an epiphany. Everyone was diligently taking notes and I said to myself, 'What am I doing here?' I was taking journalism classes but I knew I didn't want to work in journalism. I said, 'This is a farce.'"

This time, Wallace quit school and went home. Not just home to Buckhannon, W.Va., the small town where he grew up. Home to 1 Christopher Lane, the house where he was raised.

Wallace slept in the actual room, on the second floor, where he had slept since fifth grade. He started up a basketball magazine.

A year passed. Then two. The years became a decade.

Wallace lived with his parents until he was 32. He understands there's a word for people like this.

"Everyone thinks," he said, "that you're a loser."

• • •

Sometime after 6:30 p.m. Thursday, Chris Wallace, 48, will identify the player the Grizzlies will take with the No. 4 pick in the draft. He'll relay the name to New York. NBA commissioner David Stern will announce it on ESPN.

And while there will be many other, more publicized moments on draft night, maybe there shouldn't be.

"It's the American dream," said Sonny Vaccaro, founder of the famed ABCD All America Camp, who has known and worked with Wallace for years. "To put your mind to something and then go do it despite long odds, isn't that what this country is supposed to be about?"

Well, yes. How fitting that Chris and Debby Wallace named their 10-year-old son Truman, after the former president.

"I was reading David McCullough's biography of Harry S. Truman at the time, and it struck a chord with me," Wallace said. "One, Truman was from a small town like me. Two, he didn't graduate from college. Three, he lived at home until he was in his 30s. Four, he failed as an oil and gas prospector and as a haberdasher before he succeeded in politics.

"I didn't fail at the magazine business, but I didn't hit it big, either. Truman was a late bloomer. And even when he became president he was still the small-town guy from Independence, Missouri."

Wallace is rattling all this off, by telephone, well after 10 p.m. Boston time. It is the week before the draft. He has gone back to Boston to settle some things.

For instance, he has to say goodbye to Maurice Cormier, the bartender at Bertucci's, an Italian restaurant near the Celtics practice facility where Wallace had lunch just about every day.

"Chris Wallace is an unbelievably good guy," Cormier said. "He's the kind of person who will talk to anyone. Rick Pitino used to come in here, and you couldn't approach him. He'd growl at you. Chris acts like he's one of us."

There's a simple reason for this, of course: Wallace is one of us. He started out as a fan. He didn't play in college or the pros. The most memorable moment of Wallace's high school career didn't even take place during a game.

"The coach was talking to the team, and he fell asleep," said Bob Wallace, Chris's dad. "His teammates started calling him Rip Van Winkle after that."

But Wallace loved the game, loved everything about it, the way some kids do. He loved watching West Virginia Wesleyan, the local NAIA team. He loved going to the national NAIA Tournament in Kansas City every year with his dad.

"I saw Jack Sikma, I saw Slick Watts," Wallace said. "It might as well have been Paris for me."

This is why Wallace dropped out of Kansas. Not because he couldn't do the academic work. Because he was preoccupied — no, make it obsessed — with basketball.

He just had to be involved in the game. He came up with the idea of publishing a college basketball magazine.

"What do you know about publishing?" asked his father, before he helped put together an $8,500 loan.

"Nothing," Wallace said, "but I can do better than the ones that are out there now."

The Blue Ribbon College Basketball Yearbook came to be considered the best of its kind. It didn't generate enough money to move Wallace out of his parents' house or anything, but that wasn't his priority.

"I could have had a small apartment, or driven something other than my parents' old station wagon," Wallace said. "But I knew the people I needed to be meeting weren't in Buckhannon, West Virginia. So I put all my money into travel and maybe having some nicer clothes so I looked decent when I got somewhere.

"I made sacrifices because I had to make sacrifices. I'm not a live-at-home guy. But I just knew there was something in the game for me. I didn't know what it was, but I knew it was out there."

In December of 1986, it presented itself in the form of a phone call. The caller was Jon Spoelstra, an executive with the Portland Trail Blazers. Spoelstra — a subscriber to Wallace's magazine — was disenchanted with Walter Berry, the player Portland had selected in the first round of the previous draft.

"He asked me if I wanted to be a scout," Wallace said. "I just about had a coronary."

Spoelstra finally asked Wallace to send him a scouting report on any college player, as a small test.

"About a week later, I got a 70-page report on Mookie Blaylock," Spoelstra said. "I was stunned by the depth of it. But then I thought that maybe this is the one player he knows well. So I called and asked for another report, and this time I picked the player.

"Sure enough, a week later, another 70-page report arrived, and it was as good as the first. I hired him without ever meeting him."

In the Blazers' basketball department, this did not necessarily go over well. What credentials did Wallace have, really? He was the publisher of a basketball magazine for fans.

But on draft day 1987, Wallace got down on his knees — "literally on his knees," Spoelstra said — and asked the Blazers not to pick Ronnie Murphy of Jacksonville.

"In the NBA, it's very rare to go out on a limb like that," Spoelstra said. "Chris said Murphy would be out of the league in two years. We drafted him anyway, and he was out of the league in one."

The Blazers did let Wallace make their pick in the third round. He chose Kevin Gamble, of Iowa, who had a 10-year NBA career.

The rest was happily ever after, right? Wallace had finally broken through.

Except Spoelstra took a job with the Denver Nuggets in 1989. Wallace, naturally, went along.

Three months into the job, Spoelstra was fired. Wallace — just back from getting married in Hawaii — was let go, too.

"We did what I call a reverse Beverly Hillbillies," he said. "We packed up the station wagon and moved back to West Virginia."

Two years passed before Wallace got another chance. The Miami Heat invited him to come down for an interview.

"My wife — she's the practical one — said that to make it financially I needed to negotiate a certain salary," Wallace said. "They offered me $25,000 a year, take it or leave it."

This was in 1992.

"Good God, Chris, you can't live in Miami for $25,000," said Wallace's father. "What's wrong with you?"

Wallace took the job anyway. What's money when you're chasing a dream?

He spent five years in Miami. He moved to Boston — the Celtics agreed to swap second-round picks as compensation — after Rick Pitino got the Celtics job.

So when Jerry West called Wallace two weeks ago and offered him the chance to run a team on his own, Wallace had to look back in wonder at the entire, astonishing trip.

"This is what I've been working for my whole life," he said. "I go to Kansas on scouting trips a lot. Whenever I leave Allen Fieldhouse, I look across at the dorms and think about the time I spent working over there. I get a lot of letters from kids now asking how to get into sports. I laugh when I think I started picking up trash."

This is why West was so irked by the widespread assumption that he picked Wallace because of their relationship. They're not all that close, for one thing. Before Wallace was hired, they'd been to dinner together a couple times.

Beyond that, there's a lot of back-scratching in the NBA, a lot of people who have responsibilities they didn't necessarily earn.

Players go straight from the court to general manager jobs. Front office and scouting positions are filled by friends and sons who want to work in the league.

Wallace is the exception to all that. He's the guy who didn't have anything to rely on except his body of work.

Yet even after all his years in the NBA, Wallace wasn't a popular choice in Memphis, not nearly as popular as someone like Mark Jackson or B.J. Armstrong would have been.

"I give West a lot of credit and I give the owner a lot of credit," Vaccaro said. "It takes some guts to hire Chris Wallace. But, I tell you what, he's going to be a big success in Memphis."

Back in Boston, Celtics fans chortle at this idea. Bill Simmons, who calls himself The Sports Guy on ESPN, rips Wallace every chance he gets.

Of course, a basketball blogger recently pointed out that in 2001 Simmons wrote: "Joe Forte falls to the Celts at No. 21! My dad and I are fired up right now."

Forte, from North Carolina, turned out to be a bust.

"The thing is, Chris has never been the primary decision-maker," Vaccaro said. "I know for a fact he would have taken Tony Parker instead of Forte if it had been his choice. But that was Red Auerbach's choice. I know because I was on the phone with Chris, and he nearly killed himself when it happened."

OK, but how about Kedrick Brown, who the Celtics drafted before Forte in the same draft? Or how about the trade for Vin Baker? Wallace's record is not pristine.

But whose is, really? West and both made mistakes.

So did Harry Truman, for that matter, and history has been kind to him.

By the way, the draft falls on June 28, the same day Harry married Bess Truman in 1919. How's that for symmetry?

Eighty-eight years later, Wallace is faced with a big day of his own. Go on, Chris — give 'em hell.

GRIZ AND MEMPHIS STILL RIPE FOR GROWTH
DECEMBER 16, 2007

This is a story about the Memphis Grizzlies. And tomatoes.

Not just any tomatoes, mind you. Bradley tomatoes.

"They're very delicate, old-time tomatoes," said Tom Tims. "People go nuts over them."

Tims should know. He grows Bradley tomatoes on his farm in Ripley. Every summer weekend, he loads up his truck with cucumbers and squash and Bradley tomatoes and brings them to Memphis.

It's a perfect fit, really. Tims loves growing his tomatoes; Memphians love eating them.

And all it took to make this tomato trade a reality was an NBA basketball team.

• • •

Earlier this week, Andy Dolich resigned his position as Grizzlies president of business operations. Or the press release said Dolich resigned. He was actually the latest victim in Mike Heisley's recent reign of error.

The team has a hard time winning games. It has hard time drawing crowds. I could go into all the reasons and particulars but, at a moment when people are trying to remember why we wanted the Grizzlies in the first place, it seemed like a good time to talk about tomatoes.

Two years ago, Memphians couldn't drive Downtown and buy Tims' Bradley tomatoes. Then a half-dozen women, most of whom had no connection to each other, started calling around, trying to fix that.

OK, they weren't after Tims' tomatoes, specifically. They were after a farmer's market. A big, sprawling, happy, farmer's market, like the kind you can find in Brooklyn and Seattle and San Francisco.

One of those women was Ellen Dolich, wife of Andy, president of business operations for the Memphis Grizzlies.

Dolich didn't have to involve herself in Memphis when she arrived. Her husband made a robust living. She could have sat around eating bon-bons.

But, no. She preferred vegetables.

"She was passionate about the need for a market," said Andy Kitsinger, vice president of planning and development at the Memphis Center City Commission. "And she was willing to work to make it happen."

The half-dozen women gathered for a meeting after a concert at Court Square. Dolich volunteered to be in charge of vendors. Those are the people who actually sell things. Without vendors, it's not much of a market. And a market needs tomatoes, right?

Pretty soon, a phone rang in Ripley.

"I guess it's fair to say we were skeptical," Tims said.

Tims hadn't been to Memphis in a long time, see. The Memphis he remembered wasn't the best place to sell vegetables.

"Ellen had me meet me her Downtown," said Tims. "She drove me around and, I have to tell you, it absolutely blew me away. I didn't have one iota of a clue that Memphis was as nice as that."

So Tims decided to give it a shot. The rest is local produce history.

"It's been wonderful," said Tims.

Maybe the Grizzlies should have put Dolich in charge of player procurement too? Because once she landed Tims, she went after Mike Lenager, who raises Angus beef in Tipton County. Lenager remembers exactly what he said when Dolich called the first time to invite him to sell his beef at the new market.

"No," said Lenager.

So she called a second time.

"No," said Lenager.

A third time.

"No."

A fourth time.

"No."

"What exactly is your objection?" said Dolich.

"I know Memphis," Lenager said. "I don't want to go somewhere I have to bring a gun with me."

Dolich invited Lenager to come visit, just as she had invited Tims.

"I was shocked," Lenager said. "Y'all have the best-kept secret. It's wonderful."

So Lenager signed up too. Maybe it's time to retire the term "carpetbagger." People who grew up in Memphis sometimes don't understand the potential of the place. But there was Dolich, freshly arrived from the West Coast, driving farmers around, showing them all the cool stuff they've been missing.

"She was my driving force," Lenager said. "She doesn't take 'no,' easily."

Because of that, Memphis now has a thriving Downtown farmer's market. Last summer, more than 40,000 people poured into the city to buy pumpkins and cactus and pecan pies and yeast rolls.

Many of those 40,000 have never been to see the local NBA team, but their lives have been enriched by the presence of the local NBA team in a way they probably don't even realize.

Which is the larger point of this, really, and another reason to hope the Grizzlies get it figured out. No, the team isn't very good right now. No, the arena isn't close to filled.

But remember when we had that testy debate over bringing the NBA to town? Remember the list of pros and cons?

Nobody listed a bustling farmer's market as one of the pros. A market and an NBA team? One has nothing to do with the other.

Except, in Memphis, as it turned out, one had everything to do with the other. Maybe that should have been foreseeable, after all. The more a community has to offer, the more smart, passionate people it can attract. Some of those people might want to start a market. Some of those people might want to start something else. A business. A fund drive. A charter school.

In this way, a community grows richer. And a richer community attracts more smart, passionate people. And so the community continues to grow richer, even as some of the smart, passionate people who changed the community inevitably move away.

Now the Doliches are headed back to California. It's sad to see them go. But come next spring, a big, sprawling, happy farmer's market will reopen in Downtown Memphis.

Tomatoes, anyone?

GRIZ ROOT FOR MASCOT – ENTIRE FRANCHISE RALLIES AROUND GUY IN THE FURRY BLUE COSTUME
JUNE 22, 2008

Mascots don't get cancer. Think of all the mascots you've ever seen around the ballpark. They jump on trampolines. They swap high fives with kids. They mock officials and they scoot around on motorbikes and they might even trip and fall on purpose if it'll draw a laugh.

But they don't get cancer. It's not in the job description.

"Mascots are all about joy," said Eric McMahon.

McMahon is a mascot. He's the guy who runs and leaps and has a ball inside the furry, blue Grizz costume.

Only this day, he wasn't doing any of that. He was sitting in a doctor's office, listening to the doctor's words and trying to make sense of it all.

Hodgkin's lymphoma.

Stage 3B.

Yes, that's out of four.

Someone from the Grizzlies called while McMahon was still in the doctor's office. Just to make sure everything was fine.

Everything wasn't fine. He'd naturally be taking a leave from his job. The guy from the Grizzlies said they could put out a press release. McMahon thought about this for a moment.

It seemed like the right thing. But odd, too.

The mascot has cancer? Mascots don't get cancer. Everybody knows that.

• • •

It's another big week for the Grizzlies, as they set about the task of building a winning team. The NBA Draft takes place Thursday. The Grizzlies hope to get lucky this time. And, yes, absolutely, you have the right to be skeptical.

This is the team that once turned the worst record in the league into the No. 4 pick. This is the team that passed on Carlos Boozer and drafted Troy Bell. This is the team that — in the midst of one of its grimmest seasons — lost its mascot to cancer.

Can you imagine how that bit of news rippled through Grizzlies headquarters? Can you imagine what it did to morale?

The Grizzlies had already missed on Greg Oden and Kevin Durant, already seen their win totals and ticket sales plunge toward the bottom of the league.

And now the mascot had cancer?

"It was very, very hard," said John Pugliese, senior director of marketing.

Pugliese is one of the people who hired McMahon, 28, after an exhaustive search two seasons ago. McMahon had been working in Phoenix, as an understudy to the Suns' Gorilla.

"The Gorilla basically took me under his wing," said McMahon, if you can try to picture that.

So the Grizzlies hired the guy. Said he had a fabulous first year. When he came back from the preseason trip to Spain dragging, McMahon and the Grizzlies dismissed it as jet lag.

Except McMahon didn't get better. He kept losing weight.

"It went on for three months," McMahon said. "By the time it was diagnosed, it was stage 3B, which is bad."

The oncologist decided to try a particularly aggressive form of chemotherapy. At first, things looked promising.

"Then he got a bacterial infection," said Mary McMahon, Eric's mother. "Because he had lesions all through his colon, the infection got into his blood and caused blood poisoning."

Soon — his immune system weakened by the chemotherapy — McMahon was in full-blown crisis. The family was summoned to his bedside.

"His lungs collapsed, his kidney failed and his liver started to fail," said Mary McMahon. "He had two tubes to drain fluids out of his chest, more than three liters of fluid a day."

Mary McMahon remembers asking the intensive care doctor for something — anything — to hold on to by way of hope.

"All we can do," the doctor said, "is support his systems and hope his body starts to fight."

McMahon can't even remember large chunks of this time when he lay near death. His mother said he was babbling throughout much of it, talking aloud as if he were at FedExForum, giving out directions, trying to fire up the crowd.

Friends started prayer chains. The Grizzlies were supportive beyond words. They remembered McMahon talking about his "best friend Paul." So they found Paul and flew him in for a week.

Grizzlies guard Casey Jacobsen kept stopping by to see McMahon. Yes, the much-ridiculed Casey Jacobsen.

"He came to see me six or seven times," McMahon said. "A couple of times, I didn't even know he was there, I was so out of it."

Somehow, it all worked. After nearly four weeks in the hospital — two weeks in intensive care — McMahon was released. His mother took him back to Phoenix in a wheelchair. That's how weak he was.

"I had to adjust his pillows for him," she said. "He could barely lift his head."

That was four months ago, in February.

This past week, McMahon put his body through a full, relentless, 45-minute workout.

"It was a full agility workout," McMahon said. "I feel great right now."

So there's your good news, Grizzlies fans. Wasn't it about time for some? After more than 30 rounds of chemotherapy, the doctors have said McMahon is cancer-free.

"The human body is a miraculous thing," McMahon said.

The human spirit, too. McMahon can't quite believe everything people have done for him the last seven months.

"You're not even supposed to know my name," he said. "To protect the mystique, teams don't even acknowledge a person is in the suit.

"But when I got sick, the Grizzlies humanized me. They said 'Our mascot is Eric McMahon and he is dealing with a real-life issue that's more important than anything else.'"

Occasionally, someone will tell McMahon, "Isn't it too bad it took you getting cancer for people to do all that for you?"

McMahon corrects them.

"It took me getting cancer to realize what people were willing to do for me," he says. "That's what's too bad."

As for the future, all McMahon will say is that he plans to be back as Grizz sometime this year. He won't give a timetable. But people close to Grizz — and there's a phrase you don't see every day — say he'd really like to be back for Opening Night.

"I would like to thank everyone," he said. "And I'd like to show everyone what can happen in this life."

Bad things can happen. To teams and people, too.

But look at the mascot. That's all you have to do. The guy is living proof that you don't need a trampoline to bounce back.

II

PEOPLE

RAMSEY ROCKS 'EM AT THE ZONE
JULY 25, 2001

The fan waits patiently for the player to finish his warm-up. He knows not to interrupt.

He has brought along a new, white baseball, in hopes of getting an autograph. He's already collected a few signatures on the ball, but needs this last one to make it complete.

So when the player is finally finished, the fan steps forward, holding out the ball.

"Sorry to bother you," he says, "but can I get you to sign this?"

The player doesn't hesitate. He takes a pen and starts to scribble on the curved, hard surface.

"David Ramsey," he writes.

And then David Ramsey, the Redbirds organ player, smiles at the moment.

"That," he says, "doesn't happen very often."

Organ notes: There is an official Trivial Pursuit question that goes like this: Who was the only person to play for the Yankees, Rangers and Knicks in the same year? A: Eddie Layton, the organist.

Ramsey remembers precisely how it all started.

Dr. Bernard Kraus, the owner of the Double-A Memphis Blues, decided he'd like organ music at the ballpark. He knew Ramsey was a fan of the team, knew he could play the organ, and wondered if he might put the two together.

"I happened to be in Birmingham at the time," Ramsey says. "I called my mother, who played the piano, and I asked her to collect all the piano music she had that might be appropriate.

"I didn't know if I'd be doing it for one day, one week, how long."

That was 1971. That was 30 years ago.

Ramsey has played for Bo Jackson and Michael Jordan. He's played for Mark McGwire and Charlie Lea. He's played for the Blues, the Chicks and now the Redbirds.

The only time Ramsey, 61, stopped playing was when someone told him he had to.

That was in 1995. Tom Ford, the new general manager, decided that people didn't want to hear organ music anymore.

"He called me in and said he'd been very successful with another formula and he wanted to give it a try," Ramsey said.

Ramsey did not start smashing chairs or anything. He is a peaceful man who teaches music at Rhodes and plays the organ at First Presbyterian Church when he's not at the ball yard.

"I said, 'Fine, I understand,'" Ramsey said. " 'But can I still work in the press box?'"

So for three years, Ramsey worked in the press box, helping run the scoreboard. Then Dean Jernigan arrived with the Redbirds.

One of the first things Jernigan did was put Ramsey back where he belonged.

"What's Memphis baseball," Jernigan said, "without David Ramsey?"

Organ notes: In 1968, Denny McLain cut two albums featuring himself playing the organ. His comment at the time: "When all is said and done, some day in the future, I hope they will remember Denny McLain as a professional musician."

Ramsey has a theory about baseballs and organs, a theory about why they go together as well as Tinker and Evers.

"It's because there's room for commentary," he says. "The play unfolds on the field and the organ helps tell the story."

The Cubs installed the first organ in a major league park, in 1941. Roy Nelson was the organist.

Since then, the organ has become as much a part of the ball yard as hot dogs, as Cracker Jacks, as the drunk guy in the seventh row yelling at the umpire.

When the Dodgers played their last game at Ebbets Field, Gladys Gooding ended things by playing "Say It Ain't So."

When Carlton Fisk hit his game-winning home run in Game 6 of the 1975 World Series, Red Sox organist John Kiley played Handel's Hallelujah Chorus.

At the major league All-Star Game fan festival, they let kids sit at a real live Clavinova CVP98 and play "Charge!"

For Ramsey, the central challenge of the job is fitting the music to the moment.

He compares it to playing an organ along with a silent movie, the way it always used to be done.

"All the action is on the screen or on the field," he says, "but you'd notice if the organ wasn't there. You really would."

Organ notes: In 1998, the Minnesota Twins tried to go without an organist. During the first seventh-inning stretch, hearing the canned music, the Minnesota fans booed. The organ was back by the next home stand.

Ramsey begins every ballgame the same way he begins every church service. With an opening hymn.

Roughly 20 minutes before the opening pitch, as the fans are starting to arrive, he sits at the new, theater-style organ and plays "Take Me Out to the Ballgame."

This isn't a rousing version. That's saved for the seventh-inning stretch.

It's dreamy. Ethereal. All suspended notes and sweet whispers and reminders of baseball games past.

"It's never the same," he says. "Just the mood is."

After that, after drawing people in, Ramsey settles into a complementary role.

It used to be that organists carried the whole show. Some even sang the national anthem. If there was music at the ballpark, they supplied it. Not anymore.

At AutoZone Park, there's recorded music between innings. More recorded music before each Redbird player comes up to bat.

If a Redbird hits a home run, they play the theme from The Natural. Kiley and the Hallelujah Chorus wouldn't have had a chance here.

Ramsey's time, then, is the actual playing time, when both teams are on the field.

He trills at foul balls. Riffs over a spectacular catch.

Unlike some organists, who play recognizable tunes to fit the moment, Ramsey improvises.

"It's all improvisational," he says. "I create it on the spot."

Organ notes: At Harry Caray's funeral, Sal Soria, the organist at Holy Name Cathedral, played "Take Me Out to the Ballgame" as Caray's casket was carried down the aisle. Soria needed sheet music to play the tune. "I had to sort of somber it up and slow it down," he said, "to make it a little more classy."

The bottom of the ninth, a Redbird rally dies.

The fans get up. The taped, cheery Redbird theme booms over the loudspeakers as the place empties out.

By the time Ramsey has the floor again, not many fans are left.

"Do you hear how good it sounds," he says, "with the empty seats?"

Ramsey has been playing for more than three hours. Now it's time to sum up.

"We're right back where we started," he says, "'Take Me Out to the Ballgame.'"

He plays the tune slowly again, drowsy notes hanging in the still night air. After 30 years of practice, it sounds less like an anthem than a wish come true.

JOURNALIST'S HOPE: 'TO DO THIS WITH DIGNITY AND HUMOR'
AUGUST 7, 2001

The e-mail arrived one week ago today. The subject heading: "A Candid Conversation with the Oncologist."

It was from Dennis Freeland, the sports writer — and former editor — of *The Memphis Flyer*. And it was, alas, the latest in the series.

Dennis started sending the e-mails in May, to explain to friends and colleagues why they weren't seeing him around town.

The e-mails were funny, sad, sweet and philosophical. Also, increasingly ominous.

One explained that Dennis had severely blurred vision. Another raised the possibility of multiple sclerosis. Another said the doctors had found a brain tumor. Another said the tumor was malignant.

And then came last week's e-mail. Which — with permission from Dennis — you can read for yourself:

"We talked to Dr. Schwartzburg yesterday. He was kind, compassionate, patient and seems to be very informed — just as many on this list said he would be.

"I have a glioblastoma, the most malignant and fastest-growing brain tumor. There is no cure. The recommendation is to have brain surgery to remove as much of the tumor as we can, then follow that with radiation and possibly chemotherapy.

"If all that goes well, I might live 18 months. Conversely, if we do nothing, my condition will worsen and I will die in a few months.

"I know this is hard to read. It is pretty tough to write. I wish I could at least phone all of you and tell you in person. But it is my great fortune in this life to have many friends. I hope you will understand ...

"To some, these e-mails may seem strange. But you are all my friends and I have always been an open person. In fact, the list is growing (hey, it's free — who wouldn't want to receive e-mails with such uplifting subjects as 'A Candid Conversation with the Oncologist'?).

"Whatever we decide about the treatment, I want to do this with dignity and humor. I want to make this as painless as possible for my family and friends. What I do not want is for people to feel sorry for me. It is the hand I was dealt and I will play it as best as I can."

• • •

This is a story about a friend and a sportswriter. In exactly that order.

Dennis Freeland, 45, is having brain surgery Wednesday morning. It's a dangerous procedure. One doctor told him to spend today as if it might be his last. Dennis figures he'll skip sports talk radio.

Oh, that's a joke. And it's quintessential Dennis.

Funny. Smart. Able to step back and get off a wry comment even if he has a rooting interest in the subject matter.

Usually, writers don't write about other writers. But Dennis is a part of the fabric of this town. And, besides, in his remarkable series of e-mails — all written in massive, headline-sized type, so he can see what he's written — the guy has done some of his best work lately.

Take this one. Sent immediately after receiving the biopsy results.

"I was making a mental list of all the faiths that I have saying prayers for me, mostly thanks to this list," he wrote. "Baptist, Catholic, Church of Christ, Episcopal, Islam, Judaism, Methodist, Presbyterian, Unitarian and Zoroastrian ... All of this means more to me than you can know."

Or this passage, in the same e-mail.

"You know, sending out this e-mail is like casting a net in the ocean. Regardless of the day of the week or the time of day, within 30 minutes your positive messages start coming in from all over the world. It is so cool. And makes me feel better."

Can you imagine a better metaphor than that? Laptop as fishing net?

But then, this is why Dennis has always been so good at his job. Because he doesn't look at things the way everyone else does.

When something like this comes along in the sports world — when someone gets sick, when an offensive tackle dies on the field — you read a lot of stories about how it all puts sports in perspective.

Dennis never needed the reminder.

He loves his job. You can sense this in every sentence he writes. Even now, Dennis confesses he asks his wife, Perveen, to read him the sports page.

But he can talk about music or religion or politics, too. He knows where sports fit in the hierarchy. Dennis would like to live long enough to see the Tiger football team turn things around — wouldn't we all ? — but he'd really like to live long enough to see his daughter graduate from high school.

That's why Dennis decided to have the surgery, by the way. Feroza is five. Dennis figures he still has some things to teach her. If surgery will buy him a few more birthdays, how could he not try it?

But the other day, Dennis decided to make some home movies, just in case. Of father and daughter.

So he had a friend come over and point the video camera. He and Feroza sat on their backyard swing and talked about everything.

Later, that night, Feroza came in to Dennis's bedroom, where he was lying down, exhausted.

She put one of her favorite CDs in the stereo. The Beach Boys.

"I want to spend some time with you," she said. Then she climbed on his bed and started dancing.

"It was a miraculous moment," Dennis said. "Totally unplanned and totally miraculous."

Dennis doesn't think much beyond such small moments anymore. He knows there's no cure for him.

He'd just like to wake up from surgery tomorrow and shoot a few dozen more videos, share a few hundred more dances with his daughter.

Usually, there's no cheering in the press box. But there's an image we all can pull for.

MAKING THE FAIR DECISION
MAY 12, 2002

He figured he was in trouble when he was beaten up by his wife's aerobics class.

Morris Fair, the County Commissioner, decided to stop by the class one morning and explain why he supported the new NBA arena. His wife, Diane, had warned him about the mood.

"A couple of the ladies," he said, "were very irate."

Fair tried his best to make them understand.

He explained that no property tax money would be needed to finance the bonds.

He explained that most of the money could not, by law, be used for schools.

He explained that he'd run the numbers and seen the books and determined, in balance, it was a solid, reasonable deal.

"They were not all convinced," he said. "They said that everyone knew the vast majority of my constituents were against it. I said that I respected that, but it's not my job to take a survey every time we have an issue come up. I have to make a judgment, an informed judgment, on what the best thing is.

"That got a couple really mad."

Fair laughed at this. Laughed the rueful laugh of someone who had been run out of office for doing what he thought best.

On Wednesday, Fair cast one of the 11 votes in favor of the financing package that finally ended the arena debate.

On Tuesday, Fair lost in the Republican primary to John Willingham, at least in part because of Fair's position on the NBA.

Perhaps this looks to some of you like a man who got his just due. Or perhaps it looks like democracy arriving one day too late.

But let me gently suggest that maybe, just maybe, it's evidence that the arena fight — the long and passionate arena fight — was a good deal more honorable than some would have you think.

Yes, of course, there were low moments, too. The backroom wrangling over the contractor. The appalling last-minute rush to take care of friends.

But while it's fashionable to talk about the entire process as a raw and ugly lesson in politics, it was at times much loftier than that.

It wasn't just the arena supporters who distinguished themselves, either. The name Heidi Shafer is now synonymous in this town with grassroots advocacy. Commissioner Walter Bailey risked alienating his voting base when he emerged as the most vocal political opponent of the deal.

On the other side of it, Shelby County Mayor Jim Rout may have sealed his decision to step aside with his support of the project. Clair Vander Schaaf is another arena supporter who lost his Commission seat. Linda Rendtorff barely hung on to hers.

And then there was Fair, a self-confessed numbers guy, who paid more attention to the numbers that mattered to the project and less to the numbers that mattered to his career.

Fair is 72. Too old, he says, to think about running again. He knew that the politically smart thing to do was to hammer the arena as an irrational giveaway.

But Fair is a finance geek, a man who prides himself on his ability to understand the most complicated deal. His proudest moment as a commissioner came earlier this year, when he identified and helped close a loophole in the county's health insurance plans for retired employees.

"It saved the county $40 million in future costs," he said. "But nobody wrote it up, it was like it just didn't happen."

Fair studied the arena deal with the same exacting eye. To this day, he's the only legislator to get a look at the Grizzlies' books.

"I would not consider agreeing to a lease with any tenant if I didn't understand their financial condition," he said. "They said they couldn't let me see them. I said, 'Fine, you won't get my vote.'"

Next thing you know, Fair had the books. It was typical of his entire approach. Others hollered. He studied, tweaked and improved. He insisted that, if the Grizzlies were sold and moved out of town, the city and county would get the huge buyout due under the lease before Michael Heisley got a cent. His emphasis was on the dull and vitally important details.

And then, when enough of the details fit, he concluded that, yes, the deal made sense.

"I became comfortable with the whole scenario," he said. "That our bonds will get paid. That we will not pay a single penny out of city-county debt service. That the numbers work."

The problem, of course, is that it's hard to sell this to the populace. Spread-sheet analysis doesn't go far in a sound-bite world.

How do you make people understand that there was no vast pot of money to go to the arena or schools? Or that most of the dollars came from fees restricted to tourism and nothing else? Or that the Grizzlies had nothing to do with last year's heating and tax bills?

Fair invited any of his constituents to come by and go through the math with him. Exactly two of them took him up on the offer.

And then they voted him out. Then they sent this thoughtful, exacting man to the political sidelines for good.

That's their right, too, of course. Fair is as quick to say this as anyone. We elect our representatives to make decisions on our behalf. Then, if we don't like what they do, we try someone else.

So Fair's wife went back to her aerobics class late in the week, wondering what the reaction to the vote would be. Some of the women were conciliatory.

"And some said nothing at all," Fair said, "which meant they were glad."

Either way, they should understand that Fair did something you don't always see anymore, something that deserves a tip of the hat.

He used his best judgment. He paid with his seat.

An exercise in courage is what you could call that.

NO PRESSURE, AS LONG AS NEW ARENA IS PERFECT
AUGUST 11, 2002

A nine-year-old boy in Tullahoma fidgets. His family tries to distract him.

"Sit here with your uncle," someone says.

His uncle is a draftsman.

The boy picks up a mechanical pencil and starts to draw. Buildings. Houses.

Two hours later, the boy is still drawing.

"You should be an architect," someone says.

The boy looks up, curious.

"What's an architect?"

• • •

Thirty-seven years later, Frank Ricks, architect, points his car downtown and heads for the massive NBA arena construction site.

It's Sunday. There's absolutely no need for Ricks to be at the site on this day.

"I just wanted to see it," he says. "To think about some things."

Ricks studies the way the project fits into the area.

He frets about the scale of the arena compared to the neighborhood.

"There's a danger," he says, "that it will look like it just crashed here."

And a danger that people will hate it.

And a danger that they'll never stop talking about the cost.

And, well, you see the challenge facing Ricks and the rest of the architects charged with designing the biggest, most expensive public building this town has ever seen.

Like it or not, the thing is going up. Two years from now, barring disaster, the Grizzlies will move into their new home.

Will it be a triumph like Camden Yards? Will it be a flop like Comerica Park?

Will it drive a bigger wedge into the community? Or help shrink the one that's there?

A great building can do that, you know. Look at AutoZone Park.

During the construction process, many Memphians were deeply skeptical of that project. A certain disaster, some said. Why did they have to put it down there?

Then the place opened and everybody shut up.

Oh. Now we understand.

Looney Ricks Kiss — that's Frank Ricks's firm — was the local architect for AutoZone Park, too. Ricks will tell you right up front that the NBA arena is more of a challenge.

It's much bigger, for starters. In both dollars and square feet.

It's a basketball arena, not a ballpark. There's no blue sky.

Beyond all that, the arena has been the subject of a civic brawl. George Flinn's opinion notwithstanding, the recent election didn't remotely end the debate.

So all Ricks and the national architectural firm, Ellerbe Becket, have to do is get it perfect. Which, of course, Ricks understands.

"There's always pressure to do great work," he says. "We have our own standards, to begin with. But when it's a civic building, is there more pressure?

"Sure."

• • •

The subject is urban planning. It sounds a lot like lawn care.

"You know how you sprig sod?" Ricks asks. "You put in new sprigs of grass, you water it, till it and try to get it to grow together.

"That's what we're trying to do here. To plant something that will create more growth and renew the entire area."

Ricks is passionate about this topic. He doesn't talk much about all the neat stuff inside the arena. He talks endlessly about the impact it could have.

In some ways, it seems as if he's trying to build an arena that will be the exact opposite of its predecessor. The Pyramid is a building with a really cool exterior that says "Look at me." The new arena will be a building with a modest exterior that says "Look inside." Or, better yet, "Look around."

"This arena is going to be humongous," Ricks says. "What we're trying to do is find a way to blend it in the middle of this small-scale neighborhood in a way that benefits both."

They're doing this by breaking the building into smaller parts. The core will be the round court section, or the drum. It will be flashy, metallic and new. All around it will be smaller, more intimate sections, done mostly in red brick.

There will be an office building on Third, across from Gibson guitar.

There will be a tight pedestrian alley on the back side of Beale.

There will be trees and grass along Fourth, across from Church Park.

"What we hope is when you get there, you'll almost feel like you're driving through a park and the arena just happens to be a part of it," Ricks says.

"It's the same if you're walking down the Beale Street alley. We want you to feel like it's been there for a while."

• • •

When Ricks goes to a game at AutoZone Park, he still wonders how it would look with the restaurant in right.

It was in the final plans. A lively barbecue restaurant with a big deck that would have been open even when the park was not.

"There's something called value-engineering," Ricks says. "It got cut out."

Which bring us to the following point: Even in a $250 million arena, everything can't be exactly the way you'd prefer.

Take the domed roof, for example, the one that's been revealed in sketches and looks a bit too much like the Mid-South Coliseum for some tastes.

"It's a financial issue," Ricks says. "A dome is inherently rigid and self-supporting."

Ricks picks up a piece of paper to demonstrate. When he bends it into a dome, it holds. When he holds it out flat, it sags.

"If you did this with a piece of cardboard, it would hold," he says. "You need stronger material. In an arena, that means more steel.

"So then you have to make a value judgment. Would you rather put the money where fans can see it and touch it?"

The architects went with the dome. They then softened it by adding an illuminated cornice around the top of the building that will cut off the view of the dome from the street. At night, when the cornice is lit up, it will give the building a halo effect.

"It's a compromise," Ricks says. "Everything is."

• • •

Ricks moved from Tullahoma to Memphis to go to Memphis State. He figured at the time he'd get his degree and go back home.

But he grew to love the place. He saw some opportunities here. It's funny how life works.

More than two decades later, the firm Ricks started with two other Memphis graduates — Carson Looney and Richard Kiss — has designed some of the most important buildings we have. The new library. The AutoZone corporate offices. The FedEx technology center in Collierville. AutoZone Park.

Nobody can say how the new arena will rank with those, of course. Only that it will be designed with care.

Lately, for example, Ricks has been thinking about St. Patrick's. It's on Fourth, on the back side of the building. It could easily get lost.

So Ricks and his colleagues have decided to recess parts of the arena along Fourth, and to illuminate the church spire.

"I don't think anyone is going to say, 'Hey, I'm glad they moved that wall back so they can see St. Pat's,'" Ricks says. "But subconsciously, people notice small things like that.

"We're not just building an icon. We're building a city, too."

RADIO FAMILY LOSES A VOICE
FEBRUARY 22, 2004

The old woman sat in her chair, her usual chair, as her final few hours dwindled away.

She figured it was time. She had said, more than once, she figured it was time two years ago.

Her neighbor came to sit with her. At one point the neighbor asked if the old woman wanted to go to a doctor. This drew a sharp reaction.

"Why do you want to send me to a doctor?" the old woman snapped.

She preferred her chair. The two women sat together. It was quiet except for the radio, an old battery-operated model that sat on an end table.

About 1 p.m. the old woman had asked her neighbor to flip it on. She wanted to listen to her sports shows. That's how she thought of them too. As her shows.

So the two of them sat and listened as the old woman's breathing grew labored.

They listened as her color started to change.

They listened as afternoon became evening, as a day and a life slipped away.

"She never asked me to cut it off and I wasn't going to," the neighbor said. "She was Mary from Midtown. She loved that radio."

···

Bob Phillips can hear the voice in his head right now. It makes him want to laugh, to listen, to argue, to smile.

"She had that voice," said Phillips, who co-hosted a sports talk show in the 1990s.

That voice.

That raspy, insistent, logical, unwavering voice.

"Inside of two words you knew it was Mary from Midtown," Phillips said.

Anyone who has ever tuned a radio to sports talk in this city knows Mary from Midtown.

They know her inflection, her sensibility, her profound love of tradition, sportsmanship, Memphis, the Razorbacks, the Braves and — especially — talk.

She called everyone. All the time. She called local shows and national shows; she called early and called late.

"There were times I'd be driving late at night and I'd hear her on one of the national feeds," Phillips said. "I'd say, 'There's Mary. I guess she can't sleep tonight.'"

Radio permits this kind of familiarity — almost intimacy — between listeners, callers and hosts. Mary came to feel like a friend, or a grandmother, or an elderly aunt.

And yet she was an enigma too. She was Mary from Midtown. No last name.

Was she married? Was she loved? Why did she call so much? Why did we care to know?

But when her voice disappeared from the airwaves in January, when word started to circulate that she might have died, it left a mystery that seemed oddly important to solve.

"I always imagined her sitting at her kitchen table, listening to the radio and smoking a cigarette," said Dave Woloshin, who has had a talk show in Memphis for 21 years. "But I'm guessing. I didn't even know her last name."

Tobey.

That was her last name. John Stamm, executive news editor at *The Commercial Appeal*, recalled it somehow.

The newspaper's library found a Mary Tobey who lived on Stonewall in Midtown. Born on Dec. 20, 1916. With a Social Security number that said she was from Arkansas.

The library had some phone numbers of neighbors too. One of them was Lee Sanford.

"Yes, that's her, Mary from Midtown," Sanford said. "She was always calling those radio shows.

"She was private. She didn't let anyone but me inside her house. But she loved to talk and she had that voice."

Ahh, that voice again. Sanford has an explanation.

"She smoked unfiltered cigarettes," she said. "When she stopped driving I'd go to the store and buy her eight or nine cartons.

"She smoked Pall Malls, but they went out. So then I bought Markers, but they stopped making them, too.

"She finally said, 'Just buy me filtered cigarettes, I'll pinch the filter off and smoke that.' And that's what she did."

Sanford is reluctant to talk about Mary because Mary was reluctant to talk about herself.

Except for Sanford, none of Mary's other neighbors knew about her lively radio life.

"I never heard that," said Ules Mabone, who lived across the street from Mary for 20 years. "But that's how she was. If I was a child of 7 or 8 I would have thought that was the scary lady's house.

"But she wasn't scary, she just lived in her own world."

Mary didn't have children. Her husband, Ed, died in 1985.

A long time ago Mary worked as a buyer for Lowenstein's. She had a terrier and a sign on her back fence that said "Beware of Dog."

Mary loved music. Especially jazz. She listened to vinyl records and never switched to CDs.

She kept an eye on the neighborhood. She also kept an eye on Sanford's children.

"Her husband died in 1985 and my husband died in 1983," Sanford said. "We were kind of in it together after that."

Mary made cookies for Sanford's kids after school. She always remembered their birthdays.

"And then, about 10 years after her husband died, it was like she started to give up," Sanford said. "She called me and she said that if I promised never to take her to the hospital or a care home, she'd leave her house and everything to me so I wouldn't have to work anymore."

Sanford was true to her word. For the last two decades she watched out for her friend.

"We talked a lot," Sanford said. "She loved to talk, especially about sports. Sometimes she'd buy me season tickets to go to the games and then I'd tell her what I'd seen."

On Jan. 8, when Sanford went to check on Mary, she realized her friend was in a bad way.

There was no particular diagnosis. She had lived 87 years, that's all.

They listened to the radio together. Shortly after 8 p.m., Mary died.

"The radio was still on when the ambulance came to carry her away," Sanford said. "I don't know why, but I didn't cut it off."

Mary was taken from her house to a funeral home. She was cremated. There was no memorial service, no plaque or stone.

"That's what she wanted," Sanford said, "so that's what I did."

It's a melancholy end, just the same. A woman with such a deep love of history leaving no trace of her own.

No kids. No memorial. Just the memory of a voice, an ethic and a heart.

"Radio is different," Phillips said. "It almost feels like family. It's hard to think she's made all those calls for all those years and won't make them anymore."

Mary's number is inactive, by the way. The message is one she might have ordered up herself.

"The number you have reached has been disconnected," it says. "No additional information is available at this time."

ROBERTS PROVES GRACE, SUCCESS GREAT PAIRING

Decker Ploehn has a Loren Roberts story. But, then, doesn't everyone?

Ploehn is on the Board of Directors of the John Deere Classic. He's in town for the Memphis tournament.

"Last year, it rained real hard at our tournament," Ploehn said. "Loren wrote a note to our grounds crew thanking them for having the course in such good shape.

"They stuck it up on the wall. They were just ecstatic to get that note. It made them feel really appreciated."

• • •

Joan Matthews is a scorekeeper at the FedEx St. Jude Classic. The other day, she was assigned to the group that included Roberts.

"I've been doing this a long time," she said, "but I saw something I'd never seen before."

Kevin Sutherland hit a ball in the water on No. 11. At least, it looked like it was in the water.

"Loren said, 'Don't drop it yet, let me go up and check,'" Matthews said.

It was raining, hard. Roberts took off.

"He's running up to the green in the rain," Matthews said. "I've never seen a pro do that for another pro."

• • •

Skyler Clayton is 12. He plays at Pine Hill. He's a city kid trying to learn a country club game.

Clayton and some buddies followed Roberts last week.

Who's your favorite golfer, Clayton?

"Tiger Woods," he said.

Who's your next favorite?

"Loren Roberts."

Why?

"He helped me with my swing," Clayton said. "He's really nice."

• • •

Bill Fesmire is a pediatrician. He takes care of Roberts's kids. Sometimes, he follows Roberts to tournaments.

"Everywhere we go, we meet people from around the country who got to know Loren at their own tournament," Fesmire said. "It could be someone who worked the ropes. It could be anyone. They meet the guy and become instant Loren Roberts fans.

"He's huge in Milwaukee. I mean, huge.

"We went to the Major League All-Star game in Milwaukee in 2002. Loren is sitting six rows behind Cal Ripken Jr. And people are coming up to him, walking right past Ripken, and asking for Loren's autograph."

• • •

Shaun Micheel was nervous. It was Sunday at the 2003 PGA and he was tied for the lead with Chad Campbell.

Micheel had never won anything on Tour. He often struggled on weekends.

When Micheel got to his locker, he found a handwritten note from Roberts.

"You're as good as anybody out here," the note said. "Go out and win the tournament."

• • •

Early April 2004. Roberts has not qualified for the Masters. He is competing, instead, for the Dog Pound Championship.

This is something his buddies cooked up. When he plays badly, they send him dog bones.

"One year we sent a dog bone the size of an umbrella to Quad Cities," said David Sayle. "We had it delivered to his locker."

This day, they're playing at Spring Creek. To take their friend's mind off what he's missing. Four against one. They beat the snot out of him.

"He had to pick up the tab at the Rendezvous," said Sayle. "I will say he complained about that a little bit.

"But he's a great friend. He's a regular guy. Did you know that at his tournament he stuffs his own goody bags?

"Any other player would let someone else do that. Not Loren. If anybody's stuffing goody bags, he's going to be right there with them."

• • •

The year was 1999. Roberts won the Byron Nelson.

The win came with a check for $540,000. Right off the top, Roberts donated $100,000 of it to Le Bonheur Children's Medical Center.

"I thought about it on the flight home," he said. "I thought it was the right thing to do."

• • •

Roberts hits his tee shot on No. 9. He turns, gets two water bottles and gives them to a woman in the gallery.

"We go to church together," said Martha Hester, who got the bottles. "He offered them to an older man first. Then he asked me if I needed some water.

"I guess it's kind of unusual for a golfer to think about someone in the gallery during a round."

• • •

Another year, another disappointment. Loren Roberts will not win the tournament he'd so love to win. He shot a 67 Saturday and is 14 strokes behind David Toms.

But if you have kids, and you're coming out today, you'd do well to go see Roberts.

To show them that it's possible. Even in these tricky times.

You can be a pro and still conduct yourself with generosity and class.

WILEY'S GIFTS ARE WORTH LEARNING
JUNE 20, 2004

The phone rings at Melrose High School. A woman named Kathleen picks it up.

No, she has never heard of Ralph Wiley. No, there has not been any talk of him this week.

Kathleen takes a message. Could the principal return a call, talk about what Wiley meant to the place?

She writes this down. The principal does not return the call.

It's a slow week at Melrose. School is out for the year.

Kathleen does not know if or when Wiley graduated from Melrose. She can't really place him, she says.

Silence.

Wiley, Ralph Wiley.

"Is he someone special?" she asks.

• • •

How would Wiley react to this? What would he do with this revelation, this humbling bit of news?

Would he laugh? Would he shake his head? Would he come to the defense of Kathleen because, geez, what did she ever do to anyone?

We cannot know. Wiley is dead. He is dead and silenced and anyone who knew the man will tell you the silenced part couldn't have happened any other way.

So we turn to Richard Lapchick, one of the foremost thinkers about the role of sports in America, who also happened to be Wiley's close friend.

Should they know Wiley at Melrose? Should they remember this member of the Class of 1970?

"Not only should they remember him," Lapchick says, "they should name a school after him."

Pause.

"I'm not kidding. I'm serious. They should name a school after him."

Wiley died last week, of heart failure, too young at 52. The obituaries noted he was from Memphis.

Until that moment, how many knew? Wiley from Memphis? You don't say.

It's not just Kathleen, either. It's everyone, it's us.

We remember our sports heroes. We memorize them, celebrate them, know them by heart.

Let me tell you the story of Larry Finch. Let me tell you the story of Ronnie Robinson.

Hell, let me tell you the story of Tim Thompson or David Paine.

But a book hero? A learning hero?

A kid from Orange Mound who made it on the strength of his words and his thought?

"Nobody knows the guy," says Jimmy Scott. "It's kind of sad."

Scott is another Melrose graduate, Class of '90. He was captain of the track and football teams.

Scott remembers reading Wiley in *Sports Illustrated* and discovering — heart pounding in his chest — that Wiley went to Melrose, too.

"It changed my life," Scott says. "I started reading everything I could get my hands on. Ralph Wiley went to Melrose? It shows what you can do."

Scott would tell his teammates about this small miracle. They'd look at him funny, shrug.

"Richard Cooper was the guy everyone wanted to be back then," he says. "He played in the NFL.

"Those are the guys we love. Nobody has a clue about Ralph Wiley. They don't know him, but they should."

They should know that he was born in Memphis. That his father died young. That his mother, Dorothy, taught at S.A. Owen College — since merged into LeMoyne-Owen — and read incessantly to her son.

"Until I was 18," Wiley once said, "I never slept where I could not reach my hand from my bed to my bookcase."

Wiley delivered the *Press-Scimitar*. At Melrose, he played football and ran track. He went to Knox College, busted up his knee, and so much for the athletic career.

So he took a Greyhound bus to Oakland, where he got a job as a newspaper copyboy.

The copyboy became the beat writer became the columnist.

The columnist became the author became the regular on TV.

Wiley wrote 28 cover stories for *Sports Illustrated*. He wrote several books, including *Why Black People Tend to Shout*. He ghosted a book with Spike Lee, was a regular on ESPN and helped transform this country's notion of what a sports and social commentator should be.

"Not only was he a great writer with a great body of work, but we're talking about our first African-American sports writer who was in the mainstream," Lapchick says. "He was pretty much one of one."

ESPN's Tom Friend called him "the Black voice of his journalism generation."

Philadelphia Daily News columnist Bill Conlin called him "the black Dick Schaap."

And he did it all through intellect. Through learning. Think there's a lesson there?

"Since when did learning at school become 'acting White?'" Wiley wrote. "Why isn't robbing, stealing, drinking, carousing, and spreading illnesses considered 'acting White'? Who makes up the rules on what is Black and what is White? Now that's something I don't understand. I'd rather have learning at school called 'acting Black.'"

This was a constant theme to Wiley's work. He wrote a story about Penny Hardaway the year Hardaway had to sit out as a Prop 48. Here's how it ends:

"Anfernee Hardaway goes down into bright rooms marked Tiger Academics beneath the field house. Billy Smith bops in, followed by the more deliberate Anthony Douglas. There is no ball here. No cheering. Hardaway opens a book of stories. It is, by far, his best move of the day."

So yes, Memphis, Wiley is someone special. He should be remembered and celebrated and held up as a reminder that there is another way.

Name a school after him. That's a fine idea. In the meantime, there's something else.

Wiley once said that he had a credo. OK, he said he had many credos, but he singled out this one.

We should find a place for it at the Central Library. Put it on a banner at Melrose and hang it high.

It's Wiley, restless and certain.

"I know what I know, and I know it is never enough."

WITH GRACE AND HUMOR, COACH FINDS WAY HOME
AUGUST 9, 2006

The subject came up as they spread Derrick Barton's ashes in the garden at Grace St. Luke's Episcopal Church.

It was a sunny day in March, sad and beautiful all at once.

Barton had lived a grand life, brimming with friendship and adventure. He was born in London, he served as a commando in World War II, he played Wimbledon, represented England in the Davis Cup, then moved to Memphis and made it his home.

Joe Porter is the priest in charge of outreach and pastoral care at Grace St. Luke's. He was there as Barton's ashes were spread and lifted by a slight wind.

Which is when the idea came to him.

"Wouldn't it be wonderful if some of Derrick's ashes could be spread in England?" he mused.

Amelia Barton, Barton's wife, considered this possibility.

"What a lovely idea," she said. "You think we could?"

• • •

This is a small story, a story about a coach you may not have heard of, and a game you may not follow, with an ending — ahhh, the ending — you may want to keep close to your heart.

Derrick Barton coached tennis, not football. He didn't make a fortune, he made friends.

"Derrick just had a way about him," said James Megar, who played for Barton at Rhodes. "He touched everyone he met."

But that's not what Barton seemed destined for, back when he was the best junior tennis player in England.

By the time he was 14, he was 6-4, 200 pounds. At a junior tournament, his mum heard the complaints.

"This is supposed to be for juniors," said another parent, just within earshot, "not for freaks of nature."

Barton became the No. 1 junior in Europe. He had surpassing power and even better control.

He would wind up playing at Centre Court at Wimbledon, anyone could see that.

Except the Germans overran Poland. Soon, the continent was aflame.

Barton — big enough that people didn't ask questions — became a British commando at 15.

And that was the end of his career as one of the world's elite tennis players. The war occupied his prime years.

Oh, he would play again when the war ended. He made it into the field at Wimbledon and represented England in the Davis Cup.

But he never competed for titles. That opportunity had come and gone.

"He was never bitter," said Amelia, his wife. "It wasn't in his nature. It wouldn't even occur to him to think like that."

Barton would just do something else with his life. Which turned out to be teaching tennis, first at Davidson, then Rhodes.

Tommy Buford, one of his players, called Barton "the foundation for modern tennis" in Memphis, and the man was at least that.

Barton taught at the University Club for more than three decades. He coached 20 years at Rhodes.

But it's not his longevity people remember. It's his gentle, funny way.

Every tennis coach shapes forehands and backhands. This tennis coach shaped lives.

"In the last year, I talked to a lot of his old players and they all said the same thing," Megar said. "When you add it all up, we spent a relatively small time with him, but he had a tremendous impact on us.

"For me, that meant showing me how a man's supposed to act. The gentleness, the way he treated people. I wanted to be like him."

Barton retired in 1983. This spring, after 82 years of living, he suffered two strokes. When it became apparent he wouldn't recover, he asked to go home.

"Amelia and I were both with him when he died," said Margaret Chancey, Barton's daughter. "It was a beautiful day, and there was an English song playing in the background. Amelia said, 'Listen, Derrick, to the song.'"

And that would be the end of the story, except for what happened a few days later, when Joe Porter suggested spreading some ashes in England, too.

As it happened, the Archbishop of Canterbury was in Memphis for the Lenten lecture series at Calvary Episcopal Church. As it happened, Porter had met the Archbishop a time or two.

"I went to see him," Porter said. "I took some ashes in an envelope. He said he remembered me and I just told him, 'Well, I have kind of a special request ...'"

Porter explained the story. The Archbishop nodded, as if people asked him this sort of thing every day.

"I think we could get these scattered at Wimbledon," he said.

Whoa.

Wimbledon? Porter had never even considered that.

"We were just trying to get them to England," he said. "He was the next one headed out."

The family was moved, stunned.

"For him to offer to do that," Amelia said, "how do you put it in words?"

But a week passed. Then a month. Maybe the Archbishop had forgotten or something.

"We just didn't know," said Margaret, Barton's daughter.

So she sat down composed an e-mail. She thanked the Archbishop for his thoughtfulness.

"I wondered," she then wrote, "if in fact you had been able to scatter them."

The next day, she had an e-mail in her box. This is what it said:

Dear Margaret,

I am sending you this e-mail from the Royal Box at Wimbledon. I have placed Derrick's ashes directly outside the Royal Box at Centre Court.

"I was just flabbergasted," she said. "I started calling everyone I could think of. To have the ashes scattered outside the Royal Box during the tournament itself? It's the perfect ending for my dad."

And somehow, it's a lesson, too. About grace in the face of life's turns. About humility and perseverance and good-humored faith.

Barton was supposed to end up at Centre Court at Wimbledon, anyone could see that.

All these decades later — after a life of kindness and service — he finally did.

GREG HANEY WROTE THIS HEADLINE
MAY 2, 2007

But then, Greg Haney has written hundreds of headlines, thousands of headlines, although, since it's Haney, and he'll edit this column, too, he'll probably want to see the math.

As a copy editor at The CA, Haney writes 8-10 headlines a night. Call it nine, on average. Multiplied by five nights a week. Multiplied by 50 weeks a year. Multiplied by the 20 years that have passed since he gave up reporting — after a decade — to work on the editing desk.

So Haney has written approximately 45,000 headlines for you to read over your morning biscuits and coffee. This is his last.

Haney, 59, is one of those who accepted the buyout package recently offered by E.W. Scripps. He had on a Hawaiian shirt when he showed up for his last night of work at 4 p.m. He had a dinner of Chinese takeout with two fortune cookies.

First cookie: "Romance is about to blossom."

Huh. Greg's been married to Karin for 38 years. But now he won't be working nights!

Second cookie: "Your principles mean more to you than money or success."

Haney held this one up in triumph.

"There you go," he said. "That's for all of us."

Which was quintessential Haney, really. The man can't even keep a complimentary fortune for himself.

He has to try to spread it around. Make everyone else look good. Small wonder he was such a fine copy editor.

That's the essential job description, after all: Make everyone else look good.

Write snappy headlines. Catch every mistake. Take the stories sent to you by cranky, self-inflated reporters and make them read like poetry.

This last part is not always easy, but Haney's two-year hitch with the Peace Corps probably helped.

"I was a media volunteer," he said. "They assigned me to the Micronesian Islands, a place called Truk."

Haney ran a small newspaper in Truk. Half of the paper was in English, half in Trukese.

"I got so I could figure out what it said," he said. After which, editing your typical football or basketball writer was a breeze.

But you still have to want to do it, still have to care about the job.

There's not much glory in fixing someone else's mixed-up metaphor. There's no Pulitzer Prize given for outstanding work on the scoreboard or agate page.

There's the considerably subtler satisfaction of being part of an enterprise, of knowing the newspaper was better in the morning because of the work you did the night before.

Haney felt this to his bones. He was often more obsessed than the writers about getting it exactly right.

So he picked up the phone and called them. To ask for clarification, to understand a particular nuance.

"When your phone rang, you knew it was Haney," said Zack McMillin, who has worked in news and sports. "It had a special Haney ring."

The guy was just more careful than most. About pretty much everything.

One day, Haney dropped his lunch all over the parking lot. He wheeled and headed back to the car with the following explanation: "I have a backup lunch."

Tuesday afternoon, right on schedule, he reported to work, shared some ceremonial cake, then set about doing his job one last time. He edited a brief about the Cardinals. He wrote the headline about the Memphis-Ole Miss baseball game. He said he "lamented" the economic pressures on newspapers today and most of us do.

Earlier this week, Letterman offered up the "Top Ten Signs Your Newspaper is in Trouble." No. 7 was: "All horoscopes: 'Now would be a good time to get out of the newspaper business.'"

Everyone is making cuts. Los Angeles, Philadelphia, Dallas, Orlando. They're tempting or pushing their Greg Haneys out the door and it's hard to know how this improves the enterprise.

Haney himself is typically upbeat. He says he's looking forward to getting in shape and cleaning out his car. After decades of neglecting both, he figures it's about time.

He also figures he's had the best job in the world. And that journalism — and this paper — will do just fine. People need stories today as much as they ever have. They even need their scores.

Speaking of which, Haney still had some work to do. He had to proof the final changes to the agate page.

Sometime around 11 p.m., as the delivery trucks idled behind the newspaper building, he turned to Gary Mangum, the designer in charge for the night, and said it just the way he always has.

"Mr. Mangum, the agate page is gone," he said.

And then, after 30 years, so was he.

III

UNIVERSITY
OF MEMPHIS
BASKETBALL

YEAR ON THE BRINK?
NOVEMBER 24, 1996

Larry Finch eases his Isuzu Trooper into a space along Park, honks, waves, starts talking before the truck door even closes behind him.

"I told you I'd bring you one," Finch says. "Don't I always bring you one? Of course I do, and you know it."

Finch is talking to three men gathered on the steps leading up to Gooden's Hair & Skin Care, a simple, worn-around-the-edges barber shop and hair salon in Orange Mound, the part of Memphis where Finch grew up. This is where Finch gets his hair cut. This is where Finch has gotten his hair cut since before he can remember.

Finch is delivering University of Memphis basketball schedules. He goes to the back of the truck, lifts the heavy door, peels off three, four, five schedules from a pile, hands them to his friends. Then he is off again, with another wave, another honk, off to the shop where he gets his shoes repaired, or the shop where he gets his shoes shined, or a restaurant.

Finch, 45, does this before every basketball season. It's startling, really. Imagine Kentucky coach Rick Pitino delivering schedules all over Lexington; imagine North Carolina coach Dean Smith delivering schedules all over Chapel Hill; imagine Georgetown coach John Thompson delivering schedules all over Washington.

But Finch is a part of his community in a way those coaches are not; he is a product of his community in the way even these most revered of coaches can never be; he grew up in Memphis, played basketball in Memphis, coached in Memphis, has become a part of the Memphis fabric.

"Larry Finch is Memphis basketball," says his former college coach, UAB athletic director Gene Bartow. "It is as simple as that."

But as Finch stands on the threshold of his second decade as head coach of the Tigers, nothing seems so simple as that. Finch is under siege. In the same way that the 1995-96 season was about Lorenzen Wright, that the 1992-93 season was about Penny Hardaway, this season is about Finch. The team is a modest and unfamiliar collection of athletes. Finch will have to do a fine coaching job to get it to finish above .500. The pressing, intriguing questions about the season seem to surround the coach himself: Is he losing his touch? Can he still recruit? Will his 11th season as head coach of the Tigers also be his last?

Finch is in no mood to discuss any of this; not now, anyway. He's got places to go, schedules to deliver. Next stop, the shoe repair shop. Finch gets out. Peels off another schedule. Hands it across a counter. Smiles, shakes a hand, heads for the door.

"Now, you support the Tigers, OK?" Finch says, over his shoulder, on the way out. "And we'll see you next year."

• • •

The Pyramid is filling, fans shuffling in, all to get a first glimpse of the new edition of the Tigers. The players are skimming through warm-ups, the band is bright and brassy, the cheerleaders are in relentless good cheer. But on what is supposed to be a grand opening for a new season of Memphis basketball — even if the opening is an exhibition game against something called the Geelong Supercats — the mood is subdued, the talk all about Finch.

"I wish Finch was the guy," says Joey Lucchesi, a Memphis graduate, a season-ticket holder. "I like him personally. But I think he's losing control of the program. It might be getting to be time for him to go."

Time for him to go? That's a joke, right? Finch has won 204 games, averaged 20.4 wins a season, led the Tigers to the NCAA Tournament in six out of the nine years in which they were eligible. And his last two years have been two of his best, as he coached and cajoled the Tigers to back-to-back conference championships.

"Larry wins 20 games every year," says Saint Louis coach Charlie Spoonhour. "That's the kind of bad year I'd like to have once in a while."

But there have been fissures lately, cracks in the franchise. The 1995-96 season ended with a crushing loss to Drexel in the first round of the NCAA Tournament. Five players blew off the team banquet. Season-ticket sales are down more than 1,000. Tiger Club contributions were down by more than a quarter million dollars last year. Finch has had two straight drab recruiting classes and seems on his way to a third.

Beyond all this, there is a growing sense that Finch doesn't have the energy, the imagination or the media savvy to direct a basketball program in the 1990s. He is an uninspired speaker; a defensive, sometimes irritable voice on his own radio show; a man whose profound belief in individual responsibility — "I can't put a gun to a boy's head and make him do what I want," says Finch, whether the subject is academics or drugs or recruiting — sounds too much like abdication for some tastes.

Some of the criticism of Finch is plainly driven by racism; there are fans who will never accept the coach because he is black. But that doesn't obscure legitimate concerns over the direction of the program.

"Looking at it from afar, I assumed that things were in pretty good shape," says R.C. Johnson, athletic director at Memphis. "I thought that because of the success that was here, the ship was sailing pretty smoothly. Now that I'm here, I've heard more things than I thought I would about the program."

The Tony Harris recruiting saga deepened and illuminated Finch's troubles. Harris is a splendid guard at East High, blessed with quickness and touch and rare vision. Tennessee wanted him. Memphis wanted him. Every major college program wanted him.

In the past, Harris would have chosen Memphis, just as Elliot Perry chose Memphis, just as Hardaway chose Memphis, just as Wright chose Memphis. Finch has relied on that tradition — a tradition he helped start — to keep talented prospects at home.

Now, it appears, tradition is not enough. The day after the Geelong exhibition, Harris held a press conference in his high school library. This newspaper sent three reporters to cover the event. Local television stations had cameras whirring away.

"Memphis is my home," said Harris. "But the University of Tennessee is my future."

And at that precise instant — frame it, freeze it, remember it as this year plays out — Finch's own future got dimmer still.

• • •

Finch is camped out at Neely's restaurant now, eating french fries three at a time. He is talking about basketball, telling stories, explaining how he settled on 21 for his jersey number.

"When I was a boy, I cut myself real bad," he says. "I got 21 stitches. I didn't feel it, but there was blood everywhere and ..."

Just then, a waiter sails past. Trips. Spills a drink all over Finch, all over his French fries, all over his tie and his suit. Finch looks stunned, then displeased, then sympathetic.

"Look at that boy," he says, softly. "He's terrified. He can't help himself. Catastrophes happen."

This is typical Finch; sunny, sweet, forgiving. Not many relish the idea of Finch failing as coach of the Tigers, or at least not many who have met him. He is a sensitive man, a man who can't drive on the South Campus of the university without an involuntary shudder, because that is where his father died, back when Finch was a boy and the South Campus was a hospital.

Finch may also be the closest thing to a fairy tale this town has ever known. He grew up in Orange Mound, no indoor plumbing, a mother who took home $5.50 a day cleaning house, $5 for labor and 50 cents for the bus fare.

"I wanted to be a fireman," Finch says. "How many big-time jobs could black kids want years ago?"

Finch became a basketball player instead, first for Melrose, then for Memphis. He had a sweet shot, a persistent smile, a key role on the Memphis team that lost to UCLA in the NCAA title game in 1973, electrifying and unifying the city in the process.

But a strange thing has happened over the course of Finch's career. People have forgotten the Finch they grew up with. Finch the cheerful player has morphed into Finch the dour coach.

"People don't remember old No. 21," says Kenny Moody, who played on the first Memphis team Finch coached. "Even I have forgotten him. Now I think of him as Coach Finch, and that's too bad. That's wrong."

Finch is seen as an issue, more than an individual. The details of his life are lost amid the shouting. He likes horror movies ("real scary ones"), doesn't invest in the stock market ("stocks are gambling"), has a swimming pool he has rarely used ("my kids use it"), is thrifty about everything but clothes ("my wife calls me cheap") and has a listed telephone number ("the kids would give it out anyway").

He is also the sort of person who feels sorry for a waiter who drenches him with a drink. This is not necessarily a good thing for a man in his position.

"Larry hurts," says Rev. W.A. 'Bill' Adkins, a close friend of Finch. "He cries. He cries a lot.

"He does not have the kind of thick skin that a basketball coach needs."

• • •

Finch frowns at the question. He is happy to talk about basketball; happy to talk about his childhood; not so happy to talk about whether he expects to be coaching the Tigers at this time next year.

"That's negative," he says. "I won't dwell on the negative. I'm a positive person."

Finch shrugs. Topic closed. The guy has four years to go on his contract. Four years at $110,000 in base salary, more for television and radio. He is too smart to walk away from that package. Too competitive to walk away from coaching.

"One thing about Coach Finch, he wants to win," says John Wilfong, who played for Finch and his predecessor, Dana Kirk, at Memphis. "I've been around a lot of coaches who wanted to win for what it did for them: more money, the chance to get another job, the chance to be in the limelight. Dana was like that. Well, Larry doesn't care about the limelight. He just wants to win."

So maybe that is how this basketball season will go. Maybe Finch will rally his overmatched team, win more games than anyone expects, get carried off the court on the shoulders of fans with a renewed appreciation for his talents.

Finch laughs out loud at the notion. Not at the part about the wins. The part about the shoulders. After 10 years as head coach, 10 years and more wins than anyone in Memphis history, he understands he is not going to change anybody's mind about his style or his program.

Besides, the ultimate measure of Finch may not be wins and losses, but dollars and cents.

"If it's about wins and losses, of course he should be here," says Moody. "But it's about selling tickets, it's about making donations, it's about being accessible. In the end, it's like everything else. It's about making money."

In that respect, the basketball program is not doing as well as some would like. Season tickets to the basketball program have dipped from 14,003 in 1991-92, to 10,584 last season, to 9,259 by Friday. Fund-raisers for the athletic department have admitted running into resistance because of Finch.

"It's a lot harder," says Bill Koeneman, a member of the Tiger Club board of directors, who says he supports Finch. "They're just down on Larry so bad. Anybody we talked to about it, the boosters that I have got to talk to, just everybody ..."

Finch can't fight this. He can't make people buy tickets. He can't make them give money. He can't or won't or doesn't know how. So he occupies himself doing what he does best: coaching his team; teaching his players; making his rounds.

And passing out schedules for a year he knows could be his last.

GOOD GUY FINISHES AHEAD
MARCH 2, 1997

Bob Huggins strode across the basketball court, head down, scowling. The Cincinnati coach had just watched his team lose to Memphis. So he veered over toward the table where Memphis coach Larry Finch was holding his radio press conference and took the microphone from Finch's hand.

Huggins hesitated for a moment, looked at Finch.

"I just want to say congratulations," said Huggins. "To a guy who might want to think about running for mayor."

Everybody laughed. Finch shrugged. That's the sort of Saturday it was at The Pyramid, where 13,125 showed up to watch a celebration of Finch that ended better than anyone could have scripted.

Talk about a smashing exit. Finch had the wing of a building named after him during pregame ceremonies: the new practice gym, the Larry O. Finch Recreation Complex. Then he watched his team go out and whip Cincinnati, 75-63, by playing its best basketball of the season.

By the time the day was over, you half expected Memphis president V. Lane Rawlins to search out Finch and offer the guy a raise if he'd forget the whole unpleasant business.

Rawlins resisted the urge. He and athletic director R. C. Johnson must be silently grateful they canned Finch when they still had a chance. After Saturday's win (which improved Memphis's record against ranked opponents to 5-0) sentiment for Finch is running higher than ever.

"We love you," said state Sen. Steve Cohen, greeting Finch after the game had ended. "Everyone loves you."

Everyone doesn't love Finch, of course, at least not as head coach. Otherwise he'd be sticking around to practice in that new gym. But even those who are growing weary of Finch farewell games — and this was not the last one, not with the Conference USA Tournament and a postseason tournament yet to come — had to marvel at the way this one turned out.

"Historic," said Avron Fogelman.

"Tremendous," said Sunday Adebayo.

Finch arrived to a standing ovation. He took nearly 30 minutes to make his way around the court, shaking hands, signing autographs. Finch still was standing in a group of fans when they played the national anthem.

"OK," said Finch, putting down his pen. "I'll be back after."

Then the game started. What a game it was. Cedric Henderson scored 24 points. Chris Garner played 35 minutes without a turnover. Adebayo and Chad Allen helped control Cincinnati's big guys. When you're assembling a list of people who will be missed next season, don't stop at the coach.

The ball wound up in Henderson's hands with seconds left. Henderson flipped to Garner. Garner flipped to Allen. Allen hoisted up a three-pointer at the buzzer that ... well, hey, no day is perfect.

So the celebration began. The players cut down the nets. Somebody held up a sign: "Finch for President."

Finch hung around, signing autographs, posing for pictures. Joanne Grinder of Memphis asked Finch to pose for a shot with a poster of hers that read "So Long, Coach."

Finch held the poster in his lap. Looked down. Studied the words.

"That's hard to say," he said, finally.

On this day, harder than ever.

4 WORDS BEGIN NEW TIGER ERA
MARCH 11, 2000

"It's a done deal." — John Calipari.

Well, that was easy enough, wasn't it?

Four little words that made it official.

Four little words that put an end to what little suspense remained.

Four little words that put Memphis basketball back on the map again.

John Calipari is the next head basketball coach at the University of Memphis. He'll be introduced at a press conference at the Pyramid at 3:30 today. If you want to meet him, there will be an open house from 5-7 in the Tiger Club Room. And believe me, if the guy has the attendance clauses in his contract that some seem to think he has, I bet he stays to shake hands with every one of you.

But this isn't about money; not today, anyway. It's about hope. It's about buzz. It's about the sort of boundless, silly excitement that comes in the first, heady days of a big-time hire, when all you can see is a limitless future, all you can imagine are the possibilities.

You could hear it Friday night, in convenience stores and gas stations, or flipping channels on the radio.

People talking about Memphis hoops, their voices brimming with wonder and optimism.

What will this mean for recruiting? Who will be his assistants? How do I buy a season ticket, anyway?

"I think the goal here is a Final Four goal," said Memphis athletic director R.C. Johnson, "and Calipari's a Final Four guy."

Even now, even now that we know it's happened, it's still a little hard to believe the university put the deal together.

Think about it. Think about your first reaction when you heard Memphis was interested in Calipari. Ridiculous, right? Calipari just wanted his name out there. Memphis didn't have the money or the stage to hire a guy with his profile.

Well, give Johnson credit. He didn't listen to any of that. The last coaching search, he went after three guys named Ricardo Patton, Steve Robinson and, ahem, Tic Price. This time, he shot somewhat higher.

He sold Calipari on Memphis as a nice place to raise a family. He sold Calipari on Memphis as a nice place to raise a championship banner, too.

"I thought it was a good fit," Calipari said Friday, "a good place for me."

Oh, there are a handful of people who will still tell you Johnson didn't handle the search properly. Which is just a shorthand way of saying they wished Johnny Jones had been given the job.

What was Johnson supposed to do? Wait until today to get the search cranked up? So he'd just be making contacts, now, instead of holding a press conference?

As it was, Johnson refused to talk about Calipari until late Friday. He might have been the only one in the country who clammed up about the deal. When Memphis put together that late winning streak, he was determined to talk about nothing other than the current Tigers.

Finally, when the Memphis season ended with Thursday's loss to De-Paul, it was just a matter of picking the right moment to introduce Calipari. Johnson settled on Monday first. But with the craziness cranking up — and with all the contract details settled — he decided to try to move it up two days.

Melba Johnson, R.C.'s wife, picked up the phone Friday evening. Called Calipari's wife, Ellen. When Ellen said they could be here by this afternoon, that settled it.

So even now, the new coach is winging his way to Memphis, to a city he's visited for a single day, to a program he hopes to take to places it hasn't been in ages.

It's been one weird year for Memphis basketball. Today, it's about to get better.

JOY BACK IN TIGER BASKETBALL
NOVEMBER 18, 2000

So this is what joy feels like.

So this is what it feels like when a program is on the rebound.

Twenty-thousand people are on their feet.

The national television cameras are rolling.

The new coach is trying to shout something to his players, but can't make himself heard.

Shyrone Chatman, wearing a striped Tiger mask, one that makes him look for all the world like the Phantom of The Pyramid, has just buried a trey from the left corner to put Memphis up by nine. And The Pyramid is bursting with noise.

"That's how it's supposed to be," said John Calipari. "That was unbelievable tonight."

The Memphis Tigers took the wraps off the Calipari era at The Pyramid Friday. There have been better endings in the recent history of Memphis basketball, but not many better nights.

Calipari likes to talk about how at UMass his debut game was notable mostly because the scoreboard caught on fire. This time, well, the fire might spread to the whole town.

What's that? The Tigers lost?

Yeah, that's right, they did. And it's just like Temple coach John Chaney, really.

A few years ago, he threatened to kill the Memphis coach. This time, he just tried to kill the mood.

But you know what? He couldn't do it. Neither could his gutty, bombs-away, Temple team.

When is the last time you remember scalpers circling The Pyramid before a November game, charging fifty bucks a seat?

When is the last time you remember folks getting to the building early, to better soak in the mood?

When is the last time you remember 13-year-old kids wearing crazy hats shaped like basketballs, or a student section that was darn near packed, or the pointed barn on the river filled to the very brim?

Before the game, Ricky Bishop climbed the dozens of stairs to find his seats at the top of section 230. "I'm in row W," he said, "and there isn't any X, Y, or Z."

The last few years, Bishop spent maybe five minutes in his seats at the beginning of games. Then he picked one from the vast swatch of empty seats and moved down.

This time?

"Looks like I'm going to have to stay right here," he said, happily. "The enthusiasm is back."

And so he sat down. For a moment, anyway. And then came the tipoff and who could sit through a game like this?

The first half was all Memphis, an exhibition of what this team could become. Kelly Wise hauling in rebounds. Scooter McFadgon hitting hanging jumpers. Chatman burying that trey.

The second half was different; a taut, thrilling heavyweight brawl. There were 11 lead changes, all in the last 14 minutes.

"It felt like a Duke-Carolina," said Earl Barron. "It was hard to beat that."

Oh, sure, the game could have turned out better for the home team. Kelly Wise could have taken more than three shots in the second half.

Courtney Trask could have avoided the silly fouls. Lynn Greer could have missed some of those bombs.

But for the better part of three months, the Memphis marketing department has been pitching their posters and bumper stickers, the ones that say "It's Back."

All along, we figured they were referring to quality basketball. Who knew they were talking about joy?

MARCH SADNESS – WITH NCAA DREAM IN HAND, TIGERS WATCH IT FALL AWAY
MARCH 13, 2005

All zeroes on the clock. Memphis trailed Louisville by two. Darius Washington, a sweet-faced, 19-year-old freshman, stepped to the line with the fate of a season in his palms.

He was all alone.

Truly.

Because no time remained, no other players stood around the lane.

He had three shots. Make two, the game goes into overtime. Make three, Memphis wins everything.

Wins the game, wins the tournament, wins a trip to the NCAAs.

Washington swished the first shot. He pointed to the bench and winked.

Ha!

He winked! He was going to do it, wasn't he?

The second shot hit the rim and — his father still couldn't believe this, an hour later — bounced to the right.

"I don't know how that happened," said Darius Washington Sr. "He thrives on that."

The miss shook the kid. Memphis coach John Calipari saw this from the bench.

"I should have called time," he said. "But I let it play out."

Third shot. Everyone standing. Millions watching on TV.

Some Memphis players interlocked arms. Arthur Barclay draped a towel over his head. Duane Erwin sat, not looking, at the farthest corner of the court.

Washington set the third ball spinning on its way. One ball, so much at stake.

It hit the rim once, twice, then bounced off to the right.

Washington dropped to his knees, then fell to the floor.

Calipari ran to him, but couldn't pull him up. Jeremy Hunt tried and failed, too. Darius Sr. fought his way past security.

"I'm getting out there," he said. "That's my son."

• • •

Memphis forward Duane Erwin called it an instant classic. It was so much bigger, richer and more human than that.

Louisville defeated Memphis to win the Conference USA Tournament Saturday, 75-74. If you weren't there to see it, you should probably go ahead and start lying.

Tell everyone you saw the last one in the series. Tell everyone you saw that miracle of a game.

"Amazing," said Calipari.

"Incredible," said Louisville coach Rick Pitino.

"Let's party," said Louisville forward Ellis Myles.

Uh, let's not. But let's stand in wonder at the effort, at the spectacle, at the ability of college kids to summon up a game that surpassed anything that could reasonably have been expected of them.

The Tigers had played three games in three nights. Their previous game ended after 8 p.m. Friday. They tipped off against Louisville at 10:35 a.m.

Go get 'em, guys. Would you like some coffee first?

But who needs coffee when you're running on pure adrenaline?

The Tigers were fabulous. The Cardinals were fabulous. Here's an actual excerpt from the first half play-by-play:

2:27: Made 3-pntr by Rice, Anthony.

2:05: Made 3-pntr by Dean, Taquan.

1:51: Made 3-pntr by Carney, Rodney.

1:30: Made 3-pntr by Palacios, Juan.

Four 3-pointers in a row. Bang, bang, bang, bang.

The lead changed every time. That's how the thing went.

At some point it became less a game than a series of gasps. And it came down to the final minutes, which Calipari described like this: "Aw, they're going to win! ... They just lost it. ... Oh, my gosh, they're going to win! ... Oh, man, they lost it ... Oh, gosh, he got fouled, he's getting three free throws, they're going to win!"

In the middle of it all was Washington, which was fitting somehow. He has been in the middle of it all season, the good and the bad.

He had to learn how to play point guard. He had to deal with a resentful, sometimes angry Sean Banks.

"Did he think of leaving?" said Darius Sr. "No, but I did."

Father and son talked constantly, dozens of times a day. "Thank God for Nextel," said Darius Sr., patting his cell phone.

Darius Sr. was just a junior in high school when Darius Jr. was born. He later married Tarchelle — "my high school sweetheart," he said — and they had a daughter, too.

But Darius Sr. poured his love of basketball into his son, made him the focus of their collective dreams.

"He's never failed," said Darius Sr. "I can't think of when he's failed at anything."

Now Darius Sr. was watching his son lift the Tigers into the NCAA Tournament, and he wasn't exactly surprised.

Washington scored eight of the Tigers' last nine points. If Washington hadn't taken over, said Pitino, "they're not even in the game."

With six seconds left, Louisville's Brad Gianiny missed the second of two free throws. Erwin rebounded the miss and got the ball to the little guy.

He flew up the court. As he rose to shoot, Louisville's Francisco Garcia plowed into him.

"Who wants to be there more than you?" Calipari asked Washington in the huddle.

"Nobody," Washington said.

At the shoot-around before the tournament, Calipari had every player practice a game-winning shot. He somehow forgot about his point guard.

"Hey," said Washington, visibly ticked, "what about me?"

The kid can shoot free throws, too. When he went home for Christmas, he worked on it with his dad.

"He shot 200 a day," said Darius Sr. "To distract him, I would stand behind the goal and wave a mop."

Washington had five games this year when he didn't miss a free throw, including 10-for-10 performances against UAB and TCU. He was shooting 71.8 percent for the year.

Small wonder the Louisville players had a bad feeling when he stepped to the line. Earlier in the year, they lost to Kentucky when Patrick Sparks hit three straight free throws with no time left.

"Déjà vu," Myles said. "After he hit the first one, I was thinking, 'Dang, he might hit these next two.'"

That's not how it happened, of course. Washington stayed down on the court for a very long time.

He couldn't muster a comment. He couldn't take his head out of his hands.

"He's sick," said Erwin. "Anybody would be sick."

Everyone tried to console him. Memphis players, Louisville players, even the Louisville coach. Pitino told a small story about another guy who once missed a big foul shot.

"I remember UMass was playing Providence ... Sports Illustrated wrote 'UMass almost got the No. 1 seed in New England as Rick Pitino missed the one-and-one.'"

So Washington is not the first one to be in this position, but that won't make him feel better anytime soon. The NCAA Selection Show takes place this evening. Memphis doesn't need to watch.

Someday, though, Washington will understand that people don't hold him responsible, that, if anything, they want to wrap their arms around him and tell him everything will be OK.

Ana Schilling, 10, is the daughter of Memphis assistant Ed Schilling. She's a ball girl, and very wise.

As she left the locker room Saturday, she said something that might as well have been from the whole community of Memphis fans.

"Daddy," she said, "tell Darius that we love him, OK?"

A DREAM SEASON FOR TIGERS? LET THE FUN BEGIN
OCTOBER 13, 2007

The dunk contest was supposed to be between Jeff Robinson and Doneal Mack, but Memphis coach John Calipari interrupted it with a small request.

"This is for my own enjoyment," he said, summoning freshman point guard Derrick Rose to the court.

Calipari handed Rose the ball. He told him to dunk just once.

The crowd rose to applaud the new kid.

It was almost too much. This was his first public moment at Memphis. He was supposed to dazzle everyone with a single dunk?

The clapping grew louder. Rose calmly bounced the ball high in the air. Then he went up, grabbed it, brought it back down — nearly to his toes — and slammed it, backward, emphatically through the hoop.

The place exploded.

"Just a regular dunk," said Rose, afterward.

"JUST A REGULAR DUNK?" asked Memphis forward Chris Douglas-Roberts, and then he laughed.

But what a way to start this journey, this basketball trip that will wind on for seven months, and is supposed to end at the Final Four in San Antonio.

"You don't know where it's going," said Calipari, during the Memphis Madness celebration at FedExForum Friday night, "but it looks like it's going to be a lot of fun."

That's right, fun, and just in the nick of time, wouldn't you say?

This city could use a pick-me-up, something to feel good about again. Over the years and the decades, there's not much that has made Memphis feel better than Tiger basketball.

The most famous example came in 1972-73, when Larry Finch and Gene Bartow led Memphis to the championship game against UCLA.

It's the stuff of civic legend now, of municipal mythology.

The Tigers brought the city together. That's what everyone says. Black and white, rich and poor, people put aside their differences to pull for a single basketball team.

What a happy fable, eh? And what a perfect time for it to happen again.

Because, 35 years later, Memphians are divided once more. Or maybe we're just more keenly aware of the things that have divided us all along.

The mayoral race was divisive and ugly. Only one of the three major candidates — the one who finished third — was gracious about the results.

Letters to the editor are raw and bitter. People have chosen sides or, worse, chosen to leave town.

If this isn't a job for Memphis basketball, then what the heck is?

And, yes, it is entirely understandable if you are rolling your eyes right about now. It's just a basketball team, after all. Just a dozen players and a coach.

A basketball team can't put a stop to the violence. A basketball team can't lift thousands out of poverty, or make fathers act like fathers, or solve the financial problems of The Med.

A basketball team can't even bring everyone together, no matter the mythology.

Will a basketball team cause Willie Herenton to look inside himself? Or cause his opponents and detractors to see the good in the man?

Of course not. It's just a basketball team. Let's not be naive.

And yet, there is something the Tigers can do, and will do, and even started doing Friday night.

They can make people smile. You remember how to do that, right?

This month's issue of *Men's Journal* quotes a Kansas University study that concluded "sport fans suffer fewer bouts of depression and alienation than do people who are uninterested in sports."

Most sports fans don't get to pull for a team that's been to two straight Elite Eights, either. Or that comes into the season ranked in everyone's top three.

Chuck Roberts, the public address announcer, was so pumped his voice gave out after introducing just four players Friday night.

"I have no voice," he croaked. From out of the stands rushed local sportscaster Greg Gaston.

"The next player," Gaston picked up, not missing a syllable.

It was quite a moment, really. This Memphis team is so deep, it has a backup PA announcer.

"This is the best team Memphis has had in a long time," said Douglas-Roberts. "We have to get to the final game this year."

Which may or may not mean the Tigers will do it. That's the peril of sports. Nothing is certain but the opportunity, and the continuing devotion of the fans.

Sean Donaldson, 14, showed up Friday wearing a classic, white Memphis State jacket from the mid-1970s.

"I got it from him," he said, pointing to his dad.

Turns out Tim Donaldson, 49, started at Memphis in 1976. He wore the jacket to games in the Coliseum. He remembers Finch and Bartow and everything they meant.

When Donaldson graduated from Memphis, he put the jacket in the back of his closet. He married a girl he had met in the dorms. They had a son, Sean.

Years passed. Memphis changed.

Not long ago, Donaldson happened on his old jacket.

"You want to wear this?" he asked Sean.

Sean definitely did.

So Friday night, Donaldson went to work early, and left work early, all so he and Sean could be at FedExForum 90 minutes before the doors opened.

Donaldson wanted to see Rose, certainly. He wanted to see something else, too.

"This team has to help us get past the petty bickering," he said. "To be honest with you, this is the only glue the city has right now. This is the one thing, no matter your nationality or your politics or your religion, that everyone can get behind."

Father and son waited patiently for the doors to open. For the season — and maybe the fable — to begin anew.

BELIEVE IT FOLKS, THE KID IS JUST THAT GOOD
NOVEMBER 6, 2007

Chris Douglas-Roberts missed a jumper from the wing, and it was just a miss, until Derrick Rose started cutting toward the basket, and left the floor, and kept rising and rising, and reached his arm high and grabbed the ball, and threw it down, and somewhere in there that one little miss became both a moment and a memory.

Oh.

My.

God.

That's what the guy said, a professional journalist, sitting right next to me.

The dunk was thunderous and sensational, a spontaneous burst of brilliance almost exactly a year in the making, since the day last November Rose said he was coming to Memphis.

Monday, he arrived, soaring through the air, better than even the most fervent Memphis fans allowed themselves to imagine.

"That was unusual," said Calipari, deadpan.

Right. Unusual.

In the sense that watching a guy do crazy, magical, impossible things is unusual.

Oh, and by the way, Memphis defeated Tennessee-Martin Monday, 102-71, to open its most anticipated season in years with a victory. But everyone expected that. They didn't necessarily expect to walk out of the building, alternately babbling and laughing about the ridiculous things they had just seen from a freshman.

"That's D-Rose," said Douglas-Roberts.

Well, why didn't someone tell us?

OK, they did tell us, over and over, but telling has its limits.

Greatness has to be seen to be appreciated, to really have an impact. And so it happened, after a frustrating first few minutes, that Rose revealed his greatness to Memphis.

He said he was nervous at the start of the game.

"I was kind of scared, a little bit," he said.

Memphis fell behind; the other guys were hitting everything.

Then Rose grabbed a loose ball and drove the length of the court for a layup. Except, this wasn't any layup. It felt like a technological trick. How did they fast-forward one guy and leave everyone else going along at normal speed?

The next possession, it happened again. Zip. Zip. Zip. Except this time, Rose dished to Douglas-Roberts for the finish.

Then came the dunk, off the missed jumper, and now it was getting silly.

And then, ahhhhhh, Rose turned it over. The kid is human after all.

Tennessee-Martin's Carlos Wright flew down the court for the easy layup. Only, wait, this couldn't be happening, could it?

Rose was chasing him down. And Rose was catching him. And Rose was timing his leap to block the layup and ...

Oh.

My.

God.

He blocked it! Against the glass!

"I was mad because I turned the ball over," he said. "That was a hustle play so Coach wouldn't yell at me."

Rose gives a lot of credit to Coach, by the way. A TV guy asked him if he just decides to take over a game.

"It's really Coach," he said. "Coach tells me what to do."

Note to John: Keep telling him to take over games.

Anyway, the crowd was appreciative, and roared like heck, and the rest of the game felt more like a celebration. Shawn Taggart had 15 rebounds. Douglas-Roberts had a career-high 28 points. And when it was done, all anyone could talk about was the new guy.

"I think I've done a good job with him," said athletic director R.C. Johnson.

Har.

"I don't know what to say," said Doug Barron, the golf pro.

A lot of people just smiled, crazily.

In 25 minutes, Rose finished with 17 points, six assists, five rebounds, two blocks and just one turnover. And the thing is, he looked even better than that. He looked like a force, a star, the kind of player who could win a championship.

Or not. There are no guarantees. Will the team mesh? Will the shots fall? Will Rose get complacent?

OK, you probably don't have to worry about this last part. Someone asked him to grade his debut performance.

"C, C-plus," he said.

Then the kid allowed himself a smile.

"But when I get used to it, it's going to be scary."

Happily, it already is.

MEMPHIS' BASKETBALL WIZARDRY ON DISPLAY
MARCH 29, 2008

Houston — Last minute of the half, Derrick Rose sailed in for an open dunk.

It was not just any dunk, though. It was a thrilling, backward, soaring expression of everything Memphis fans have wanted to say since this tournament began.

First No. 1 seed to lose, eh? Can't shoot foul shots? Not sufficiently tested to compete on the big stage? Not from a BCS conference like the Big Ten?

What a hoot that last one is today.

Rose's emphatic slam put the Tigers up by 30 against Michigan State. Thirty! In the first half!

"I've never been involved in a first half like this anywhere, high school, anywhere," said Chris Douglas-Roberts, "we really played out of our minds."

So much for the theory that the Tigers would be done in by the coaching wizardry of Tom Izzo.

Final score: Tigers 92, Coaching Wizardry 74.

It's not that Izzo isn't a great coach, either. It's just that the Tigers are — and this is a technical basketball term — really, really good.

They have Derrick Rose, maybe the best player remaining in the tournament. They have Chris Douglas-Roberts, who could score on an octopus. They have Joey Dorsey, who can bench press Pierre Niles.

Robert Dozier is just a guy on this team. Willie Kemp comes off the bench.

He comes off the bench. Get your mind around that. The kid was a starter as a freshman on the team that went to the Elite Eight last year. This year, he's coming off the bench.

Then some national guy drops in and writes that "all John Calipari does is roll the basketball onto the floor."

It's ludicrous, really.

The Tigers may or may not win the national championship — they may or may not beat Texas in what will essentially be a home game for the Longhorns Sunday afternoon — but every coach should roll the basketball onto the floor the way Calipari did Friday night.

"That first half of basketball was one of the best I've been involved in as a coach," Calipari said. "I was proud to be a part of it."

Remember, Michigan State was supposed to have this big, tough, collection of players that would push the Tigers around on the boards. They didn't get a rebound in the first five minutes of the game.

Michigan State was supposed to have this lethal offensive duo, Drew Neitzel and Raymar Morgan. They didn't score a point in the first half.

That's not some accident, either. It's what the Tigers do. They're bigger than the other guys, and they're faster than the other guys, and they play better defense, and they don't care who gets the glory at the end.

Does that sound like a team that rolls the ball out? Or does that sound like a team that has worked within a system for years and has a superbly defined sense of itself?

By the end of the first half it felt more like a celebration than a contest, a national coming-out party.

Dorsey picked off a pass and unleashed a soaring dunk that would have gone nicely with a Superman cape. Antonio Anderson and Rose combined on a blur of a fast break. Kemp threw an alley-oop to Niles. Yes, an alley-oop. Niles converted. Even if there wasn't much oop.

"Awesome!" said Memphis athletic director R.C. Johnson at the half, and don't be fooled by what happened after that.

It was a mess, certainly, but it was a largely irrelevant mess.

Rose got poked in the eye. That produced the only suspense. He ran into the locker room and took the longest time coming back.

Could he have been hurt more badly than anyone thought? Was something terribly wrong?

Uh, no.

"He's not real good with needles," Calipari said. "They had to try to glue it."

Mind you, Rose has tattoos. Which he got voluntarily.

"But these needles go all the way inside you," he explained.

Arrrrrrrgh, kids!

The Spartans actually got it under 20, whereupon Calipari started to fret.

"Another four minutes and I'm getting him myself," he said.

Just like that, Rose re-appeared. And hit two free throws. And got a bucket. And order was restored.

All that was left was for Izzo to start fouling, and fouling, and fouling some more. Michigan State went to the hack-a-Tiger with six minutes left in the game.

Let the record show the Tigers hit 15 of 20 foul shots from that point on.

"I just want to know," said Douglas-Roberts, "what's the knock on us now?"

Well, you still missed nine free throws. And you didn't get every rebound. And — wait, this is it! — the point guard doesn't like needles. How can you win with a guy like that?

"I can't believe they won't pick against us," said Calipari.

After Friday, maybe not.

BELIEVE IT OR NOT, MEMPHIS, IT'S THEIR TIME TO CELEBRATE
MARCH 31, 2008

HOUSTON — They held up four fingers. Four glorious fingers. One, two, three, four.

Andre Allen held up four fingers. Pierre Niles held up four fingers. And then it was everyone.

Derrick Rose, the breathtaking guard who's terrified of needles. Chris Douglas-Roberts, the sly, smiling pride of Detroit.

Joey Dorsey. That's Joey, to you. Who in the world would call him Sir?

Three minutes and fifty-five seconds remained in the Elite Eight game between Memphis and Texas. It was all over but the cutting of the nets.

So they held four fingers in the air. High in the air. Triumphant. And yes, close followers of Memphis basketball will tell you the team always does this.

"We want to win the last four minutes," Allen said.

Well, why not? They won everything else.

Thirty-five years after the 1973 Memphis Tigers left this city on their way to the first Final Four in the history of the university, the 2008 Memphis Tigers are headed the same way.

The 1973 team lost to UCLA in the national championship game; the 2008 team will play UCLA in one of the national semifinal games Saturday.

"I feel like a million dollars right now," said Allen, one of two native Memphians on the roster. "The third time's the charm."

Allen was talking about the team's losses in the Elite Eight the previous two years, something Memphis coach John Calipari addressed in the quiet of the locker room before the game.

"It's your time," he said. "Don't worry about the last two years, it's your time. You've been given a tough road, you have to beat Texas in Houston. Don't worry about that. It's your time."

Time to win this game that had stopped them each of the last two years. Time to do the only thing this team hadn't done.

"A year ago, I promised the city a Final Four," said Dorsey, the massive forward. "I wasn't going to let the Texas players stand in the way of that."

Or let them breathe, either. Or give them any reason to hope.

This Memphis team is supremely talented, physically gifted at every position. But what took place this weekend in Houston was about something more than that, something larger than physical gifts.

The Tigers hammered Texas, 85-67, just as they hammered Michigan State two days before.

"We wanted to make a statement," said Douglas-Roberts.

Possible statement: "Y'all believe in us now?"

And let's go ahead and concede that, yes, absolutely Calipari has used the us-against-the-world stuff to his advantage. But if it weren't out there, he couldn't use it at all.

It's out there. It's real.

So when Dorsey gathered in a long pass in the first half against Texas, he wasn't just thinking about two points.

"I wanted to tear the rim down," he said.

Because then maybe people would notice. Maybe then they'd stop yammering on about free throws and Conference USA and actually look at the Memphis team.

They'd see a team filled with players who hang together, who like each other and who play as hard and as cohesively as any team in the country.

"If you can ball, you can ball," said Rose.

Oh, and Rose can ball.

The kid hit an otherworldly 7-of-9 shots and finished with 21 points, nine assists, six rebounds and the Most Outstanding Player award. Naturally, he somehow missed the part about the MOP award, until he was asked about it after the game.

"I was the MVP or whatever?" he said.

Yeah.

"That's wonderful," he said, "but one of my teammates deserves it way more than me."

It's not unusual for a player to say something like this, really. It is unusual for the player to be blushing at the time.

That's Rose, though. He has the best performance-to-ego ratio in the game.

He scored the Tigers' first bucket Sunday by backing down Texas point guard D.J. Augustin.

"I was just trying to show them my height would be a problem," he said. "It was a mind thing."

Meanwhile, on the other end of the floor, the Texas players were discovering that playing against the Tigers is a whole lot trickier than, say, talking about playing them.

"They are so long and athletic," said Texas forward Connor Atchley, still a little stunned by it all.

The score went from 2-0 to 5-0 to 18-8 to 29-13.

And, no, it wasn't technically over or anything. Texas even cut the margin to five in the second half. But it never felt like Memphis was in danger of losing the game.

"It was our time," said Douglas-Roberts, as if it's explanation enough.

Their time to watch another team scramble in desperation. Their time to grind on to the end.

Their time to hit their foul shots, nearly all their foul shots (30-of-36), and how about that?

Texas coach Rick Barnes went to the hack-a-Tiger in the final minutes, which then lasted a year.

"The longest three minutes ever in my life," said Allen.

All the more to enjoy.

It is not always easy being a Memphis Tiger. If the team seems to take things personally — and it does — it is a perfect reflection of the city it represents.

The Tigers wonder when they'll get the breaks?

Memphians can relate.

The Tigers feel overlooked?

Well, Memphians can feel that way, too.

So it was just fine to have to wait a bit to celebrate this one. Just fine to watch the long parade of foul shots.

It gave everyone a chance to stand and watch in wonder, whether they were on the court or in their living rooms back home.

Could this really be happening to the Tigers? Could a team from Memphis be headed back to the Final Four?

"Not a lot of people believed it," said Allen, "but it is our time."

TEAM TRAGEDY – '85 TIGERS HAD LOTS OF TALENT, BUT TROUBLES HAUNT THEM
APRIL 3, 2008

The grave lies far from Memphis, to the south, in Mississippi, a good hour-and-a-half drive.

Down I-55, away from the old Coliseum, which is forlorn and empty now.

At Batesville, Highway 278 curves to the east. At Marks, Rte. 3 picks up south again, past chained dogs and slanting porches and finally, on the right, Quitman County Elementary School.

The cemetery is behind the school and its big, commercial Dumpsters. The chain-link fence is rusted and falling down.

The grave is just in there, to the left and then right again, beyond the weeds and the bottles and the three decrepit basketball hoops.

It is an unremarkable headstone, with an unremarkable granite flowerpot.

Except the flowerpot bears a name. It says, in large, block letters:
BATMAN

•••

Can you remember when that nickname meant something? Can you remember the spring of 1985, when it meant the world?

Batman. People smiled just to say it. They smile, even now.

"Batman," says former Memphis coach Dana Kirk, sinking his fork into a stack of pancakes. "Baskerville Holmes. That's a sad story, right there."

Kirk does not have much use for sad stories these days.

"I only do positive," he says.

So Kirk should not read this column about his old team, which is only as positive — and as tragic and as messy and as complicated — as real life will allow.

Is cocaine positive? Is prison? Is murder-suicide?

Is an unsolved murder positive? Is a debilitating stroke?

"Why don't we talk about what it used to be like?" says Kirk who, just in case, has brought some notes.

He wants to remember what it felt like when his Tigers owned the town, when the people bought his bumper stickers, when they shouted his name.

"I used to take the players out to the Hickory Ridge Mall," Kirk said. "There would be 10,000 people or more out there, just to meet the team."

The Tigers won three tournament games by a total of five points that year, including a 63-61 win over Oklahoma to go to the Final Four.

"This was when you could meet us at the gate at the airport," says John Wilfong, a backup guard on the team. "When we walked off the plane in Memphis, there were thousands and thousands of people there."

And why not? This was the year, at long last. The Tigers had the team that could win it all.

Keith Lee, William Bedford and Holmes in the front court. Vincent Askew and Andre Turner at guard.

"I played 10 and a half years in the NBA," Askew says, "and I never had as much fun playing basketball as I did back then."

Then, the fun stopped. Memphis lost to Villanova, Rollie Massimino's Villanova, which went on to beat Georgetown in the championship game.

Back in Memphis, the Tigers quietly cleaned out their lockers. They would keep in touch, of course. They would all go on to do great things.

Twenty-three years later, two of the players are dead. One has been in and out of prison. A couple of others have scuffled through life.

According to the NCAA record books, the Tigers never even appeared in the Final Four. Their appearance was vacated for NCAA violations. Kirk was forced out after the 1985-86 season, spent four months in a minimum-security prison and never coached Division 1 basketball again.

Now he sits at a table at a Perkins Restaurant, explaining why he won't tell a reporter his age.

"I have a presence to maintain," he says. "Good, bad or ugly, I have a presence in this town."

He grins at this. He will maintain his presence, two decades later, whatever it may be.

"No hard feelings," he says. "I only do positive."

• • •

On March 18, 1997, Baskerville Holmes opened the door to his house in Frayser and, frantic, thrust the telephone at his girlfriend's brother, Gerald Franklin.

"Talk to the lady," he said.

Franklin put the phone to his ear.

"Hello," a woman said, "911, can I help you please?"

Franklin then saw his sister, Tanya Crossford, lying against the wall, blood pouring down her face.

"I'm sorry, I didn't mean to do this," said Holmes, pacing now.

Franklin desperately tried to clear the blood from his sister's throat. While he was doing this, he heard a bang.

Holmes, 32, had shot himself in the head. Police ruled it a murder-suicide.

"Was I surprised?" said Wilfong, "I was surprised and not surprised."

He says this matter-of-factly, as a man who understands the realities of the city in which he lives.

"I guess, if you grow up in Memphis, you realize there are situations where people die at early ages. I guess you're never surprised."

Wilfong thinks for a long moment. He would like to be able to neatly explain it all away. Why did Holmes end up like that? Why did Aaron Price? Or William Bedford?

Price was shot and killed in West Memphis in November, 1998. The killer took his green Dodge Intrepid. West Memphis police call it an "unsolved homicide."

Bedford was taken sixth overall in the 1986 draft. He floated around the league for six years, as various teams would fall in love with his gifts (7-feet and athletic) and fall out of love with his habit (cocaine).

"I had a very close relationship with William," Wilfong says. "I played on his AAU team and roomed with him freshman year. He was a sweet, sweet kid. What happened to him was that he got involved with drugs and it wrecked his life."

This happened in the NBA?

"Before," says Wilfong says.

How do you know?

"I know," he says. "It happened at Memphis, I'm sure."

The federal prison system confirms there's a William Bedford in prison in Fort Worth, Texas, scheduled for release in 2013. This William Bedford is 7-feet tall and was born in Tennessee.

"He was a follower," says Andre Turner, on the phone from Spain. "I don't know how you can explain it beyond that. Life happened to William, I guess."

And there is something to this, of course. Life happens to us all.

Larry Finch, one of two assistant coaches on the '85 team, had a debilitating stroke in 2002. Life happened, and it can be hard.

Keith Lee, the unquestioned star of the team, lasted just three years in the NBA because of bum knees. The same body that gave him such glory ultimately took it away.

"I do think being in the limelight, having attention like that, is hard to let go of for some people," Wilfong says. "I think it was difficult for my uncle (Tiger great Win Wilfong), who played in the NBA. He looked back at his 20s as the best period of his life. If you do that, you cheat yourself out of the next 40 or 50 years. The key is to look out in the future and say, 'Now I'm going to make the next 40 or 50 years great.'"

Wilfong did that; he's a senior vice president at an investment firm.

Turner did that; he's still playing professional basketball in Spain.

Dwight Boyd did that; he's spent the last 18 years with Pepsi.

"I'm not a millionaire, but I'm happy," he says.

Isn't that the ultimate victory?

To find happiness in the unexceptional life. To enjoy life on life's own terms.

That sort of contentment apparently eluded Bedford and Holmes.

As for Lee, few really know. He keeps to himself. He declines interviews.

"I'm sad for him that his NBA career didn't work out," Wilfong says. "What I'm even sadder about is that I don't think he understands how much the community loved watching him play basketball and how much they still love him."

Back at Perkins, Kirk is talking about grandchildren. He will talk all day about his grandchildren. It is good to hear him so happy. Grandchildren are positive.

One grandson, Grey, is crazy about the Memphis Tigers.

"He's a Joey Dorsey freak," Kirk says. "He's 6. And he's got more Dorsey jerseys than Joey has."

Grey has his entire class doing a Joey cheer. There is something wonderfully sweet about this.

The grandson of the deposed coach is caught up in the moment. But it is just a moment, as fleeting as it is glorious.

This time, the name is Joey. May it ring forever. Last time, the name was ... well, here is a small test.

Dorsey has just finished practice. He is bathed in sweat. He is brimming with confidence for the task at hand. He will even talk about free throws. Ask him anything.

"Joey, ever hear of someone named Baskerville Holmes?"

Joey thinks about this.

"The name sounds familiar," he says. "Who is he?"

CAL: LOOK DEEP WHEN CONSIDERING MY TEAM
APRIL 4, 2008

SAN ANTONIO — Memphis coach John Calipari sat at the podium, fresh off his team's breathtaking victory over Texas. He listened to his players answer questions from the media. When they stood up and left, it was his turn.

"I want to say something before I get started," he said. "The reason I turned around Chris Douglas's hat, I get disappointed when I look at what it looked like in that TV over there, and I get disappointed when these young people are judged by how they wear a hat.

"These young men that I'm coaching have unbelievable hearts. I'm proud of these guys, and I'll be honest, I get offended. I had to turn the hat around because I saw what it looked like on the TV. These are good kids."

And then Calipari took questions.

It was a striking moment, really, especially in the flush of victory. Calipari could have talked about his players' impeccable foul shooting or their defensive dominance. Instead, he talked about their hats, and how they wear them, and what that says — or shouldn't say — about the kind of people they are.

Naturally, nobody wrote about it. Calipari's soliloquy didn't fit anyone's storyline. But it's useful to revisit it today, in San Antonio, as the Memphis players prepare for the biggest media day of their lives.

It will be the first time most reporters have ever talked to the Memphis players. It will be the first time the Memphis players will have to talk about their teammate, Andre Allen, who will miss the Final Four because of a failed drug test.

So how will they be judged? And are they judged unfairly?

"They are judged by a tattoo," Calipari said. "If you ask me about my team and who has a tattoo and who doesn't, you won't believe this, but I look at their eyes. I look at their eyes."

OK, and their ability to dunk the ball.

Let's not fool ourselves about that part, either. Calipari, like any coach, cares about more than character.

Did he look in Sean Banks' eyes? How about Kareem Cooper's?

Calipari's rhetoric can be so out there — and so self-serving — that skeptics roll their eyes and ignore the truth in it.

This is a mistake. Because there almost always is truth in it.

And there is absolutely some truth to the notion that people have a preconceived notion of what it means to be a Memphis basketball player.

C'mon, you know the stereotype. They're not all that bright. They don't speak the King's English.

"They just jump, run around and shoot balls," said Calipari.

They have tattoos everywhere.

Like Chris Douglas-Roberts. He has one on his neck, of all the crazy places.

You know what it says?

Judy.

As in Judy Roberts, Chris's mother. She's a strong woman, is Judy. She has her own story.

The Roberts family moved to Detroit from Kentucky, where they were slaves. Judy's father was in the first wave of African-Americans to work in the Ford plant. He died when Judy was 10, leaving Judy's mother, Laura, to raise eight children by herself.

Laura Roberts worked as a domestic, cleaning people's houses. Four of her eight kids went to college. None of them went to jail. Judy honored her own mother by insisting that her son, Chris, continue to carry the Roberts family name.

Now Chris honors his own mother. Maybe not in the way you or I would choose to do it, but is that so bad, really?

He's a great player. He's a good kid, too. The same way most of the Memphis players are good kids.

Antonio Anderson is a good kid. Derrick Rose is a good kid. Joey Dorsey is, well, Joey Dorsey.

After the Texas game, a reporter from *The Los Angeles Times* asked Dorsey about playing against a young guy like Kevin Love.

"He's a freshman," the reporter said, "he's 19. How old are you?"

"I'm a senior," said Dorsey, "22, 23."

Huh? Twenty-two, twenty-three? Who answers the question "how old are you" with two numbers?

And by the way, Dorsey is 24. What a knucklehead.

Except, see, he's not really a knucklehead. Or wasn't one there. He was embarrassed of his age. He was embarrassed to be a 24-year-old senior in college.

This is one of the reasons Memphians love Dorsey so much. It's why they love this team. Because the players aren't perfect. Because their struggles are out there for everyone to see.

The Tigers players have some rough edges?

So does the city they represent.

The Tigers players have a tendency to screw up?

So do most of the politicians in town.

This is the backdrop of our lives, isn't it? Perfection isn't the Memphis way.

But if people would just take the time to look — at the team or the city — they might find there's plenty of good in both.

PLAYERS, FANS HAVE REASON TO BE GIDDY
APRIL 5, 2008

SAN ANTONIO — At precisely 2:10 p.m., the public address guy at the Alamodome fired up his microphone.

"Please welcome to the floor, from Conference USA, the Memphis Tigers ..."

The band played. The players jogged onto the court, and it was like any court, 94 by 50 with goals at both ends.

Memphis guard Antonio Anderson said it didn't feel all that different, really. Until he looked down.

"In the center of the court, it doesn't say NCAA any more," he said. "It says Final Four."

Anderson's stomach fluttered a little over that one. And why wouldn't it?

The Memphis Tigers are in the Final Four. Pinch yourself as much as you like, it's still true.

At 5:07 today, the Tigers will play UCLA, the most storied program in the country, for the right to advance to Monday's championship game.

"It's perfect," said Memphis forward Joey Dorsey, who knows all about the history. Thirty-five years ago, UCLA and Bill Walton ended the 1973 Tigers' championship run. Two years ago, UCLA defeated Memphis in the Elite Eight.

"It's a chance for vindication," said Dorsey, which is only partly right.

Those teams don't need vindicating. They gave Memphis fans memories they carry with them today. This team is doing the same thing now, for Memphians everywhere.

"It's not just the grandmother from Orange Mound," said Memphis coach John Calipari. "It's the white mother from Collierville."

Or the displaced Memphian watching on the Internet in Japan. Or the Marine from Bartlett serving in Iraq.

Two days ago, I sent a text message to a friend, saying I was headed out of town.

"Bound for SA," it said.

"Who is this?" said the return text.

I had punched in the wrong number, sent my text to a random stranger.

"Wrong number," I texted back.

"No problem," came the reply, "I'm headed for SA, too. Go Tigers!"

All this after punching in a wrong number. A random number, out of millions of possibilities, belonging to a Memphian utterly caught up in this team.

What are the odds, eh? Actually, probably pretty good. This is how widespread the interest in this team has become.

"For our city and all that it's been through — and the feeling the city has for itself sometimes — this is good," Calipari said.

As he spoke, a nearby television ran coverage of the Martin Luther King Jr. ceremony. It was striking, the timing of everything.

Memphis reliving 1968. Memphis reliving 1973, too.

"It's about hope," said Calipari. "I think there are the kids in the city who think, 'I can't, I won't, I don't deserve ... '"

It is a stretch to say Memphis basketball can change the course of these kids' lives. It is not a stretch to say Memphis basketball players feel that obligation, just the same.

"It's a city with problems," said forward Robert Dozier, "a city with crime."

None of the other Final Four teams answered questions Friday about the places they represent. UCLA center Kevin Love was not asked about Watts.

Does this mean that Memphis fans care more about their program than UCLA fans care about theirs?

Of course not. But it does speak to the bond between the city and the team, a bond unlike almost any other you'll find. Louisville, maybe. UNLV in the glory days. But UCLA does not have a grip on Los Angeles the way the Tigers have a grip on Memphis this morning. Los Angeles has the Lakers, for one thing. And the beach.

Memphis has this basketball team, and this trip to the Final Four, and who knows when it will happen again?

It's been 23 years since the last journey. A lot has taken place in those 23 years.

The Pyramid came and went. Larry Finch was promoted to head coach, set a record for coaching victories, lost his job, and suffered a debilitating stroke.

"This would be huge for Memphis," said Dorsey, and by "this" he meant winning it all.

So they might as well win it all, right? At least, that's how they're looking at it.

"We're here to win," said Memphis guard Chris Douglas-Roberts.

Only problem?

"We're here to win," said UCLA point guard Darren Collison.

It would be easier if UCLA were here to get some good Tex-Mex.

UCLA is every bit as talented as Memphis. Both teams claimed to be loose. The UCLA players spent their practice laughing and launching shots from full court.

Love is a master at this, by the way. He can launch a full-court shot from his chest. He hit one Friday, from beyond the far goal, as the Tigers watched on a TV in their locker room.

"He's good," Dozier said, "but I don't think he's allowed to shoot them from out of bounds, is he?"

Ha.

Although, with the way the officials have been helping UCLA these last few weeks ...

"We will see," Calipari said, which was honest, at least.

We will see how this goes. We will see where this ends. We will sit in the arena, or in front of our televisions, and watch a game that will be savored and talked about for decades.

Your children will talk about it; it will be a tie to their youth.

"I became a Memphis fan watching the 1985 team," said Lindy Long. "I was a little bitty kid, and they about broke my heart."

Long is the guy on the other end of my errant text message. I called him Friday afternoon. He had just pulled into San Antonio.

"We left around 3 a.m.," he said. "Drove through the tornadoes to get here."

Tornadoes. Next up, locusts. Maybe this really is the year.

Or maybe it's already been the year. Maybe this day, this fluttering, is its own reward.

The Memphis Tigers are in the Final Four. Go ahead, say it again.

"It's right there on the logo," said Anderson.

Come 5:07, you can see for yourself.

U OF M PLAYERS TAKING COACH, FANS, CITY ALONG ON JOYOUS NCAA RIDE

APRIL 6, 2008

SAN ANTONIO — Chris Douglas-Roberts cut in along the baseline, took the slick pass from Antonio Anderson, soared in for his customary layup and thought, you know, why not dunk?

So he dunked.

He dunked for Larry Finch, watching from a Memphis hospital. He dunked for Larry Kenon, sitting in the Alamodome. He dunked for John Calipari, who wasn't supposed to be clever enough to win this game. He dunked for Detroit, which will always be his home.

Mostly, though, he dunked for Memphis, for the city and the school, and for the collection of players who never let the expectations of others shape their expectations of themselves.

"They didn't think I could get that high," he said.

Someone put that on a T-shirt, quick.

They didn't think Memphis could get this high, either, clear into Monday and the national championship game.

Thirty-five years after UCLA defeated Memphis in the 1973 championship game, the Tigers earned a second shot at the title Saturday night with a resounding 78-63 victory over UCLA.

"Revenge is sweet," said Vickie Finch, watching from the stands. Finch was at the Final Four in St. Louis 35 years ago, when her true love, Larry, scored 29 points in the loss. Now she was dancing and laughing and taking pictures with her son, Larry Jr.

"It's awesome," she said, "you can't beat this."

Not far away, former '73 forward Larry Kenon sat with Gene Bartow, his old Memphis coach, and exulted in the win.

"If they go, we all go," said Kenon.

Put that on a T-shirt, too.

Because they're going to the national championship game, these Tigers, and they're carrying all of Memphis along.

"I think we'll win it," Kenon said, "we have the best team."

And who can doubt that this morning, after watching the Tigers dismantle a UCLA team that so many thought was perfectly designed to stop what the Memphis players do best?

UCLA had the size, the experience and — this was the big thing — the genius on the bench.

That would be Ben Howland, the smartest kid in the coaching class, who is to timeouts as Mendel was to peas.

"There was a column in *The Los Angeles Times* today that said this was a coaching mismatch," someone told Calipari after the game.

Calipari pondered this.

"I don't think Ben is that bad," he said.

Big laughs all around.

What a wonderful moment that had to be for Calipari, even if he won't admit to it publicly. The guy is not a favorite with the national media. He has never met a fight he couldn't pick. But saying Calipari can't coach is like saying Derrick Rose can't run.

Can't coach?

Then why do his guys play so hard?

Can't coach?

Then why do they defend better than anyone else?

Can't coach?

Then why does he have an entire city believing in this team and, maybe, even themselves?

Calipari has never thought coaching is about proving you're smarter than the other guy. He thinks it's about recruiting great players, teaching them a system, helping them to believe in themselves, and then unleashing the result on an unsuspecting world.

It's almost hilarious, at this point. Every game is the same. The wise guys figure out all these reasons that Memphis might lose. Then the game starts and the wise guys are suddenly muttering and shaking their heads and drawing up post-game questions like these: "Derrick did some things on the court today that left a lot of us slack-jawed ..."

Slack-jawed.

Put that on a T-shirt, too.

They were slack-jawed over Rose (25 points, nine rebounds, four assists and one turnover), they were slack-jawed over Douglas-Roberts (28 points), they were slack-jawed over the free-throw shooting (87 percent) and they were slack-jawed over Joey Dorsey's single-mindedly ferocious game (zero points and 15 rebounds).

Dorsey did write another story for this one, by the way. It was called "No Love for UCLA." It could have been subtitled, "No Collison, either," because that's the way it worked out.

UCLA's Kevin Love had 12 points, but just 2 in the second half. Point guard Darren Collison had two points on 1-of-9 shooting from the field. Calipari might not be much of a coach, but for the 832nd straight game he figured out how to make the other team's best players disappear.

"I coached like I do in every game," he said.

Pause.

"According to some, in a very poor way."

More big laughs. Could it be that Calipari is the genius now?

It certainly can't be Howland who, in addition to ordering up Collison's fifth foul, went out of his way to "credit Memphis State."

Memphis State? Yo, Ben. It's been 14 years!

But this isn't a time for gloating, just dancing, and chest-bumping, and toasting a team that set a national record Saturday with its 38th win of the year.

CBS analyst Billy Packer reminded Calipari about the record in his postgame interview. The Memphis players, circled around Calipari, wondered if they'd heard it right.

"That's it, that's the most wins?" one of them asked.

"No," Calipari said, "you've got to get to 39."

MEMPHIS LEFT TO SING THE SADDEST OF BLUES
APRIL 8, 2008

At the end, Chris Douglas-Roberts pulled his jersey over his head. At the end, Antonio Anderson hid under a towel.

At the end, the Memphis Tigers collapsed on the bench, in visible, undeniable pain.

They had the title; they gave away the title.

I guess that's why they call it the blues.

On a night when Memphians everywhere were poised to celebrate the ultimate victory — when they had finally, truly allowed themselves to believe in the possibility that everything would turn out right — they instead watched, in sickening horror, as the Tigers blundered it all away.

"I thought we were national champs," said Memphis coach John Calipari.

Instead, the Jayhawks are national champs, 75-68, in overtime.

W.C. Handy would know what to do with this moment. B.B. King could play it on Lucille.

But hundreds of thousands of Memphians will take a good long time to get over this, to make some sense of what they witnessed at the Alamodome Monday night.

Free throws? They lost because of free throws? Could this game be any more cruel?

Calipari reassured everyone his players would make them when they counted. Instead, they missed.

And missed. And missed. And missed.

"It hurts," said Douglas-Roberts, speaking for Memphians everywhere.

For Clavon Barney, watching from Korea, where he serves in the Army. For Steve Williams, a FedEx employee watching from Hong Kong.

For the men and the women at the Memphis Mission, watching the game on a big screen. For the sick kids and families at Le Bonheur Children's Hospital, who had a watch party with blue punch.

"A lot of people have been waiting a long time for this," said Will Taylor, in the midst of the massive Memphis pep rally in San Antonio earlier in the day.

And by "this" he didn't mean a pep rally, either.

He meant victory. Not moral or otherwise. Victory. Butt-kicking victory. How about one of those?

Never mind the history of Memphis disappointments. Never mind everything else that had gone wrong for this town.

The failed NFL drives. The crushing NBA lottery.

This would be different. People believed it to their bones.

"Expect good things to happen" is what Calipari had said, and somehow, people did.

They expected the Tigers to make free throws; they expected Calipari to draw up the right plays; they expected Derrick Rose and Douglas-Roberts to rise to the moment; sure enough, they all did.

Rose heaved in an impossible, banked jumper with 4:15 left. That would be the play of the game. The signature shot! The shining moment! The one you see forever in your dreams.

The Tigers were up by five, after that one. Not only that, they were making their foul shots. Just like the coach had promised. With 2:12 left, Robert Dozier swished two to put Memphis up 60-51.

That's a nine-point lead. With slightly more than two minutes left. It was all over but the endless party on Beale.

The city of Memphis would finally have a title, would finally get to stick its big, foam blue finger in the air.

It was perfect. It was worth the wait. It was ...

Unbearable.

Utterly, completely unbearable, for anyone with a heart.

Kansas made plays. It's true, there's no denying it. But that's not why the Tigers lost. The Tigers lost because they stepped to the line five times in the last 1:15 and missed four times.

With 1:15 left, Douglas-Roberts missed the front end of a 1-and-1.

With 16.8 seconds left, Douglas-Roberts missed two more foul shots.

With 10.8 seconds left, Rose, the incomparable one, had a chance to end the thing. Memphis up by two. Hit both shots and it's done.

Rose hit the second but he missed the first.

"We were trying to make them," he said.

Yeah, Derrick, we know. Everyone knows. Everyone understands. Y'all wanted to win more than Memphians wanted you to win. But that's not going to make this easier for anyone in the years to come.

"We still led by three," said Douglas-Roberts, and that's true, too. The Tigers would foul. Kansas could only get two.

"We were fouling," said Calipari. Except, suddenly, his players couldn't even do that right.

"The kid got away," Calipari said.

And with it, the night. The game. The endless party on Beale. The championship. Everything.

Kansas guard Mario Chalmers rose to take the shot and released the ball and, wait, didn't Calipari say to expect good things?

This was not a good thing. This was beyond cruel.

"Ten seconds to go, we're thinking we're national champs," Calipari said. "All of a sudden, we're not."

He looked dazed, more than anything. Dazed and crushed. He said it was all his fault.

This is silly, of course. Calipari did not miss the foul shots. As for his bluster in the past months, well, what was he going to say?

That his players would miss them when they counted? That it was this city's destiny?

That good things do not happen in Memphis? That Memphians are born to lose?

Whatever Monday night comes to mean in the long haul, it cannot be that. The players played too well for too long. The season brought too much joy.

Yeah, it ended badly. It ended in a way that buckles the knees.

"We should have won," said Calipari.

That's why they call it the blues.

HE DIDN'T EVEN STOP FOR A FINAL GOODBYE
APRIL 1, 2009

He never stopped to say goodbye.

Everyone was assembled there, too. Outside John Calipari's big house on Galloway. With their signs and their flowers — yes, someone sent flowers — and their urgent and desperate chants.

"S-T-A-Y," they chanted.

It was sweet, really. And mournful, too.

Someone stuck a "Not For Sale By Owner" sign on Calipari's lawn. It will give way to a different sign soon.

Because at 4:22 p.m., the big gates swung open. A three-car motorcade pulled out.

"S-T-A-Y," the chant resumed again.

You would have thought Calipari might have stopped for a moment, wouldn't you? If only to say thanks and farewell?

Except, of course, he might have had to explain why he was ransacking the Memphis program on the way out. And why he didn't have it in him to make the same hard choice he's been asking recruits to make for years.

The three cars gunned it. It actually makes sense.

How could he look anyone in the eye?

Calipari will be introduced this morning as the new basketball coach at the University of Kentucky.

This is not surprising, really. It is not even the wrong choice.

Kentucky is Kentucky. It is a better program than Memphis. You can't blame a guy for taking off for bluer pastures after nine glorious years.

But, gee, did he have to leave quite such a mess behind him? Did he have to leave a program that will struggle to win 15 games next year?

Calipari may or may not be successful in getting all of his elite recruits to follow him to Kentucky. But you can be darn sure he's given it his best shot.

Otherwise, why have them sign Letters of Intent that included a release if Calipari bolted for the door?

UAB wouldn't agree to such a clause for DeMarcus Cousins. Calipari — shockingly — had no such qualms.

He's never been a big qualms guy, actually. He had no qualms about bringing Jeremy Hunt back from permanent dismissal. He had no qualms about package deals. He had no qualms about handing his program over to the mysterious William Wesley. He had no qualms about using the threat of other jobs to get raises from a strapped Memphis program nearly every year.

Look inside this paper, at today's sports section. In addition to the usual timeline you see on days like this, CA reporter Ron Higgins put together a Calipari-job-flirtation time line.

Everyone remembers the Calipari-to-North-Carolina-State money grab. And the Calipari-to-Kentucky-last-time-around money grab. But do you remember the Calipari-to-South-Carolina money grab? That came in 2001. An early one. Ahhhh, the good old days.

There is a chance, at this point, that some of you may be thinking this column is borne of bitterness. Kentucky fans — desperate to believe in their new savior — will think this most of all.

It's not true, though. Some of us just understood Calipari all along. We would even write about his flaws from time to time.

"Miserables!" Calipari said.

"Miserables," came the echo from the more besotted Memphis fans.

It's those people who are the angriest and most disappointed today. Because for nine years, they believed the fictions. But the Calipari they now revile — and they do revile him, with almost frightening intensity — is no different than the Calipari they adored for so many years.

He's a basketball coach. A highly gifted basketball coach who will do wonders for you as long as your interests align with his.

For nine years, Calipari's interests and Memphis's interests were identical. In the last few days, that changed.

So Calipari relentlessly watched out for his interests, of course. If that means Memphis will be a Conference USA bottom-feeder next year, well, that's the kind of price the guy has always been willing to pay.

It's who he is. It's part of the whole complicated deal. It's why the flowers and the rest seemed so achingly sad.

"S-T-A-Y," came the cheers, from Calipari's most fervent believers. But he didn't even stop to say goodbye.

BLUE ALL OVER – TIGERS FANS FILL THE HOUSE WITH SUPPORT FOR TEAM

OCTOBER 17, 2009

As many times as David and Janet Raper had been to Memphis Madness, they had never seen anything as eye-popping as this.

"Incredible," said David.

"Fantastic," said Janet.

"I got shivers," said David. "It's hard to put into words."

No, they were not talking about the slam-dunk contest. Or the 3-point contest. Or anything else involving a basketball.

They were not talking about Yo Gotti, the rapper. Or Antonio Burks, the recovering former Tiger, who sat in a wheelchair, smiling to the fans.

They were not talking about the collection of world-class recruits. They were not talking about the Memphis Grizzlies who came to watch the show.

They were talking about the crowd. My, what a crowd.

An unprecedented crowd. A breathtaking, heart-stopping and utterly affirming crowd.

Six months after the University of Memphis lost its coach and its recruits, six months after people questioned whether Memphis basketball would survive, more than 18,000 fans answered that question in the best way possible.

By showing up. By waiting in line. By massing in the plaza outside FedExForum, beginning as early as 3:30 p.m., to get into a building that wouldn't open until 7.

By 6:30, the plaza was jammed, lines running clear to the street, hundreds deep, more arriving all the time.

"Oh my gosh," said Michelle Connelly.

"It's crazy," said Jennifer Gay.

"I'm not very good at judging this," said Ed Horrell, "but I think there might be more people than seats."

This was impossible, of course. Memphis Madness had never filled FedExForum to brimming, even in the best of years.

But the people kept coming. And coming. And shortly after 7:30, Memphis athletic director R.C. Johnson wandered over to the press table.

"We just closed the doors," he said. "We're having to turn people away."

Then, deadpan: "I should have charged."

Johnson broke into a wide grin at that one. If he seemed giddy — if everyone seemed giddy — you could understand why.

This wasn't a celebration of any one era or recruiting class. This was a celebration of Memphis and Memphis basketball.

The 18,000 people who showed up Friday didn't fall in love with any one coach. They fell in love with Larry Finch or Elliot Perry, with Joey Dorsey or Baskerville Holmes, with Win Wilfong or Rodney Carney or Penny Hardaway or Derrick Rose.

Give Josh Pastner, the new coach, credit for understanding this. For making it the unmistakable theme of the night.

He built it right into the highlight video, which opened with the following words: "Not one player, not one coach, not one season."

The last few years, it was always John Calipari and the Memphis Tigers. As if the coach created the program, built it up from scratch.

Pastner, by contrast, seems to think he has been given temporary responsibility for something that was already special and rare.

He beamed every time he looked up at the crowd. He beamed when he took the microphone to speak.

"If there's any second thought that this isn't the best fan base in the entire world, they don't know what they're talking about," he said. "This is Memphis State, the University of Memphis, and you showed it tonight by supporting your team."

The rest was fun. The way these things tend to be. Yo Gotti rapped. Will Coleman dunked. What other madness event could have assembled a trio of slam-dunk judges like Allen Iverson, Penny Hardaway and Rudy Gay?

But that's not what made the night. What made the night was the crowd.

"I'd like to hug every one of them," said Pastner, still beaming.

It would have taken a good long time.

HE LOVED HIS CITY; MEMPHIS RECIPROCATED

APRIL 3, 2011

Vickie Finch remembers the day he made his decision, the day Larry Finch decided to stay in Memphis to play college basketball.

There wasn't some great big ceremony. Finch didn't try to keep everyone in suspense.

He picked Memphis.

He was always going to pick Memphis.

"He loved Memphis," said Vickie.

Right till the very end.

Larry O. Finch, 60, died at Saint Francis Hospital Saturday afternoon, family and friends gathered around his hospital bed.

"I just lost my best friend and my husband," said Vickie. "The last thing he did was squeeze my hand."

That would be typical Larry, wouldn't it? Offering one last bit of reassurance for the road?

"He just loved this city so much," said Vickie.

The feeling was mutual.

And, yes, it's possible that if you're just passing through Memphis, if you're picking this newspaper up at the airport, you're wondering what all the fuss is about.

The entire front page for a basketball player? A player who never made it to the NBA?

Yes.

Emphatically, yes.

"I've always said the two greatest Memphians were Elvis and Larry Finch," said Memphis coach Josh Pastner.

And Elvis was born in Tupelo. Finch was born right here in Orange Mound.

But, then, you know his story by now, know it the way you know all the fables we hold most dear.

He was born into the segregated South, the eldest of seven kids. His mother earned $5.50 a day cleaning houses — the two quarters to pay for bus fare.

He became a brilliant basketball player. He and his friend, Ronnie Robinson, starred for Melrose High. And then they disregarded pressure from some in the black community — who viewed Memphis State with justifiable suspicion — and decided to stay and play for their local university.

Once there, they brought black and white together, carried Memphis State to the Final Four in 1973 and caused a city riven by racial hatred to see past its differences and ...

Oh, c'mon. It's preposterous to even read it, isn't it?

Except it's all true!

Finch and Robinson played their first varsity game for Memphis State in December 1970, just 32 months after Martin Luther King Jr. was shot on the balcony of the Lorraine Motel. They weren't the first black players to play at Memphis — that was Herb Hilliard, who transferred in — but they were the first real home-grown stars.

And if the cliché about sports stars "bringing people together" is wildly overdone today, there's no other way to describe what Finch and Robinson did for this city from 1970-73.

"I remember sitting on my floor and watching him play," said Hank McDowell, who would go on to star for the Tigers. "We didn't know he was bringing the city together or anything. We were just all cheering for the same team."

Leonard Draper, Finch's longtime friend, says that was part of the secret of Finch. He wasn't trying to reshape society. He was just being Larry Finch.

"He was a basketball player," said Draper.

And he was a magnificent basketball player. After that, he was a magnificent basketball coach.

But his legacy will always be more than that. In a city that still struggles with self-doubt, Finch never doubted this was where he wanted to be.

So Memphians today will tell you they loved Finch for his smile, or his laugh, or the way his lean-in jumper always seemed to drop in.

Vickie knows the deeper truth.

"They loved Larry," she said, "because Larry loved them."

JUMP FOR JOY
MARCH 9, 2013

The first dunk. D.J. Stephens was a junior in high school.

It was on the road. During warm-ups. One of Stephens' teammates suggested he try to dunk the thing.

"He threw me an alley-oop," said Stephens. "When I jumped, I surprised myself. I honestly had no idea I could fly that high."

And, yes, you may consider that the theme of this story. Did anyone ever believe he could fly this high?

Did anyone think the kid who couldn't get a scholarship at North Texas could become one of the most valuable players on a Top 25 team?

Did anyone think he could become one of the most consistently electrifying players in the land?

Did anyone believe the 6-5 post player with aching knees and debilitating asthma could turn himself a legitimate NBA prospect and the overwhelming favorite for Conference USA defensive player of the year?

Did anyone imagine a guy who couldn't do more than two pushups in a row as a freshman — a fact Stephens revealed earlier this week — could lift his team to an undefeated conference season?

Did anyone believe that an essentially un-recruited player who landed at Memphis only because the previous head coach strip-mined the roster of talent would become one of the most beloved players ever to wear the Tigers uniform?

"It's actually indescribable," said Stephens, and it is all that, and more.

It is the kind of story that restores your faith in college athletics. It is so sweet, and so affirming, only the hardest of hearts can make it through without shedding a tear.

"I've been hearing all week that people are going to be bawling when D.J. steps on the court Saturday," said Memphis coach Josh Pastner. "I know exactly what they mean."

• • •

D.J. Stephens is not just a basketball player. He is a fable and a bed-time story. The kind you want to tell your kids.

"When I called North Texas, they told me that they no longer had a scholarship available," said Stephens, beginning the story once again. This was earlier in the week, in advance of Saturday's game between Memphis and UAB, which will be the last time Stephens, a senior, plays in front of his home fans.

So the reporters asked Stephens to tell them how he wound up at Memphis in the first place. Because some stories you can hear again and again.

"North Texas told me they no longer had room for me," Stephens said. "I called the other schools that had offered me scholarships, and they said the same thing."

Enter Pastner, who was scrambling to fill the Memphis roster after John Calipari took much of the previous one with him to Lexington.

"I got a mass e-mail from his AAU coach," Pastner said. "I called him and offered him a scholarship."

Stephens remembers crying when he got the call from Memphis.

"A week later, he was here, and I watched him work out, and I was the one crying," said Pastner, laughing.

Except — remember — this fable is true. Well, maybe not the part about Pastner literally crying. But the guts of it. Pure truth.

Stephens really was overmatched when he got to Memphis. He really couldn't do 20 pushups without breaking them into 10 sets of 2. Heck, as late as this past November — just four months ago — Pastner held Stephens out of a closed scrimmage against Alabama because he was thinking about redshirting him this year. And Stephens, for his part, was thinking about giving up the game for good.

"I was just going to be a regular student," said Stephens. "I thought God was telling me it was time."

Thankfully, former Memphis Tiger Will Barton had a different opinion.

"I called him for advice, and he said I was nuts," Stephens said.

So Stephens and Pastner decided they'd go ahead and give it a whirl and see what happened. What has happened is that Stephens has become a star. He leads the conference in blocks. He's shooting a ridiculous .669 from the field. More than that, he's become the emotional leader of a team that may win 30 games before the NCAA Tournament, and has hopes to do some serious damage after that.

"I cannot imagine what we would have done without D.J. this year," said Pastner. "Redshirt him? I have never been so happy to be wrong."

• • •

Here's the thing about the Stephens story: there are more where that came from. More stories, I mean. Your kids should know these, too.

Like the one about the Harvard game. Pastner told it earlier this week. Stephens — who sprained his shoulder during the early-season trip to the Bahamas — went down hard against Harvard and injured his shoulder again.

"He went back to the locker room," said Pastner. "They told him he was done for the day. And then he heard the crowd, like he could tell something was going wrong, and he told the doctor, 'I gotta go out there and play.'

"He could tell from the crowd that his team needed him. And he came out the last seven or eight minutes and he was unbelievable — he helped us win the game. That sums up D.J. Stephens, right there."

Except, of course, it doesn't. Because then there's the story about how Stephens spent his Fridays last spring. He and former Tiger Drew Barham realized they didn't have classes on Fridays, so they decided to devote those days to making people happy. Every Friday, they would find two or three schools or nursing homes or hospitals to visit, on their own.

"We had the time, so why not do it?" said Stephens. "To be honest, I think we got more out of it than anyone."

Which leads to the story about how Stephens met his girlfriend, Stacie. He had volunteered to help out with Mustang Madness at Houston High.

"She had a brother who went there, and she was in the stands," he said. "I guess she thought that I was really sweet the way I interacted with the kids."

The next day, Stacie told a friend about the kind-hearted Memphis basketball player she had seen.

"It turns out I knew her friend," Stephens said. "We started texting, and then, about a year ago, we realized we had something special between us."

Oh, and that leads to another story. About Stephens, sitting in the locker room in Knoxville before the Tennessee game.

"Stacie (who was back home) told me she needed to go to the emergency room," Stephens said. "I'm like, 'What's with this girl, telling me this right before a big game?' But as soon as the game was over, of course I checked my phone, and there was a text that said, 'Call me ASAP.'"

Stephens called.

"She said 'You're going to be a dad,'" Stephens said. "There was an awkward silence on the phone for a moment, and I was waiting for her to say, 'Just kidding.' But she never said it. And I said, 'Really?' And I was just happy. I was so happy. My face started glowing, right there in the locker room."

Stephens understands that some of you may not approve of this last story, by the way.

"People ask me if I'm going to marry her," he said. "Of course I'm going to marry her. The only reason that we're not married yet is that I'm not financially stable. But it's all part of the plan."

Final story, a small one: Stephens does not own a car. Once, it seemed like every Memphis player drove an Escalade. Stephens hasn't had a car since his sophomore year.

"I had a Chrysler Concorde, but it got a bad oil leak, and its engine locked up on me," he said. "Let's just say that Stacie has been very important this year in getting me from point A to point B.

"When I finally make some money, you know what I'm going to do? I'm going to pick her up and take her to the movies for once."

• • •

When Pastner called Stephens one of the five greatest Memphis players in history earlier this year, people hooted. Stephens is not one of the five greatest Memphis players. But he is absolutely one of the five most beloved.

Think about the reasons particular players are embraced by a fan base. Some players are loved because they play harder than anyone else. Some players are loved because they play with a sense of joy. Some players are loved because they have a great rags-to-riches story. Some players are loved because they seem like wonderful human beings. Some players are loved because they help the team win big games. Some players are loved because they are eye-popping athletes who make plays that nobody else can make.

Stephens is loved for every one of those reasons. He is also what we wish college athletics could be. At a time when some players can't wait to leave after one year, Stephens is having a hard time adjusting to the idea that he has to leave after four.

So of course there will be crying. There already has been.

"I'll be happy, but I'll be sad, too," said Lisa Erwin. "It's going to be that kind of day."

Erwin is the mother of Trey Erwin, the local high school football player who died of pancreatic cancer a year ago. When Trey was first diagnosed, someone asked Stephens if he would visit him in the hospital.

"I went that same day," said Stephens. "You could tell he was dealing with some things, but we really hit it off."

They started texting back and forth. They talked nearly every day. When Trey died, Stephens walked with the family at the funeral.

"He became like a little brother," said Stephens.

Said Erwin, of Stephens: "He's one of my children now. I love him. Honestly, we all do."

Erwin wasn't speaking for the entire city, but she may as well have been. Memphians don't love Stephens just because they have seen him jump. They love him because they have seen his heart.

That's why Saturday will be so emotional. That's why the ovation will be loud and long. For all the great leapers who have come through the program, there aren't many the fans look up to more.

IV

MORE
PEOPLE

STAN'S THE MAN, JUST ASK RECORD KEEPERS
MAY 5, 2007

It was another day at the ballpark, another seventh inning done, another moment for Stan Bronson Jr. to be introduced as the Memphis Tigers batboy of 49 years, another chance for Bronson to walk to home plate and take a deep bow.

This happens after every seventh inning at Nat Buring Stadium. Bronson, 79, would stay planted on home plate if he didn't get his applause.

"Forty-nine years as a batboy, that must be a record," said someone in the group of Tiger fans.

Everyone agreed that it absolutely must be.

And that could have been that. Except Beverly Dunn, longtime Memphis fan, took the thought home with her.

She pondered it. She looked on the computer. The longest serving batboy? What organization would keep such a record?

"I'm know what I'm going to do," she said, finally. "I'm going to get in touch with the people from Guinness World Records."

• • •

This is a story about perspective. About how life depends on what you see.

Do you see the rain or the rainbow? Do you see the pony or the manure?

Do you see a handicapped kid who's going to be nothing but a pain or a chance to give someone a boost?

Memphis football coach Billy "Spook" Murphy saw a chance to give someone a boost. How, it's hard to say.

The year was 1958. A mother walked into his office with her 29-year-old son. The mother was crying. Her son, Stan, needed somewhere to go.

Stan didn't have the natural gifts that most of us have. He walked with a limp and he slurred his words. He was special, is the way some people put it. And he loved sports.

The mother thought it would be great if Murphy would let her son work with the Memphis teams. He didn't even need to get paid. He just needed somewhere to go.

Murphy could have said no. What coach wouldn't have said no?

"Just show up tomorrow," Murphy told Stan.

So Stan showed up. And showed up. And he's been showing up for 49 years now.

Murphy is long since departed from the university. Stan has worked under nine football coaches, seven baseball coaches and six presidents.

He lives in a small house down Central Ave. He used to walk to the university every day. Now he takes the bus. He spends his mornings at the library.

"I look at books," he said. "I study hard."

Stan eats his meals at the Tiger Den. After lunch, he walks over to the athletic office building to hitch a ride to South Campus, where the football and baseball teams hold their practices.

"At 1 p.m., I usually find him leaning against my car," said Memphis baseball coach Daron Schoenrock. "In the fall, he leans against (Memphis football coach) Tommy West's car."

Schoenrock remembered Stan from the days he used to play Memphis as a baseball player at Tennessee Tech. But he had his first conversation with Stan his second day in the Memphis job.

"I hadn't even unpacked," he said. "Stan came in to my office and said, 'Coach, are you going to hire me back?'"

"Well," said Schoenrock, "the first thing I'm going to have to do is look at your salary schedule."

Stan laughed at that. He likes to laugh.

"Ever since then," said Schoenrock, "I tell him that if they're bringing me back, he can come, too."

So Schoenrock is the latest Memphis administrator to wrap his arms around Stan. But it's a long list. Former president V. Lane Rawlins awarded Stan a diploma. That prompted some to ask Stan what he was going to do next.

"Graduate school," said Stan.

Once, an auditor wondered who this Stan Bronson was who always ate for free.

The auditor was told to find another place to cut costs.

"I admire the university for allowing him to be a part of this program for so many years," said Schoenrock. "But the players get something out of it, too. They learn not everybody is as gifted as they are. They learn to treat everyone with respect."

And to think: All because a football coach looked at Stan and saw something most wouldn't have seen.

Which brings us back to Dunn, the longtime fan, who did much the same thing.

She saw Stan as a nice addition to Memphis baseball games, sure. But she also saw him as someone worthy of wider recognition.

"I just couldn't believe there was anyone who had done it longer," she said. "Most employees don't stay on the job for 49 years when they're getting paid. Here is a man who loves this institution enough that he's come out for 49 years without getting paid."

Dunn found the Guinness website. She learned the procedure for submitting a record claim. She compiled affidavits and newspaper clippings. She even tracked down a copy of Stan's birth certificate.

Then she shipped the packet of materials off to England. And waited. And waited.

"I'd check the website two or three times a day," she said. "It always said the claim was being investigated."

Until April 26. That day, Dunn logged in to find a message that said, "Congratulations, your record has been approved."

Dunn leapt from her chair. She called everyone she could think to call.

Eddie Cantler, the longtime trainer at Memphis, gave Stan the good news.

"Have you heard of the Guinness Book of Records?" Cantler said.

"No," said Stan.

"Well, they keep it in England," Cantler said. "Where the Queen is from. You're going to be it."

Stan considered this for a moment.

"How much will it cost to buy the book?" he said.

Cantler assured Stan he'd get him a copy. In the meantime, Stan will receive a certificate before today's Memphis game.

Dunn isn't sure he'll understand the significance. Here's hoping the rest of us will.

Life depends on what you see. Do you see the birds or the carwash? The mud or the Memphis music festival?

Do you see a handicapped kid who's going to be nothing but a pain or someone who could be the first holder of a Guinness World Record in the history of the school?

His name is Stan. He's the longest-tenured batboy that's ever been.

And, absolutely, you can look it up.

RHODES STAR TRULY SUPER IN AREAS THAT MATTER MOST
APRIL 27, 2008

By the time they went for the MRI, Scott and Tracy Patterson felt a little ridiculous.

Scott was having some problems with his balance. Well, he was legally blind. Why wouldn't he have problems with his balance?

Just four days earlier, he had celebrated Easter with his family. Then he watched — as well as he could watch, at least — the Memphis Tigers' second-round win over Mississippi State.

He worried about the Tigers' foul shooting; he didn't worry about his health all that much.

Patterson felt a little crummy. He decided to go see his doctor. That's how he and Tracy ended up at the MRI place.

"We felt stupid," Tracy said. "Like, why are we bothering them with this?"

It was nothing. Plainly, it was nothing. The machine did what MRI machines do.

They waited. The doctor finally emerged.

"I want you to see this," he said.

• • •

Four years ago, Randy Bruce, the deputy sports content editor at this paper, came to me with an idea for a column.

"It's about the all-time leading scorer at Rhodes," he said. "He's blind now."

Well. That was interesting. I asked Randy for the guy's name.

"Scott Patterson," he said.

I wrote the name on a piece of paper, then I put the paper in the manila folder where I keep all sorts of column ideas.

Then I ignored it. Or, I suppose, time passed. The Grizzlies went to the playoffs. The Tigers started to win big.

DeAngelo Williams left; Derrick Rose arrived. With big stars like that to write about, who had time for anything else?

So Scott Patterson and his story sat in my folder. This is the way of the world, isn't it?

We care about our celebrities. We care about our prime-time heroes.

We do not care about a guy who used to play basketball at Rhodes, even if he has an inspirational story to tell.

Patterson had an inspirational story. Inspirational and devastating, too.

"We called him 'Superman,'" said Tracy, his wife, who met Scott when they were both students at Rhodes. "He bore a striking resemblance to Christopher Reeve. He was 6-4 with black hair, pale blue eyes and dimples. He was gorgeous."

Patterson didn't drink and didn't smoke. He taught Sunday School for 5-year-olds during all four years at Rhodes.

"His mother always wrapped his presents in Superman wrapping paper," said Tracy, and she did this only partly as a joke.

He was that good. At just about everything. Patterson was MVP of the basketball team at Memphis University School, then a two-time MVP of the College Athletic Conference while at Rhodes.

For a time, Tracy wondered what if there was anything he couldn't do. Then, one romantic night, he told her to sit down, that he was going to serenade her.

"It was the song, 'If Ever I Should Leave You,'" Tracy said. "He opened his mouth to sing and, honestly, it was horrible."

Tracy listened, stunned. Was it a joke? But if it was a joke, why was he going on and on and on?

"It was the worst thing you ever heard," said Tracy. "It turns out, he was taking voice lessons."

Which was quintessential Scott. If he had a weakness, by golly, he was going to work on it.

He trained harder than anyone else. He scored more points (1,989) than anyone else. He drove a spiffier car than anyone else.

"A gold (Datsun) 280Z convertible," Tracy said, "with vanity license plates."

He would cruise, top down, through his days. Some guys get all the luck. Private high school. Private college. A golden car and a golden life.

Except shortly after he graduated from Rhodes — just as he was beginning his career as a financial advisor at Merrill Lynch — Patterson started to feel just a bit odd. He struggled during pick-up basketball games. Driving became tricky, too. He side-swiped another car.

"His vision started to go," said Tracy. "For a year and a half, the doctors didn't know what was wrong with him. He went to the Mayo Clinic. At one point, he was told he had a month to live. Finally, technology progressed to the point that he was diagnosed with a brain tumor."

The doctors were able to subdue the tumor with surgery, radiation and chemotherapy, but Patterson's vision never returned.

The best scorer in the history of Rhodes basketball could see only shapes and shadows.

"It was hard," said Brett Patterson, his younger brother. "I will tell you he never felt sorry for himself and he didn't, really. There was a period of adjustment that really got him. You have to understand, he was 215 pounds and built like Atlas. Literally. You just wouldn't believe. And all of a sudden he was totally bald, dents in his head, and one of his eyes kind of wandered. He struggled with that. There were times he didn't want to go anywhere. Just the pride of it all."

Patterson could have spent the rest of his life like this, holed up, self-pitying, angry at God and medicine and the entire world. Nobody would have blamed him. Everyone would have understood.

"But that's not Scott," Brett Patterson said. "After that initial period, he decided to attack his blindness the same way he had attacked everything else in his life, with relentless energy and undying optimism."

Patterson kept teaching Sunday school; he married Tracy, had three kids and built a life.

It was certainly a different life than the one Patterson had imagined. He needed a narrator at movies, for one thing.

"I'd have to go and tell him what was happening," said Tracy. "That could get to be a problem at times. At the end of 'Little Miss Sunshine,' I was laughing so hard I couldn't talk.'"

Patterson found himself laughing just as hard. Even though he had no idea what was happening. He was laughing because Tracy was laughing. Sometimes, that's enough.

"He would still go jogging." Tracy said, "but he'd come back with scrapes and bruises you couldn't believe."

Patterson kept playing golf, too. His partners would have to tell him which way to hit.

"For putts, I'd put my feet on either side of the hole and talk to him," Brett said. "He'd figure out where I was and hit it toward me. I'd tell him which way the green breaks. A couple years ago, he sank a 40-foot putt to win a golf tournament."

Then came the kids: Emma, Joshua and Samantha.

"He always said that the best things in his life happened after he lost his vision," Brett said. "He married the love of his life and he had three beautiful children."

He coached them in basketball, too. Even if that meant directing his instructions to the wrong player from time to time.

At night, instead of reading bedtime stories, he'd have to dream them up.

"He told these elaborate fairy tales," Tracy said. "Cinderella was always crazy in them. Or drunk. I'd be the one sticking my head in and saying 'Judgment! Use good judgment!'"

In this way, the years went by. Productively. Joyfully, too.

Often, he and Tracy would take long walks. She'd tell him about the beautiful moon.

"I'd tell him where it was in the sky, that it's at 2 o'clock," Tracy said. "I have no idea if he ever saw it, but he said he did."

Because what's the point of missing the moon? Even if you can only see it in your head?

"Scott believed in the importance of attitude," Tracy said. "He would get phone calls, out of the blue, from people who had cancer and he'd talk to them for hours on end about how to beat cancer and the importance of staying positive."

This was his central lesson: Don't ever give up. Laugh whenever you can. Find happiness in the small things.

Like, say, the Tigers. As a good son of Memphis, Patterson was crazy about the Tigers. Easter Sunday, he watched the Mississippi State game like everyone else.

Four days later, he went in for that MRI, and felt a little ridiculous about it, until the doctor showed them the results.

"You have a brain tumor," he said.

It was a completely different sort of tumor than the first one. It was impossibly cruel.

"This stinks," said Patterson, which is about as gloomy as the guy could get.

It did stink, too. It seemed hideously unfair. He had survived one brain tumor and figured out how to live a happy, bountiful life in darkness. Now he had to start again?

OK, then, he would start again. On the drive home from the MRI place, he and Tracy were already cracking their morbid let's-cheer-each-other-up jokes.

"I'm still getting my new kitchen," said Tracy.

"Can't you wait until the life insurance?" said Scott.

They laughed. Because why miss a chance to do that? Three days later, Patterson had to be taken to the hospital by ambulance; this tumor was growing fast.

Patterson couldn't even remember he had a tumor most of the time. His short-term memory was shot.

"I sat with him during the UCLA game," Tracy said. "That's one of the last times I saw him smile. I told him, 'Scott, they made 20 out of 23 from the line. That's Scott Patterson shooting right there!'"

The last conscious moments came during a visit with the kids. Emma is now 14, Joshua is 12, Samantha is 7. Together, the family said the Lord's Prayer and held hands.

Patterson died on April 17, at age 44.

"Forty-four was his jersey number," said Tracy.

Pause.

"He should have picked a higher number," she said. "Like 99."

More laughter. Subdued, though. Her husband would have liked that one.

He would have found the good in this, too. He would have pointed back to a full, remarkable life.

He had those wonderful kids; he loved a woman who loved him back; he laughed loudly and he sang badly; he reminded us of something we too often forget.

Heroes come in all shapes and sizes. They're not always the people we expect.

To all the world, Scott Patterson may have appeared to be a Division 3 basketball player who was dealt a bad hand. To anyone who knew him, he was Superman.

THANKS FOR THE MEMORIES – ARMSTRONG HAS BEEN U OF M'S ATHLETIC ROCK — FOR 46 YEARS
NOVEMBER 6, 2008

It is a crisp, sunny day on the Memphis practice fields, and Murray Armstrong pulls up in his battered golf cart.

"Get in," he says.

Who could resist an invitation like that?

I get in.

Armstrong, 71, drives us across the bright, green fields.

"Looks good," I say.

"Sure does," he says. "It looks Cadillac now."

Armstrong wheels around, searching for imperfections. He stops to talk to one of his employees, Reggie Miller, about getting a new shipment of weed killer.

It is an utterly ordinary day in the life of a man who has been coming to work at the University of Memphis for 46 years. And it is utterly extraordinary, too.

Murray Armstrong has lung cancer. He's been battling it — as only Armstrong could battle anything — for more than four years.

On Oct. 6, the doctors transferred him to hospice care.

"What does it mean?" says Armstrong. "I'm worse."

Murray's eldest son, Sterritt, just shakes his head at this.

"It's what the doctors do," he says, "when they feel they've exhausted all treatment options."

• • •

Thirteen years ago, I moved to Memphis from another newspaper. I had never been to this city before my job interview.

It's an adjustment, writing a sports column in a new city, maybe even especially this city.

"You're not from Memphis," is something I heard a lot.

And I wasn't from Memphis. Worse, I was from the North.

So I was uncertain, as you might expect. I didn't know if it would work.

Then one day, on the Memphis football fields, a big, gruff, older guy pulled up next to me in his golf cart.

"That was a heckuva column you wrote," he said.

I don't even remember what the column was about. But I remember feeling better, almost instantly. I remember thinking it would all be OK.

The guy in the golf cart was Armstrong, of course. He had gone out of his way to do something nice. He had taken the time to think about somebody else.

And if it's taken me a good long while to get to Armstrong's job description during his years over at Memphis, maybe it's because it's impossible to describe.

How do you describe 46 years of unyielding decency? How do you describe an entire career of everyday thoughtfulness?

Armstrong interviewed for a job at Memphis in 1962, a strapping, former Tennessee football player in need of work.

"What can you do?" said Spook Murphy, the Memphis football coach.

"Coach, I can do anything," Armstrong said. "I can kiss butt, I can shine shoes, I can do whatever you want me to do."

"You're hired!" said Murphy.

It was Armstrong's last real job interview.

"The more they found out I could do, the more I did," Armstrong said.

He coached the freshmen. He coached tennis. He served as academic adviser, and not just for the football team.

In 1967, Armstrong and his wife, Joan, moved into the athletic dorms to watch over everyone.

They raised their two boys in those dorms. They raised maybe a thousand other boys, as well.

These are not just empty words, either, the sort that people tend to say about any person who is ill.

Remember what it felt like going to college for the first time? Remember the gnawing fear?

"As a kid coming out of Illinois, I was scared out of my mind coming to Memphis State to walk on the football team," wrote JJ Hickson, in a blog set up for members of the Memphis community to communicate with Armstrong. "When I walked in the South Hall, you were the first person I saw and I felt at ease. You made me feel welcome and I knew everything would be all right."

The blog goes on like this for pages and pages. Go read it for yourself at collegetime.wordpress.com.

Dimitri Delgado: "Currently, I am a commander in the United States Coast Guard and perform international engagements in the world of anti-terrorism. I am what I am, in very large measure, because of who and what you are."

Derrick Burroughs: "Coach, I never told you, but if you have the opportunity to read this, you were the father I never had. Even though I grew up with eight sisters and one brother and none of us knew what it was like to have a father, for five years, I did."

Jeff Harrison: "Thank you so very much for all the wonderful things you did for me while I was a walk-on football player for the 1983-84 seasons. You treated the walk-ons with the same respect, compassion and toughness as the scholarship players."

This may be the most remarkable thing about the blog: the vast range of people who took the time to write.

Sure, DeAngelo Williams submitted an entry. But so did Bill Daniels, who played club handball. And Susan Day, who works in the ticket office. And Charlotte Peterson, who coached tennis. And Tim McCormack, who served as a trainer.

They wrote with humor and nostalgia, with little details that draw a picture of a man.

Jim Rapp: "I will never forget the Christmas I was allowed to stay in the dorm by myself to help with the Liberty Bowl. I woke up Christmas morning to find a small gift outside my door."

Mike Anderson: "I remember my first night in Memphis. It was freezing cold in the room and I arrived with only a razor-thin blanket. I was having problems getting adjusted from being away from home and cold when he opened the door for the nightly checks. Like a daddy, he recognized that I was cold and missing home. He closed the door and came back minutes later with a nice warm blanket."

Sherry Weaver Goad: "Do you remember in the early 1980s the parent who made a frantic 'mommy' phone call to you that there was an uncaged boa constrictor SNAKE in her son's room? You promised you wouldn't tell anybody AND that you would personally take care of the snake. If I remember correctly, you said, 'I will go up and machete the SOB to pieces.' All I know for sure is that he disappeared and you became my hero."

A football player named Steve King wrote about the time Armstrong made him a milkshake to help him keep his weight up. Dozens wrote about Armstrong banging through the halls in the morning, waking everyone up with the loud reminder that it was "College Time!"

It must have been painful, in those mornings. But now?

Stan Weaver: "I wish just one morning Coach Armstrong could wake up my son for college."

Which can't happen, of course, and not just because Armstrong is ill.

College football is an industry now. No coach works at a place for 46 years.

But if you think this notion depresses Armstrong, you've missed the whole point.

He understands that tomorrow's jobs won't necessarily look like yesterday's jobs. But somebody has to do them, right?

Somebody has to teach. Somebody has to make things go. So figure out what needs to be done and then go do that.

Do it every day, if possible. Do it with joy and kindness and thoughtfulness.

You might not get rich — Armstrong never did — but, well, you should have seen what happened before the Memphis-Southern Miss game.

Armstrong drove to the team hotel to organize the buses, just as he always does. He doesn't have the strength to sit through the games any longer, but he still has to see the buses off.

Only, this time, the players didn't walk straight onto the buses. They walked, in a line, over to Armstrong instead.

"Coach, we want to tell you that we love you and we want to thank you for what you've done for the university," said the first player. And then they did. Every player walked up to Armstrong. Every player shook his hand.

Maybe decency begets decency. Maybe that's the legacy of the man.

Some people spend their lives chasing success. Armstrong defined success a different way.

Not long ago, Armstrong tried to explain why he stayed at Memphis for all these years, why he didn't take a bigger job in a bigger place.

"It just seemed like when I got down there, everybody loved me," he said.

Yep, and still do.

GRIEF CAN'T SLOW DOWN SJC'S CANNON
JUNE 7, 2009

Two days before Christmas, they awoke like they always did. She headed for the shower, he headed for the coffee pot.

"It was our custom," said Phil Cannon, 56, tournament director of the St. Jude Classic. "I would make the coffee and Alyce would start her shower."

Cannon went out and got the paper. He read through much of it.

"I wonder what's taking her so long?" he said, to nobody in particular.

After 20 minutes or so, he got up. He wandered back toward the bathroom.

"The water was still on," he said. "I knew as soon as I rounded the corner that things had changed forever."

• • •

The St. Jude Classic will be different this year, and not just for the reasons you imagine.

Yes, the title sponsor is gone. Sir Allen Stanford is no longer available to underwrite his dreams with other people's money. But those of us who cover the tournament will miss someone else a lot more than that guy.

Alyce Cannon will not be at the front media desk, signing us in and then welcoming us back each morning. For the first time in 29 years, someone else will be sitting in that spot.

So this is a tribute. Not even to Alyce, really, because Phil Cannon would not permit it. To all the Alyces out there. To all the people who have taken the Memphis golf tournament — whatever it's been called — into their lives and their hearts.

It just happens that two of those people met in the University of Memphis athletic office nearly 30 years ago and, well, better let Cannon tell the story.

"I was in the athletic ticket office, she was in the bursar's office," he said. "I'd take my deposits over there every day."

Of such things are great romances born. Or not, if Cannon hadn't gotten some serious help.

"I was chicken to ask her out," Cannon said. "A student-worker in the office kind of figured this out. She left me a note one day that said 'Call Alyce, something about a date,' So I called Alyce and she said, 'I didn't say anything about a date.'" They went out anyway. To an opera, of all things.

A year later, Cannon asked Alyce to marry him. Although, there was another go-between on this one.

"We went on a Metro Conference basketball trip and Coach (Spook) Murphy asked us out to dinner," Cannon said. "He said, 'Little man, if you ask that woman to marry you, I'll be your best man.'" So that was that. Who could turn down an offer of a best man like Spook?

"We got married at her parents' house," Cannon said.

They didn't have a honeymoon.

"We went out and had a picnic at Shelby Forest," he said. "We bought a house instead of a honeymoon."

They had simple tastes. They never traveled outside of the country. Their one indulgence was the golf tournament.

This may seem strange to those of you who think of the golf tournament as, well, a golf tournament. To many Memphians, it is more than that.

Cannon started volunteering in 1968, when he was a sophomore at White Station. He'd ride his bike to the tournament.

In 1980, even before they were married, Alyce joined him, working in the media center. It became a regular part of their lives, as certain as the changing of the seasons.

Neither one of them even played golf. That wasn't the point.

"We loved the hospital, loved the cause," Cannon said. "In 2000, my first year as tournament director, Maw Maw (Alyce's mother) died on Sunday, the day before the tournament. We buried her on Tuesday. Alyce and Paw Paw (Alyce's father) were at the media center at six o'clock the next morning."

It wasn't just selflessness, either. They always figured they got more than they gave.

Cannon will tell you that the Alyce he first met, the one he wooed in the Memphis athletic office, would have been happy to spend her entire life in an accountant's cubicle.

The tournament changed her, caused her to grow beyond herself. She wound up buying a frame shop in Germantown, creating art for strangers who wandered in the door.

As it happens, Dec. 23rd is the busiest day in the life of a frame shop. So last year, as Alyce started in on some Christmas wrapping the night of the 22nd, Cannon urged her to get to bed.

"She said, 'I'm going to have to, because I have a headache from here to here,' and she touched the front and back of my head," Cannon said. "It was the last thing she ever said to me."

He rose the next morning to make coffee; she headed for the shower.

"After about 20 minutes I sort of looked around the corner," Cannon said. "The shower water was still on, but she was passed out on the floor."

The ambulance carried Alyce to the hospital but Cannon already knew it was hopeless.

"An aneurysm," he said. "She was 51. They finished harvesting her organs about 7:30 Christmas Eve. We know seven people got a heck of a Christmas present."

Cannon cannot get through this story without breaking down. He has not read the letter explaining who received Alyce's organs. He goes to work. He does his best. He grieves and he wonders — how can he not? — if there's a grand plan to the whole deal.

Everything was going along so well. With Alyce and with the tournament, too.

Then Alyce was gone. Then Stanford.

"I actually think," Cannon said, "that maybe God gave me the difficulties here at the tournament to take my mind off it."

It works, but only sometimes. Cannon has been working desperately to save the tournament he loves. But, inevitably, he goes home. He watches the Cardinals on TV.

"A lot of times, I get in my car, put on jazz, drive up and down 385 and talk to Alyce," he said. "About three weeks ago, it was pouring down rain one day, I was probably at a low spot, I got in and started driving and ended up at the cemetery. Somebody had put a stuffed bear on the gravesite. I took it and kind of tried to wring the water out of it. Metaphorically, I think I was trying to wring the tears out of my soul."

He sagged. Metaphors only take you so far, you know? And now comes tournament week. The tournament they built their lives around.

How can he work the tournament without Alyce? How can he possibly go into the media center?

"I'm dreading it," he said. "I'm expecting a seven-day funeral. But I gain strength, and I quit crying real quick when I think of the St. Jude children that are facing this every day of their entire lives. It's real easy to stop crying and quit feeling sorry for yourself when you remember the sick little bald-headed girls."

Which is maybe the lesson here, if there has to be one. The tournament is not about one volunteer or about one sponsor. The tournament is about this city and this cause and the tens of thousands of people who have made it a part of their lives.

Alyce Cannon may be a symbol of those people. It is hard to believe there will be a tournament this week with someone else sitting at the front media desk.

But there will be a tournament. And someone will win. And the fans will have a blast. And at the end of the whole deal, a miraculous hospital will get a check.

That is why Alyce did what she did. That is why her husband will give it his best shot this week. And then, when it's over, he already knows what he'll do.

He'll get in his car. He'll turn on the jazz.

"Me and the little bear," he said, "we're going to bring her the final results."

WHEREAS WE HONOR A REGULAR NICE GUY – HE'S MAKING MEMPHIS A BETTER PLACE, ONE DOUGHNUT AT A TIME
JUNE 10, 2009

The ceremony took place under a bright blue sky, with doughnuts as hors d'oeuvres.

Yes, doughnuts. What exactly did you expect?

Bagels? Or croissants?

The ceremony was to honor someone who answers to the name "Donut Man."

So of course they served doughnuts. Glazed doughnuts. Some coffee would have been nice.

"OK, we ready? asked Councilman Kemp Conrad.

All said they were ready, if suddenly sticky of hand.

"WHEREAS," Conrad started, and it got so quiet you could almost hear the yeast rise.

• • •

This is not a big breaking story. It is not about politics or corruption or budgets or crime.

It is about one man who makes doughnuts. That's the beauty of it.

His name is Don DeWeese and he grew up in Philadelphia, Miss., and he once told his wife Rita that he'd never, ever want to live in Memphis.

"True story," he said. "We were living in Jackson, Tenn., at the time."

A year later, DeWeese was transferred to Memphis. Isn't it funny how life works?

DeWeese worked for JC Penney in what he calls "the new Raleigh Springs Mall" store.

"I had a bunch of departments," he said. "Boys, girls, infants, lawn and garden, and toys."

Some mornings, DeWeese stopped at Gibson's Donuts at 760 Mt. Moriah. Being the social sort, he and Mr. Gibson came to be friends.

"They called me the official tester," he said. "I got to know if the doughnuts were cooked right."

In 1996, Mr. Gibson retired. Heart problems. Go figure? The official tester then promoted himself.

"I bought the store as investment," DeWeese said.

Yeah. An investment in kids. Because under DeWeese, 62, Gibson's does not just sell doughnuts. It sells memories and experiences.

It sells hot glazed doughnuts eaten in your pajamas.

It sells Saturday mornings with your mom or dad.

"For a lot of people, it's the only time of the week a daddy can go one-on-one with his child," DeWeese said. "It's quality family time and we don't care if you spill milk on the floor."

As it happens, one of the fathers who took his kids to Gibson's was an aspiring politician named Kemp Conrad.

DeWeese didn't know Conrad. He treated him like everyone else. Which is to say, fabulously.

"We started going every Saturday," Conrad said. "And then, as a member of the City Council, you're given the opportunity to name a road after one member of the community each year."

This was Conrad's first choice. Whom should he pick? A wealthy donor? A mover and shaker? A genial doughnut man?

"It was my wife's idea," Conrad said.

Someone, elect his wife.

Conrad may have other inspired moments as a member of the City Council but they won't be any more inspired than this one.

A street named after a doughnut man. Well, why not?

Why not honor someone who makes this a better community one cruller at a time?

Why not shine a light on a person who has turned his own little piece of Memphis into a magical place?

So often, we reserve our honors for those who do extraordinary things. But isn't there as much value in doing ordinary things — like making doughnuts — extraordinarily well?

DeWeese didn't wait for a new mayor to help him create a fabulous doughnut shop. He didn't move his doughnut shop to Mississippi in a huff.

He hung a flying cow from his ceiling. He decided to have a blast.

So it was that last Saturday morning, before a gathering of kids of all ages, Conrad started to read.

"WHEREAS, Don DeWeese is known for his love of people and Memphis ...

"WHEREAS, he single-handedly operates his own type of boys and girls club ..."

The man said "WHEREAS" 11 times before he was finished. Followed by one joyful "NOW THEREFORE." Then Conrad unveiled the sign on that little stretch of Mt. Moriah outside the shop: "Don DeWeese Boulevard."

Maybe it was the doughnuts, but you should have heard the people clap.

"I said I'd never live in Memphis," DeWeese said. "Now I'd never leave."

LAWYER RE-EVALUATES LIFE, LEAVES N.Y. STREETS FOR RHODES SIDELINES
SEPTEMBER 10, 2011

He remembers the smell of burned cement, the way it hung in a haze. He remembers the McDonald's trucks, driving up and down Second Avenue.

"They're refrigerated," he said.

For the bodies. Or pieces of bodies. Dan Gritti watched the trucks come and go, come and go. He was an attorney with the firm Littler Mendelson. He was on top of the universe. He shopped wherever he wanted to shop. He had a driver to take him wherever he wanted to go.

His income: substantially more than half a million a year. His favorite perk: free tickets to every home Yankees-Red Sox game.

As it happened, the Red Sox were in town the night before. He and his brother saw them get rained out. So he woke up, put on a suit, walked out to hail a cab, reveled in the glorious morning, and then watched, standing right there on the corner, as the world forever changed.

The North Tower. The South Tower.

"I saw both of them go down," he said.

He remembers the oddest things. The two clouds in the sky. The girl, collapsing in tears.

Gritti returned to his apartment. He started making calls. Which friends were alive? Which friends were not?

The phone rang. It was work. A message to all members of the firm.

"It said that this is a great tragedy but that the clients of the firm still have to be served and we were expected to be at work the next morning," Gritti said. "It took every fiber of my being not to throw the phone against the wall."

• • •

Sometime before 1 p.m. today, Gritti will run out onto the field as his Rhodes Lynx get ready to play their first game of the season. Yes, his Rhodes Lynx. Gritti, 37, is a head football coach now.

He is a football coach because planes brought down two buildings. He is a football coach because he has seen how swiftly life can end. He is a football coach because — yes, this is really true — he would like to spend his days doing good.

Not good like his boyhood hero, Mario Cuomo, necessarily. But maybe that's a reasonable place to start.

"I did my seventh-grade book report on the diaries of Mario Cuomo," he said, as if that explains everything.

Gritti was a dreamer, a political junkie, a working-class son of Massachusetts in the time of the Kennedys. He liked hockey, football and Democrats, and makes no apologies for any of it.

But he was going to work in politics. He knew that part for sure. He went off to college at Vanderbilt, got a job as a student assistant under Gerry DiNardo in the football office, but reserved his deepest passions for political campaigns.

As a freshman, Gritti worked as a college coordinator for Sen. Tom Harkin in New Hampshire. When Harkin lost, he joined the Clinton-Gore campaign. He could see it all unfolding ahead of him. He would finish up at Vanderbilt, move to Washington to work for Sen. Jim Sasser, and build a career in government.

Except, Sasser lost. Practically every Democrat lost that year. Gritti threw up his hands and opted for the path well trodden: he went to law school.

People like to say you can do anything with a law degree, but the dirty little secret is that you tend to become a practicing lawyer. It seduces you, the law. Not necessarily the work, but the life. The next thing Gritti knew, he was living and working in Manhattan, defending investment banks in sexual harassment cases. There was one case, in particular. Gritti flinches from it even now.

"The guy who ran the mailroom took all the doorknobs off the doors," he said. "If someone wanted to come in and pick up their check, he'd put his penis through the hole and they'd have to stroke it to get in."

Gritti's job was to go after the accusers. Dig through their histories for anything to indicate they might really enjoy opening doors that way.

"The idea was to make it so painful they'd want to settle," he said.

So that's what Gritti did. Until he walked outside one morning and watched more than 2,600 people die. Gritti looked at his life, looked at what he had intended his life to be, and realized they didn't match.

He thought about going back to politics. He volunteered for more campaigns.

"The final straw for me was Sen. Max Cleland, in Georgia," he said. "That was my last campaign. When a guy who lost his limbs for his country is considered not patriotic enough because he wanted TSA employees to have civil service protections, well, I called my dad and cried."

Then he called DiNardo, his old boss. Looking for a job. DiNardo had moved on to become the head coach at Indiana and said he'd be thrilled to have Gritti back.

It would be nice to report that it was all smooth sailing from that point forward, that Gritti found instant contentment and bliss. The pursuit of dreams doesn't go that easily. After two years, DiNardo was canned and Gritti — with seven years of college and law school behind him — wound up sleeping on his parents' couch.

But then came four seasons as an assistant at Middlebury. Then two more at the University of Chicago. And then — a decade after Gritti found the courage to really look at his life — he got a call from Rhodes president Bill Troutt, offering him a job as head coach.

It is not particularly glamorous, Gritti acknowledges. He keeps an inflatable mattress on his office floor. On one wall, there's a photo of him shaking hands with Clinton. On another, there's a photo of Adam Vinatieri, kicking the field goal to beat the Raiders in the playoffs in 2002.

"I was at that game," he said, remembering. "Then my brother and I went to the Super Bowl."

Gritti paid $2,000 cash for each ticket. He flew through Memphis on the way to New Orleans. So life has come full circle, in a certain way. Even as curious a life as his.

Gritti has thought a lot about what he'll say to the Rhodes players before today's game. He's going to tell them about some firemen he once knew.

"There was a station a few blocks from my building," he said. "I walked past it all the time."

Often, Gritti wore his Red Sox cap. The firemen let him hear it about that. Or maybe, in the evenings, he'd walk past them with a date. They let him hear about that too.

All those firemen raced to the World Trade Center. All those firemen died. While Gritti won't pretend to be able to find some grand meaning in their deaths, he knows what they have come to mean to him.

"It's important to do what you love," he said. "And it's important to do what you love as well as you can. Not just for yourself, but for all the people who never got the chance. My friends who died, a lot of them were in the same boat I was. They were doing OK, but they weren't doing what they loved.

"Those firemen. You know what they loved to do as much as anything? They loved to play softball. And you can bet, when they played softball, they played it with everything they had."

Gritti shrugged. He was wearing an old shirt bought at the Manhattan Brooks Brothers.

"The glory days," he said, laughing at the fib.

The glory days are not the days when you can buy whatever you want.

The glory days are the days when you can be the person you intended to be.

LAPIDES BATTLES ILLNESS BUT SAVORS LIFE
JULY 11, 2013

George Lapides showed up at the radio station the same way he has for more than four decades now, taking his seat in front of the microphone. Lapides wouldn't think of doing a show without extensive notes. Wednesday was no exception. So he was ready to talk about the Grizzlies, or NBA free agency, or his beloved St. Louis Cardinals or whatever else happened to come up.

First, though, he had something he had to say. Something he had been putting off as long as possible.

Lapides, 73, has been diagnosed with something called idiopathic pulmonary fibrosis, a lung disease for which there is no cure. So he is moving the show from 8 a.m. to 10 a.m., which will give him more time to get going in the mornings.

He can't say how long he will be able to continue at 10 a.m. IPF makes it progressively harder to breathe.

"I've got an illness that killed Marlon Brando and Mal Moore and essentially killed Reggie White," is how he described it to me on the phone. "Sometimes I have a hard time believing it. I was the person who wanted to be the one exception and live forever. That's how much I love living."

• • •

This is not a sob story. It is not because Lapides insists that it not be. "I don't want anyone feeling sorry for me," he said.

So call it an appreciation then. An appreciation of a man who has been the voice and conscience of Memphis sports since he became sports editor of the Press-Scimitar at the age of 27, who has been as much a part of this city as the men he has covered — Finch, Bartow, Calipari — for more than four decades.

Lapides is, in fact, an institution, though he resisted the description the other day.

"I know people talk about my ego and stuff," he said. "But I'm just me. I've been lucky to do a bunch of things I've really loved."

Like the newspaper job. He was the sports editor and columnist. He would have happily done that forever except the paper closed in 1983.

So Lapides reinvented himself. And kept reinventing himself. He served as the athletic director at Rhodes for a year. He worked for Fogelman Properties. These days, people tend to think of Lapides as old school, but there was nothing old school about Lapides' career. He did television before newspaper types did television, and did radio before newspaper types did radio.

Of course, the radio wasn't exactly his idea. Lapides will tell you that himself.

"The editor of the paper told me he wanted me to do a talk show," he said. "I asked him, 'What's a talk show?'"

Lapides figured it out. Boy, did he figure it out. He's been talking in Memphis ever since.

At some level, it seems utterly mystifying. You've heard about people who have a "face for radio" right? Well, Lapides has a voice for newspapers. He has a slight stutter. Sort of a tremulous pitch. There isn't a sports fan in Memphis who hasn't at least tried to do a Lapides imitation, the same way that, nationally, sports fans once imitated Howard Cosell.

But everybody listened to him. Because Lapides had the goods. He really could get Bear Bryant and Archie Manning on the phone. He really could tell you what was going on behind the scenes. Lapides left the newspaper business, but he never stopped being a reporter. He understood that the key to good talk radio is having something to say.

Yes, he could be harsh at times. Or prickly. You pick the word. But Lapides was never mean, in the way that some radio hosts are mean these days. And he always used his influence in the service of his hometown.

Remember, not so many years ago, when the Memphis Chicks were leaving town? It was Lapides who called his old friend Dean Jernigan and enlisted his help. Because of that call, Memphis got a Triple-A franchise and a downtown ballpark. Because of that ballpark — and the civic enthusiasm it sparked — a bunch of Memphians decided to try and bring an NBA team to town.

Does all that violate some purist's view of the proper role for a journalist? Maybe it does. But Lapides doesn't much care. He grew up here. He went to games at Russwood Park. If he could do something to make Memphis a more vibrant sports town, he figured that was part of his job.

And, yes, I note that I have shifted to past tense, as I type this. That's probably not right. Lapides will still be on the radio, just starting a bit later in the morning. And the last thing he wants is for everyone to call in and wish him well.

"What kind of show would that be?" he said. "Beyond that, I really don't think I have any right to complain. I really don't. I've done what I wanted to do. I've had a great life."

Lapides returns to this theme, again and again. He was diagnosed with IPF in April. He's handled it with astonishing grace.

He carries an oxygen tank with him now, wherever he goes. He sometimes sounds out of breath on his show.

But complain?

"Why would I complain?" he said. "I've got nothing to gripe about. I've loved my work. I've got two wonderful sons. My wife, Barbara, is five times smarter than me. I'm an incredibly lucky guy.

"The one sad thing to me, other than leaving this world that I love, is that I won't get to see my grandchildren grow up to be young adults. I've got a drop-dead gorgeous 6-year-old granddaughter and I'm dying to know how much trouble she's going to cause her parents when she's 16 or 17."

Lapides laughs at this. It's remarkable how it always works. You can spend your days laboring at a job you love, but family still matters most.

Which brings us to one last topic. Does Lapides have a bucket list? Anything he'd still like to see or do?

"Yes," said Lapides, and he starts to talk about Barbara again.

They met, he says, "shortly after she was hatched." Their families were longtime friends. There's a picture out there somewhere of Lapides pushing Barbara in a stroller. But they didn't actually date until Barbara — then a freshman in college — had to return to White Station High School to discharge some final responsibilities at a sorority dance.

"My mother told me I had to take her," said Lapides. "I said, 'She's too young.' I was already out of college. She was just a freshman. But I took her and that was that."

They married in 1964. Meaning, next year, it will be 50 years.

So, yes, there is something Lapides still wants to do.

"I've been holding a 1964 bottle of Bordeaux," he said. "Next year, I want she and I to sit together and drink some of it."

HALL OF FAMER PRESCOTT ANSWERED CALL FOR REDBIRDS
MAY 18, 2014

Allie Prescott remembers where he was when he learned he would not be the athletic director at the University of Memphis. He was sitting on his patio, by the pool, talking to his wife, Barbara.

"The phone rang and it was Lane Rawlins and he said that although I had been recommended, he was going to reopen the search," said Prescott. "He said that he really felt the university needed someone with Division 1 football experience."

Rawlins was president of the university at the time. He asked Prescott if he would remain a candidate while they searched for other possibilities.

"About 10 minutes later I called him back and said I was grateful for the opportunity, but that I would remain in my position with MIFA," Prescott said.

So that was that. Prescott would not get his dream job.

And you know what?

The city of Memphis is better for it.

I bring this up because Prescott was inducted into the Tennessee Sports Hall of Fame on Saturday night in Nashville. The plaque must have had the longest inscription ever. Fireballing pitcher at Kingsbury High School and the University of Memphis. Longtime college basketball official. General manager of the Memphis Chicks. Executive director of the Memphis Parks Commission. Executive director of MIFA. But all you really have to know about Prescott is that the biggest accomplishment of his career came after his biggest disappointment.

He was stung when he was passed over for that Memphis gig, especially because he had been selected by the search committee.

"They cut it down from 36 to 10 to three of us," he said. "And then I was told I was the one identified."

But Rawlins wanted to hire someone else anyway. He wound up hiring R.C. Johnson.

"It was really disappointing," said Prescott. "I had lived in Memphis all my life, I had played there, I thought I had prepared myself, but these things happen."

These things do happen, of course. To each and every one of us. The reason there are so many clichés about bouncing back, and getting up, and trying again, and getting back on the horse, and dusting yourself off, is that disappointment — even bitter disappointment — is universal.

We all get smashed by life. We all get disappointing phone calls.

The question is what happens next. The answer, for Prescott, was another phone call.

Prescott remembers getting that one, too. He figures he was back on his patio with Barbara.

"Dean (Jernigan) called and said 'I'll go after this if you'll do it with me,'" said Prescott.

By this, Jernigan meant he'd try and buy a Triple-A team to replace the departing Double-A Memphis Chicks. And he'd put that new team in a new, downtown ballpark.

"I remember the skepticism very clearly," said Prescott. "People thought we had lost our minds."

Put a ballpark in downtown Memphis? Why in the world would anyone do that?

"There was the perception at the time that it wasn't the safest place to put something so beautiful," said Prescott, being kind. The actual perception was that no suburban families would dare bring their kids to a scary place like downtown Memphis.

Seriously, that's what people thought. It was up to Prescott to explain why this thinking was misguided. He had to sell a different vision to politicians and corporate sponsors and suite holder and season-ticket buyers.

"I remember looking in the mirror one day and seeing the only employee of Redbirds Baseball," said Prescott.

So the only employee got after it. He met with any group that would listen to him. He described how a deserted piece of land at Third and Union could become the very heart of Memphis.

A year or so later, Prescott was named the "Communicator of the Year" for his efforts. It was an unexpected but telling bit of recognition. When we think of professional communicators, we tend to think of professional word-spinners. Prescott is nothing like that. He is modest. He is gracious. Prescott was an effective communicator because people believed — really believed — what he was communicating.

So the ballpark got built. That deserted piece of land at Third and Union was transformed, just the way Prescott said it would be. Suburban families brought their kids downtown. The Pursuit Team decided, hey, if it can work for baseball, why can't it work for the NBA? Then even more suburban families brought their kids downtown. And so the trajectory of a city was altered.

Nobody is pretending AutoZone Park hasn't had its boom-and-bust moments over the past decade. The place simply cost too much to build. But there are very few projects in Memphis that have had the catalytic impact of that baseball stadium. It has done everything Prescott promised.

So here's to the newest member of the Tennessee Sports Hall of Fame. Here's to a Memphis kid who has spent his lifetime trying to make Memphis better.

It wasn't always easy. Prescott had his disappointments. But you know what happens when God closes a door, right?

Turns out, he opens a ballpark.

HALL OF FAME INDUCTION BITTERSWEET FOR HUMPHREY
JULY 27, 2014

The speech starts with Sandra. That part, Claude Humphrey knows for sure. He will be inducted into the Pro Football Hall of Fame next Saturday, and he will stand in front of the greatest players who ever played the game, and he will use his time on the stage to talk about the girl he met when he was a student at Lester High School and she was a student at Manassas High School and she walked on up and introduced herself.

"We had a basketball game at Manassas," he said. "She just walked over to me and said, 'Hey, I know your niece.' And I said, 'OK.' And she said, 'I'd like to meet you.' That's how it started. She's been with me all of my life."

Sandra was with him when he went on to be a college star at Tennessee State. She was with him when he was selected by the Atlanta Falcons with the third pick in the 1968 draft. She was with him when he was named NFL Defensive Rookie of the Year, and when he became a perennial All-Pro, and when he briefly retired before returning to help carry his new team, the Philadelphia Eagles, to the Super Bowl.

Sandra was with him after all that, too, when he waited for the Hall of Fame to call.

"She was my biggest publicist," he said. "She always thought I deserved to make it and she always thought I would make it, no matter how bad it looked sometimes."

So yes, of course, the speech starts with Sandra. She died of cancer a year and a half ago.

"It's hard," said Humphrey, 70, contemplating the weekend ahead. "I have mixed feelings. I'm proud we made it. But without her there, it won't be the same."

• • •

This is a love story most of all. But it is a Memphis story, too.

This city's first Pro Football Hall of Famer grew up in Binghampton, across from Lester High School, in a shotgun house with exactly four rooms.

"It really wasn't a street we lived on," said Humphrey. "It was more of an alley. Kids at school called it Humphrey Alley. They named it after us."

Millie Ann was the mother of the house and the bread-winner. She worked at C & M Bagging Company, sewing burlap bags that would hold corn and coffee that was shipped overseas.

As luck would have it, Lester started a football team right about when Claude arrived.

"We were terrible," said Claude. "But we got better. Tennessee wasn't recruiting black players, but I did get recruited by Nebraska. Illinois came to see me. Eddie Robinson sent a recruiter and I went down to visit Grambling, but I found out there was nothing in Grambling but Grambling. And it put me too far from Sandra anyway."

By then, Humphrey and Sandra were a regular item. They'd go on dates Sunday afternoons.

"We used to walk down Main Street, and then down Beale Street," said Humphrey. "We would go to the movies Sunday after church, and then we would walk down to the river. We weren't allowed to go to most of the movie theaters, but we could go to the Princess, up on Main Street. We could sit up top — that's where they put us — and get a cone of ice cream."

Humphrey decided to stay close to Sandra and play football at Tennessee State. During Humphrey's sophomore season, the couple got married at Sandra's family house in North Memphis.

"On Christmas Day," said Humphrey. "We celebrated Christmas and our anniversary on the same day every year. For a honeymoon, we went to my brother-in-law's house and kind of shacked up for two or three days."

Love is a many-splendored thing.

And then came the NFL years. Humphrey was a blistering presence off the end. It was a time of fierce, almost legendary pass rushers. Guys like Bubba Smith, Carl Eller, Elvin Bethea, Jack Youngblood and L.C. Greenwood. But even with that group of contemporaries, Humphrey made first-team All-Pro five times and second-team All-Pro three times.

He was Dwight Freeney before Dwight Freeney. He is credited — in retrospect, because NFL statisticians didn't even keep the stat before men like Humphrey forced them to — with 122 career sacks.

Small wonder Sandra had faith that Humphrey would be selected for the Hall of Fame when he retired in 1981. Sure enough, Humphrey made it to the final 15 in 2003, 2005 and 2006. But he never quite got the 80 percent of the vote required. He was left on the verge three times.

"Sandra used to cry with me when I didn't make it," Humphrey said. "When we didn't make it, we sat down and hugged each other and cried."

Then, a couple of years ago, they were on their way to Atlanta when Sandra said she had stomach pains.

"You ought to get that looked at when we get back," said Humphrey. "It could be an ulcer or gallstones."

It was ovarian cancer. Humphrey accompanied his sweetheart to every round of chemotherapy.

"It went quick," said Humphrey. "Less than a year. I miss her every day."

• • •

The week of the 2014 Super Bowl, the NFL invited Humphrey to New York. He was a finalist for the Hall of Fame again, this time as a senior candidate.

"They said to wait in our hotel rooms, that they'd call around 1:30 p.m.," Humphrey said.

"It got to be about 3 or 4 and they still hadn't called. So I told my daughter, 'Well, call everybody and tell them we didn't make it.' But just about the time I got the 'We didn't make it' part out, the phone rang. I was waiting for someone to say I was passed over. Instead, they said, 'Congratulations.' I darn near passed out. I was holding the phone and I felt lightheaded."

At last, Humphrey was in.

He's still not sure what to think.

He's thrilled, and humbled, and grateful, certainly. But it's just ...

"Sandra would have loved this," he said. "My wife was a socialite. She would have loved every minute of this. And she'd make sure I don't show up in a polka dot shirt."

As it happens, this last detail is being taken care of. Humphrey's three daughters — Claudia, Cheyenne and Cherokee — have already pestered him about his clothes.

"I told them all I need is a black pair of slacks to go with a gold jacket," he said. "And they said, 'We're going into your closet tonight.'"

But it's not really about the clothes, of course. It's everything else.

"If you walked in my house right now, you would think Sandra was still there," Humphrey said. "We've changed absolutely nothing. I know eventually that's going to have to change, too, but I'm still living with Sandra right now. That's the way it feels."

Humphrey shrugs. He's not in a depression or anything like that. He has his quiet pleasures. He plays checkers at the Springdale Checkers Club. He has a 12-year-old grandson, Archie Robinson Jr., and the two of them have quite a time.

"We go to church on Sunday, and then after church we go find some chicken wings, and we fill up on chicken wings and then we go home and fall asleep," said Humphrey. "We do that every Sunday."

Yes, quite a time.

But it's a bittersweet moment for the kid from Humphrey Alley. What's a lifetime achievement without the person with whom you created that life?

Humphrey is asked if he has a favorite picture of Sandra.

"Every picture she ever took," he said. "She never took a bad picture. My wife was beautiful."

'BREAD MAN' CONLEE ACED GIFT FOR LIVING ON HIS TERMS
AUGUST 12, 2014

He died at the golf course. Of course he died at the golf course. Because how else could this preposterous, heartwarming, heart-rending, hilarious and altogether impossible story have ended?

A bread delivery man who became a country club champion? A life-of-the-party salesman who married the same woman three different times? An unwanted infant who was abandoned in a police car by his mother, who then grew up to be one of the best amateur golfers in Memphis? A father whose 18-year-old son was killed in a collision with a train, who then turned that loss into a golf tournament that helped hundreds and hundreds of other sons from all across the country?

Larry Conlee was not going to go out just any old way. So, sure enough, he showed up at Quail Ridge Golf Course on Friday for his usual 12:30 game.

"Typically, in our group, on the first tee, everyone is taking some kind of pills," said Eddie Patterson, who has been playing golf with Conlee for more than 40 years. "But he said, 'I'm feeling great. I couldn't feel any better.'"

Conlee birdied No. 2. He found himself 120 yards out, on a side hill, and dropped the ball 3 feet from the cup.

"He's the best I've ever been around from that distance," said Patterson. "And I've been around a lot of pros."

Conlee wound up shooting 69 on the afternoon, which isn't too bad for a 73-year-old man. He two-putted No. 18. That would be the last hole he ever played.

Not long after, Conlee fell dead from a heart attack.

"He never regained consciousness," said Chris Conlee, Larry's youngest son and the pastor at Highpoint Church. "He was still in the clubhouse."

So it is tempting to say that Conlee went the way he would have wanted to go. Because that's the comforting sort of thing we tell ourselves at a time like this. Even though, truth be told, Conlee would have preferred to go after shooting a 64, like he did a few months ago.

But even that misses the point. Because the end of Conlee's story — as eerily fitting as it may have been — isn't close to the best part of it. The best part is what came before. The best part is the struggle and the redemption and the constant, irrepressible laughter throughout.

"It wasn't an easy life," said Chris Conlee. "He had his ups and downs. But he used that as a platform to make other people feel good. He had a way of making people smile."

• • •

He would take your money on the golf course, mind you. Breadie — everyone called him Breadie or Bread Man — would certainly do that.

"They called 16, 17 and 18 the triangle," said Chris Conlee, talking about Germantown Country Club. "He'd challenge you to play the triangle and he'd give you two strokes over three holes. 'But I get one throw,' he would say. Then it would be on.

"Anyway, No. 18 had an out-of-bounds all the way down the right side. The guy he was playing would be in the fairway. And he'd walk over and pick up their ball and throw it out of bounds. 'I said one throw,' he would say. 'I didn't say whose ball.'"

That was Breadie Conlee. Always one step — or gag — ahead of the rules. But you don't live the kind of life Conlee led by doing what the world expects of you. He really was abandoned in a police car by his mother when he was just a 1-year-old. He really did bounce from foster home to foster home in Covington.

"At 13, he went out on his own," said Chris Conlee. "He dropped out of school. He moved to Memphis. Then he got a job at Hart's Bakery delivering bread and cookies and stuff."

You'll notice that the game of golf wasn't any part of that narrative. Foster kids don't typically spend a lot of time at country clubs. But Conlee's bread route included a stop at Galloway. The next thing you know, Conlee was playing the game. Then he was playing it well. Then he was playing it just about as well as anyone in the entire city, winning club championships, and raising his two boys — Bubba and Chris — to play golf too.

Conlee still wasn't a conventional golfer or anything. He'd come tearing up in his bread truck right before an important tee time.

"He didn't finish high school, he was a blue-collar man, but at 1 o'clock he was on the No. 1 tee at Galloway," said Chris. "He lived in a blue-collar world but his charisma and his golf game made him welcome in a white-collar universe."

And then, on April 20, 1981, everything in Conlee's carefully constructed life went dark.

Bubba, 18, was killed when the car he was driving collided with a train.

"We were at a gas station at Byhalia Road," Chris said. "My brother was coming to tell Dad he just shot a 64. The train track is 100 yards behind Byhalia. We heard the collision and the sirens. I was 10 years old and I was walking around the corner to see what happened and Dad literally grabbed me by the shirt and said, 'Get in the truck, I don't want you to see.'"

How do you recover from a moment like that? Anyone who knows Larry Conlee will tell you he never really did. He and his wife, Janice, divorced, their marriage unable to withstand the weight of the grief. On the day he died, Conlee's phone number for himself was listed in his cellphone under the name "Bubba Conlee."

So this isn't about recovering or moving on or anything quite so neat. But it is about somehow getting through. And the one way Larry Conlee got through was to recognize and help others who were having a hard time.

Over the weekend, Chris Conlee got a card from a girl at his church. The girl has Down syndrome. The card read: "Dear Chris. I miss Mr. Conlee. I loved him. He was so nice to me."

"He used to take her to get Mexican food," said Chris. "Dad did things like that all the time."

He threw a tournament for a friend diagnosed with cancer not long ago. Raised $12,000 just like that. He traded bread and chips so golfers without a lot of money could get reduced rates on tee times.

And then there was the Bubba Conlee National Junior Golf Tournament, which began in 1981. The initial idea was to have a one-time tournament to celebrate the life of Bubba. But over the last 34 years, the tournament has become one of the best junior tournaments in the country.

At the last Bubba, Eddie Patterson was with Conlee when a call came in from the director of another junior tournament.

"This guy was mad," said Patterson. "He was telling Larry that he was giving the junior golfers too much stuff, giving them too nice a time. And Larry yelled back, 'I don't care about your tournament. I care about the kids. If it weren't against the rules, I'd give them even more.'"

• • •

Stories. They will be telling stories when the life of Larry Conlee is celebrated at Highpoint Church at 6 p.m. Tuesday. So don't be surprised if the service runs long.

There was the time Larry told Chris he'd get him a Camaro convertible if Chris shot 69 in his first high school tournament. But Larry didn't just promise a convertible, he went to the dealer and borrowed one.

"He was driving it around the course during the match," said Chris. "Sure enough, when I shot 70, he drove it right back to the dealership."

There was the time Chris desperately wanted to go see Karl Malone play at the Mid-South Coliseum. But the game was already sold out.

"So he got three or four trays of hot dog buns," said Chris. "He's like, 'C'mon!' We run up to the door and he says to them, 'Concession is out of hot dog buns! Concession is out of hot dog buns!' They wave us in, and as soon as we get through the door we put down the trays and go watch the game."

There was the time 13-year-old Chris invited an African-American player to join him for a round at Germantown Country Club. One of the pros took Chris aside and told him that wouldn't fly.

"I went and got my dad. He marched right down to the pro shop," Chris said, "and he had his finger in the pro's chest, and he was saying, 'I'll pull out of this country club right now if you don't do what's right.' I couldn't hear what the pro said, but we played golf that day."

Oh, and then there is what may be the sweetest story, from Father's Day last year, when Larry Conlee went before the congregation at High-point Church to be baptized.

Conlee had never been mistaken for an angel. He played as hard as he worked. When he married Janice for the third time a few years ago, Chris whispered to him during the service, "If you do this again, I'll kick your butt."

So you'd have to consider it an upset to see the 72-year-old scrambler up there, humbling himself before family and before God.

"For the first time in my life I'm at peace with myself," Larry said.

With that, 15-year-old Mark Conlee pushed his grandfather's head beneath the waves.

• • •

This past Friday morning, Chris Conlee was on Poplar, driving to his church, when a familiar face pulled up behind him at the light.

"It was Dad," he said. "He waved and smiled and carried on."

As it happens, Chris Conlee has a weakness for fast cars. He gunned his convertible — yes, he finally got one — and left his father behind.

"But the next light caught me," he said. "There was Dad, pulling up behind me again. He was pointing at me and laughing. When the light turned, I gunned it again. That was the last time I ever saw him. What are the odds of that? I consider that moment a little gift."

Larry Conlee drove on to his golf game. The last one he ever played. But after he signed his card, he went to the refrigerator at the clubhouse and pulled out a sheet cake. It was for a young woman named Paige, who worked at the golf course. It was her last day before returning to college for the new academic year.

"He was showing it to her when he fell out," said Patterson. "He collapsed right then and there."

So let the record show that the last thing Conlee did in this life was not play a round of golf. As romantic an ending as that may have been. No, the man they called Breadie was engaged in something he considered an even higher calling. He was doing something nice.

ONE LAST ROUND PROVES TO BE PERFECT MEDICINE
NOVEMBER 7, 2015

He told the kids last Thursday.

"I'm going to play golf tomorrow," said Bruce Lamey, 64.

His kids were understandably surprised. It's not that Lamey dislikes golf or anything. That wasn't the surprising part. It's that Lamey is dying of liver cancer. He's in hospice care.

But last Thursday, he announced to the assembled that he was going to join his buddies and play golf at Glen Eagle Golf Course in Millington.

"It's going to be a beautiful day," said Lamey.

Said Jestein Gibson, his daughter: "We thought it was the meds."

• • •

Ultimately, we will all have a whole list of final times. We'll have final birthdays and final anniversaries, final trips to the Gulf Coast and final

Christmas Eves. But how often do we know, in advance, it's the last time for any particular thing? Especially a particular thing we have come to love?

Bruce Lamey loves golf. He has always loved golf. He doesn't love golf as much as he loved Mary, his wife, who died three years ago. He doesn't love golf as much as his five kids.

But beyond that?

There's not much else that Lamey loves more than golf. Except the Memphis Tigers, and that depends on the day.

It never even mattered to Lamey that he wasn't particularly good at golf.

"He's an average golfer," said Gary Hoffman, aka Pookie, who has been playing with Lamey for a couple of decades now. "He's what I'd call a bogey golfer. He just loves the game."

He loves the camaraderie on the golf course. Loves the sunshine and the green grass. Lamey made his living with a succession of small businesses — a printing shop, a plumbing outfit, a place that made industrial valves — but that's not where he was happiest.

"He just liked being out on the golf course," said Jonathan Gibson, his son-in-law. "But I honestly didn't think he'd ever play golf again."

Lamey was diagnosed with liver cancer in January. It has gone the way these things too often do. Chemotherapy. Visits to the doctor. Bad news from the doctor. Hospice care called in.

"It's been hard," said Nick Lamey, one of Bruce's sons. "The Tigers have helped."

Ahhh, the Tigers. That other Lamey love.

"He was a Memphis football fan before it was cool to be a Memphis football fan," said Nick. "He hasn't missed a home game in a solid 10 years."

So the Tigers' miraculous season has been a happy distraction, even as Lamey has continued to fade. He made it through the whole Missouri State game. He left the Cincinnati game at the half. The Ole Miss game, he watched from a television on Tiger Lane. The Tulane game, he finally stayed home.

As for golf, he hadn't made it out to the course for months. Everyone assumed that was done. But then, last Thursday night, Lamey made his announcement.

"I was in bed when I got the text," said Jestein. "He said he needed a ride. I'm like, 'Dad, you're on a walker. You can't play golf.' He said, 'Jess, it might be my last time.'"

So she gave him a ride. Of course she did. Which is not to say she didn't have some misgivings about the whole deal.

"I was thinking, 'I can't believe I'm going to drop him off with a bunch of people I've only heard stories about,'" she said. "But we got there early. I met Pookie."

With a man named Pookie in charge, what could go wrong?

Nothing, as it turns out. It was exactly as sweet as you would have hoped. Randy and Steve and Gary and all the guys were there.

"I'm sure there were at least 20 of us," Pookie said. "I told him, 'It's a beautiful day in the 70s and the sun is shining, let's just enjoy the day.' He said that's exactly what he wanted to do."

As for the golf itself?

That was never the point. It was always about everything that came along with the golf. But for the record, Lamey played 11 holes before his energy ran out.

"He was a little slower than usual," said Pookie. "But he had a couple nice holes. Everyone was glad to see him out there. It was a perfect day."

Since then, the cancer has continued to do its work on Lamey. He has bad days and only slightly better ones. He fades in and out of consciousness. Nick, the son, laments that his father likely won't be around to see how this glorious Tiger year ends.

But he had that final round on the golf course, and all the rounds that came before. He had friendship and laughter and the occasional putt that broke just the way he wanted. He had Mary, and the kids.

And unlike most of us, he had the opportunity to play one last round, knowing exactly what it was about.

"I picked him up and drove him back from the course," said Gibson, the son-in-law. "He was over the moon."

V

UNIVERSITY OF MEMPHIS FOOTBALL

HOLLERS, HUGS AND GOAL POSTS
NOVEMBER 10, 1996

Lane Rawlins hugged R.C. Johnson. Hugged him, squeezed him, picked him up in the air.

"Whoo-hoo!" Rawlins hollered. "Whoo-hoo!"

Rawlins is a distinguished guy. The president of the University of Memphis. A published scholar. But this was no time to stand on ceremony, not with goalposts tumbling and tens of thousands dancing and a final scoreboard that read Memphis 21, Tennessee 17.

So Rawlins saw Johnson coming toward him, Johnson extended his hand, and then the handshake became a hug, the hug became a lift, the lift became a twirl.

Rawlins put Johnson down. Finally. Merrily.

"I'm not sure I can find the words to explain this," Rawlins said. "I don't know."

Memphis beat Tennessee.

Memphis beat Tennessee for the first time, on national television, in front of the largest crowd in Liberty Bowl history, in a way you had to see to believe.

"I'm glad I lived to see this," said Paul Hartlage, the Memphis radio guy, who has been fighting cancer of the esophagus, who made it back to call the most dramatic win in Memphis history. "That was a great game to call."

Funny thing. It didn't start out that way. It started out drab and cold and uneventful.

Tennessee scored a touchdown. Memphis scored a touchdown. But Memphis generated exactly 2 yards of offense by the end of the first quarter, 32 yards by the end of the first half. When Tennessee slammed the ball down the field to take the lead at the start of the third quarter, Memphis looked to be finished.

"We needed something," said defensive back and kick returner Kevin Cobb. "A lift."

The kickoff tumbled out of the sky to Cobb. He sprinted right, got hit somewhere around the 25, spun around, appeared to go down.

So why was he still running? Why was he wasting his breath? Why was he ...

"GO!" Cobb heard from the sidelines. "RUN!"

Cobb had not gone down. Impossibly, he had not gone down. He had done an involuntary pirouette, a full 360, touching his hand to the grass, then his elbow to the grass, then popping upward and onward and, a few seconds later, into the end zone.

Suddenly, everything had changed. The game felt different. A sloppy game turned interesting. An interesting game turned unforgettable.

"They were always this team you saw on television that was bigger than you and stronger than you," said Ken Newton, the Memphis center. "Well, now we knew they weren't."

Everybody stood. The rest of the way, they stood. Tennessee got a field goal. Memphis got the ball back with six minutes left and 69 yards to go to take the lead. But Memphis had generated just 83 yards of offense the whole game.

"We needed someone to step up and make plays," said quarterback Qadry Anderson. "That last drive, it seemed like everyone was stepping up."

There was Andre Woods, skittering for two yards on a fourth-and-1.

There was Anderson, slinging the ball 41 yards down the right side for Chancy Carr.

There was Jeremy Scruggs, rambling up the middle for 13 yards.

And there was Anderson again, lobbing the ball to Chris Powers for the winning touchdown.

"I looked down and saw the end zone line underneath me," said Powers. "I was just praying I got in."

He got in. Memphis led. Then Memphis hung on. Tennessee's last play looked like a typical Memphis play, crazy, desperate, futile. Peyton Manning pitched the ball over to Jay Graham. Graham ran around, then pitched the ball back to Manning. Manning went down in a defeated heap.

And then it was bedlam, pure bedlam, an emotional blend of hugs and hollers and tears and falling goalposts.

A cluster of Memphis basketball players danced at the 30.

Someone ran around with a sign that said, "Where's Knoxville anyway?"

Rawlins found Johnson and gave him that twirl. Johnson's feet were swinging, he was walking on air.

On this day, in this city, he wasn't the only one.

A VOICE THAT LIVED SIGNS OFF
MAY 31, 1997

The Vanderbilt basketball game was one of the toughest, his friends say. Paul Hartlage had checked himself out of the hospital so he could do the radio play-by-play. He was weak, frail, drained by both the cancer and its cures.

"I picked him up at his house an hour after he got home," said Hank McDowell, Hartlage's friend and sidekick on Memphis basketball broadcasts. "He lay down in the backseat while we drove."

The Vanderbilt press box is high above the court. Hartlage struggled up the steps. Then he proceeded to call the game with the energy, passion and joy that had become his trademark.

Hartlage, 43, died Friday morning. He had been sick for more than a year. But if you only knew him from his voice on the radio, from his big, merry, growling, partisan voice on the radio, you might not have suspected the guy was ailing.

That was the remarkable thing about this past year; that was his gift to the rest of us. Serious illness has a way of making sports look pretty trivial. Serious illness has a way of making everything look pretty trivial. But the simple pleasure Hartlage took from games — the enormous effort he made to get to games — put things neatly in perspective.

If Hartlage was going to be upbeat, then why shouldn't we?

If Hartlage was going to focus on living, then why shouldn't we?

And if Hartlage was going to enjoy the ballgame, then why shouldn't we do that, too?

He broadcast 10 years of games for the Tigers, basketball and football. He embraced every win, suffered every loss, blasted every marginal call.

"I think he came to us thinking he was going to be this unbiased reporter who was going to report everything he saw," said Bob Winn, assistant athletic director at Memphis. "I guess you know how well that worked."

Hartlage felt the way you felt; he saw what you saw; he said what you thought, only Hartlage seemed to say it better and louder.

This last year was a struggle from the start. Hartlage was diagnosed with cancer of the esophagus in April. He spent most of the basketball season receiving treatments that often felt worse than the disease.

"I remember the game against Missouri," said Winn. "He was just starting a combination of chemo and radiation."

"After the game, the team voted him a game ball. It was very emotional. And then I followed him under the darkness of the stadium, because I didn't think he wanted anyone to see him cry. And he was just standing there retching. Retching and crying. All you could do was put your arm around him."

Hartlage missed some games after that. But he made it back for the big ones, the football win over Tennessee, the basketball win over Michigan, the last game of the year against Cincinnati, where Hartlage was given a thunderous standing ovation.

Hartlage broadcast all those games. He called them, savored them, celebrated them. And in the process, he reminded us of an old truth: Dying is easy. Everybody does that. It's living that's the trick.

A STORY OF FATHER AND SON
OCTOBER 8, 2000

In the end, Rip Scherer would not let go.

He put his arm around Scott's shoulders. Together, they ran from midfield through the end zone and underneath the stands.

The scoreboard read: Memphis 17, East Carolina 10. You didn't have to look very closely to see the coach's eyes were rimmed with red.

"I'm just so proud of him," Rip said, voice cracking. "To do what he did ...

This is a story about football only in the sense that Field of Dreams is a story about baseball. It's about a father. It's about a son. And it's a good thing there were 23,496 witnesses because, otherwise, who would believe it today?

Father dotes on overachieving son.

Son wants to make his father proud.

Father won't give son the chance.

Son waits and waits and waits.

Circumstances finally force father to turn to son.

Son comes through to save the father and the day.

"It was," said Rip, when he could say anything at all, "the perfect script."

Did you see it? And did you think you were watching something from Hallmark instead of Fox?

"It was a dream," said Michele Scherer, Rip's wife, Scott's mother. "I can't begin to put it into words."

Understand, for starters, that as a football coach, Scherer has always made one heckuva dad.

Every coach says this, of course. Every athlete, too. They hold out for bigger contracts in the interest of family. They demand trades in the interest of family. They retire so they can be with their kids, then come back so their kids can see them play, then retire so they can be with their kids again.

Scherer really believes it, to the bottom of his shoes. And if he ever wondered which was more important, job or family, it was cleared up for him one tumultuous day in 1987.

Scherer, the offensive coordinator at Alabama, had a meeting in Tuscaloosa. The same day, Michele had a meeting at an Atlanta hospital with seven-year-old Scott. For nearly two years, Scott had suffered from something called Perthes disease, a blood disorder that stopped blood from flowing to his leg. He wore a huge brace to support the leg.

Well, at the Tuscaloosa meeting, Scherer learned he'd been fired. At the Atlanta meeting, Michele and Scott learned the brace could come off.

So the family met that day at a Toys R Us in Birmingham to celebrate by buying Scott a toy.

"I think that put it in perspective for me," Rip says. "You're reminded what counts."

Since arriving at Memphis, the Scherers have ordered their life that way.

When Scott played quarterback at Collierville, Rip was almost always in the stands.

When Rip coached C-USA games, Scott would stay with him at the team hotel and then, come Saturday, trail after him on the sideline, carrying his headphone cord.

And then came decision time, time to choose a college for Scott. Scott wanted to come to Memphis. His father said no, go to Davidson, go to a place where you can thrive and play.

But two weeks before Scott was to leave, the kid sat down and wrote a long letter to his father, listing all the reasons Dad was wrong.

"He convinced me," Scherer said. "He's the one who changed my mind."

Still, for two-plus years Scherer didn't get near the football field, except for some special teams play. Neil Suber got a chance. Travis Anglin got a chance. So did Kenton Evans and Stephen Galbraith and anyone else with a willing arm.

But Scott?

The kid is 5-9 in his wildest dreams. And, as his father puts it, "he's got my speed."

Scott got a straight 4.0 in the classroom, worked slavishly on the field and threw exactly two passes (completing one) for eight yards.

"He began to doubt," says Rip, "that he would ever play."

Then, a few weeks ago, Anglin hurt his ankle. Then, last week, Suber hurt his shoulder. Then, finally, the coach didn't have a choice.

"He called me Monday morning," Michele says. "He said, 'Are you ready for your son to start?'"

As it happened, Rip may have never coached a bigger game at Memphis, may have never coached a bigger game in his life. The Tigers were 3-2 but teetering on the brink. The three wins were against teams that were a combined 1-13 heading into the day. Beat a good team like East Carolina, and people might start to believe. Lose, and they'd wonder anew why Scherer's contract had been renewed.

So what happened?

The impossible happened, of course.

The first time Scott got his hands on the ball, he drove the team 84 yards for a score. He hit 4-of-4 passes for 59 yards. Sugar Sanders finished the job.

The next time Scott got his hands on the ball, he drove the team 23 yards for another score. He completed two more passes for 20 more yards. This time, he scored the TD himself.

And on and on it went, a story impossible to believe. The kid completed 11-of-16 passes to six different receivers for 141 yards in the first half. Memphis led 17-0. Scherer madness, is what it was.

"I kind of surprised myself," Scott says. "It hasn't sunk in yet."

The second half was tougher. East Carolina either figured the kid out or — and Scott should take this up with his dad — the Memphis coaches sat on the lead. East Carolina scored a late touchdown to get close, and had a final chance to tie.

With 13 seconds left, East Carolina quarterback David Garrard fired a final pass high and deep. Memphis safety Glenn Sumter came down with it. From opposite places on the sideline, father and son met at the center of the field.

Afterward, in the locker room, Rip talked to his football team. Which is when the cheer went up.

Rip rarely gives players game balls. That's just not something he does. But the players kept chanting for Scott, Scott, Scott, Scott.

So Rip called his son to the front of the room. And put the game ball in his hands.

Yeah, it might have been just a football game. But there wasn't a dry eye in the house.

TIGER QB DANNY WIMPRINE IS TAKING CHARGE OF THE OFFENSE
AUGUST 25, 2002

The story begins with Miss Jean because the story began with Miss Jean. Shaking her head. Not budging. And, boy, was Danny Wimprine crushed.

He had been looking forward to the day for as long as he could remember. OK, he was just 6, but it felt like forever.

The local playground sponsored a football team. Called the Mustangs. Open to kids 6 and over. Wimprine, age 6 — finally age 6 — and his mother marched right down to sign up.

Then, a crisis. The age of eligibility had been raised one year. Miss Jean, the woman in charge at the park, delivered this news to young Wimprine.

Who responded by crying. And crying. And crying. And crying. And... Miss Jean just shook her head.

"We came back one year later, and he started playing," said Danny's mother, Barbara Wimprine. "But that's Danny. He just loves football. He's always been crazy about it."

• • •

The University of Memphis football team kicks off the 2002 season Saturday. A lot of people — perfectly sane, clear-thinking people — believe this is the year the Tigers will finally go to a bowl game.

Some of this is because the head coach seems to know what he's doing.

Some of it is because the receivers are big and fast and the tailback is big and shifty and the offensive linemen are big and experienced.

But mostly it's because of Wimprine.

Because the guy lining up behind center is an exclamation point instead of a question mark.

How long has it been at Memphis?

Since Steve Matthews, anyway.

Rip Scherer coached at Memphis for six seasons and never had a sure-fire starter.

"Historically," said Memphis coach Tommy West, "I guess there has been some uncertainty there."

And now comes this sophomore from suburban New Orleans who can power lift 355 pounds, run the 40 in 4.77 seconds and throw the ball a little, too.

Who doesn't drink. Doesn't smoke. Who can't remember the last time he had a carbonated drink because (and this is how he really looks at it) how would that help him win football games?

The only video games he likes are the football kind. He is the only player on the team to have his own pair of weightlifting shoes.

He also could find work as a Brett Favre look-a-like someday, if nothing else pans out.

Wimprine's a dead ringer for Favre. You don't have to take our word for it, either.

A few years ago, Barbara Wimprine — she used to be a Delta flight attendant — was on a flight with Favre's aunt. The proud mom happened to mention that some people said her son looked a little like Favre.

"She asked me to show her a picture," Barbara said. "She took one look and said, 'Oh, my gosh, he really does!'"

Wimprine, 21, smiles when asked about the resemblance. It's the kind of secretly pleased smile that suggests he's glad you noticed.

Because Favre is exactly the kind of quarterback Wimprine aims to be.

Not always pretty. Not a 6-5, rocket-armed guy who fills the air with tight spirals. But maybe the one quarterback you'd like on your side when a game is on the line.

"He oozes leadership," said Randy Fichtner, the Memphis offensive coordinator. "He's a winner. It's not anything you can necessarily put your finger on. It's just the way he carries himself."

This is what everyone says about Wimprine. Witness this informal survey.

Here's Steve Curtis, Wimprine's best friend: "He's the most competitive guy I've ever met."

Here's West, his head coach: "He's the kind of guy you naturally follow."

Here's Barbara Wimprine, his mother: "He's lazy. And sometimes he's a pig."

Geez, Mom.

"But he's a real good kid!" she said.

The point is, Wimprine really likes to win. He rolls out of bed each morning thinking of ways to beat the other guy.

At anything.

Including a nerd contest if it comes to that.

Wimprine's high school, J.T. Curtis High, used to have goofy contests throughout the year. Best costume. Best nerd. You get the idea.

So one year, for the nerd contest, Wimprine rummaged deep into his father's stuff.

"He had the high waters, the argyle socks, the glasses with the tape, the zipper undone with the shirt sticking out," said Barbara Wimprine.

Understand, this is a boy who took a city bus to school.

"He won," Barbara said. "The next year, all the other boys wanted to borrow my husband's clothes."

• • •

The dream was Notre Dame. Wimprine is Catholic and the Irish were on TV all the time and Michael Stonebreaker, who played at Notre Dame, grew up right across the street.

So that was the dream. Touchdown Jesus, Knute Rockne, the whole golden deal.

People even called Wimprine "Rudy."

"It's the place I always dreamed about," Wimprine said. "I didn't have any doubt that's where I was going."

Wimprine wasn't the kind of kid that failed, either.

He suited up for J.T. Curtis for four years, three as the starting quarterback.

Curtis won the state title each and every year.

His senior year, Wimprine sprained his ankle in the semifinal game, just eight days before the championship.

The school headmaster brought his La-Z-Boy from home so Wimprine could keep his foot elevated between classes.

So it came as something of a shock when the Notre Dame coaches waffled.

"He had shoe boxes of letters from Notre Dame but they really hadn't contacted us in a personal way," Barbara Wimprine said. "They finally called the week before Christmas. You should have seen his face.

"But even then, they said they couldn't guarantee he'd play quarterback. They said they might have a scholarship for an athlete."

The Wimprines scheduled a trip to South Bend for late January. The Monday before, Wimprine's high school coach called the family and asked them to take a call in his office.

It was from Scherer, the coach of Memphis at the time. He was on the speakerphone.

"He said he had Danny's tape, he had watched it and he could really use him," Barbara Wimprine said. "He said he was offering a quarterback scholarship, right now, over the phone."

The only catch: Scherer wanted Wimprine to visit that weekend. That would mean canceling the trip to South Bend.

Wimprine called the Notre Dame coaches to tell them he had another visit he had to take.

"He made the decision and canceled his trip to Notre Dame," Barbara said. "He had the maturity to know."

It would be nice to report that after such a mature, far-sighted decision, Wimprine was rewarded by an effortless transition to Memphis.

This would mean ignoring things like math. And geology. And the sick, churning feeling Barbara Wimprine still gets when she sees Fichtner's number on her caller ID.

"She knows I'm calling because Danny didn't go to this class or Danny blew that test," Fichtner said. "We've got quite a relationship."

Wimprine is not dumb. But when it comes to school work, he's a master of the last-second comeback.

His first year, he fell so far behind, he was thisclose to losing his eligibility.

"It came down to having to pass math or geology," Wimprine said. "I was failing both of them, badly."

Wimprine went to the math professor first. He asked if there was any extra work he could do.

"I cried in his office," Wimprine said. "He said all I could do at that point was get a 105 on the exam, and he didn't see how that was possible."

Wimprine shifted his attention to geology. He didn't like his chances there, either.

All semester long, a woman sat in front of him. They became friends.

"We'd get our exams back and she'd say, 'I got a 93, what did you get?'" Wimprine said. "I'd say, 'Never mind.'"

Wimprine needed an 82 on his final to stay in school. Otherwise, he'd be headed back to New Orleans for good.

He took the exam. He figured he failed. A few days later, he walked, with growing dread, over to check on his score. His friend from class was walking out of the building, in tears.

"She said she got a 55," Wimprine said. "When she said that, I started crying right there."

Wimprine dragged himself to the wall where the scores were posted, listed by the last four digits of the students' social security numbers.

"I'm like, OK., here we go," Wimprine said.

"0397 ... 88.

"0397 ... 88!

"0397 ... YESSSSS!"

Within seconds, everyone on campus knew Wimprine had made it. He screamed the news out the window. He ran up and down the halls.

"He was closer than he should have been," Fichtner said. "Sometimes he's just stubborn."

Fichtner is both frustrated and bemused by this. When Fichtner was hired, Wimprine was in such tenuous academic shape that Fichtner called every morning, just to make sure his quarterback had left for class.

Wimprine is getting better about attendance. Fichtner calls every day, anyway.

He likes Wimprine, for one thing. He also knows that if things go well, Wimprine could be his starting QB for the next three years.

Wimprine ascended to the job last year, after opening the season behind Travis Anglin. His first game as a starter was against Houston. Memphis scored 52 points.

Wimprine wound up throwing for 1,329 yards and 14 touchdowns for the season, both freshman records. He looked so good, so natural, Anglin was moved to wide receiver.

"When you've got a quarterback, you go into every game feeling like you have a chance," West said. "We've got a quarterback."

A quarterback who should be better this year, too. More in command, more comfortable.

The other day, Fichtner gathered the quarterbacks and receivers in the film room. Wimprine sat right up front, handling the questions as fast as Fichtner could ask them.

"What do we have to do here?"

"Turn it to Mike."

And:

"If they're bailing three deep, does that mean nobody's open?"

"Not if you under-throw them."

And:

"What's the check here?"

That answer is classified, but Wimprine nailed it, too.

After 45 minutes, Fichtner ended the meeting. Wimprine stuck around anyway. So did Maurice Avery and Patrick Byrne, the two new freshman quarterbacks.

"Did you see how that worked?" Fichtner said, later. "None of those QBs left because Danny didn't leave.

"That's Danny. People follow him."

• • •

A college football season is a long, grinding enterprise.

Bad things happen. Footballs get tipped. Receivers drop balls. Safeties come out of nowhere to make interceptions.

So while swagger is great in August, it's not necessarily real. What happens when Memphis loses a couple games? When Wimprine has another game like the one he had against UAB last year, throwing two interceptions? Will he still be able to lead then? Will he still have that confidence?

Barbara Wimprine tells one last story about her son. She's the mom, forgive her.

"I think it was in fourth-grade," she said. "They had a self-esteem program they were going through in school. You know, to try to get the kids to think good things about themselves.

"At the end of it, you had to complete a sentence, 'This is the one word that describes me.' And you know what he wrote?"

She laughs at the memory, at the little boy who always figured he'd do great things.

"Awesome!"

WORTH THE WAIT – AFTER 32 YEARS, IT'S TIME TO CELEBRATE
DECEMBER 16, 2003

After more than three decades of waiting, Larry Tucker called the ticket office and bought 30 seats to see the Memphis Tigers play in a bowl game.

One ticket for himself, twenty-eight for friends and family.

And one special one.

For his father, James Tucker, who died three years ago at the age of 85.

"I'd give anything for him to see this game," said Tucker, 55. "Everyone called him Tiger Pop.

"We went to all the games together. We had some caps made up, flat caps, you know like they wore in the old days.

"We wore those caps to every Memphis game. My idea was to bring his cap and hang it on the back of his seat."

• • •

The Tigers are playing North Texas tonight in the New Orleans Bowl. It's not the biggest bowl game of the year, but it's the first.

Which is perfect, really. Why make Tiger fans wait one day longer? Isn't 32 years enough?

This game is about them, after all. It's a celebration, an exclamation point and a fitting reward.

Memphis coach Tommy West will tell you this straight out. He understands.

He loves what his players accomplished this season. He's proud to bursting of nearly every one.

Acknowledging that this game is larger than any of them doesn't change that at all. It only magnifies what they've done.

They've given Memphis a winner. They've given Tucker and his father the season they talked about for years.

Tucker isn't unusual, by the way. There are thousands like him. Which is why his story is the story of this day.

He was born a Tiger fan, the same way people are born brown-eyed or blond or short or square.

He can't remember his first game anymore than he can remember his first breath.

He remembers Crump Stadium. He remembers a car.

"We'd go to games in a 1959 green and white Rambler station wagon," he said. "With blue and white streamers on it."

The road games were the best. Didn't matter where they were.

You hear all the time about how Tiger fans have suffered for so many years. Tucker says that's flat wrong.

"Me and my dad drove to Florida State together," he said. "That was 10 hours down and 10 hours back. What could be better than 20 hours with your dad?

"We went to a lot of games together. Just the two of us. I listened to his music and he listened to mine. The way I look at it, me and my dad never had a losing season, no matter how many games the team won."

This is what some people don't understand about sports, of course. How the love of a team becomes entwined with the love of things that matter more.

The love of family. The love of shared moments, of times spent together and times yet to come.

James Tucker the Tiger fan begot Larry Tucker the Tiger fan.

Larry Tucker the Tiger fan begot Angie and Amy Tucker, Tiger fans.

Angie was on the Memphis pom squad. She married a Memphis baseball player. There's a sweet inevitability to it all.

It was Aug. 8, three seasons ago, that James Tucker died.

"He'd been in the hospital for three months," Tucker said. "It was hard.

"He wasn't a big donor or anything, just a regular guy. He was the chief clerk for the Missouri-Pacific. But he loved his Tigers. He was one of those who would sit on the hill and watch 'em practice.

"He was always there."

And then he wasn't. The seasons slip on past.

This summer, Tucker headed out to Memphis fan day with his wife, Mary Helen. She stopped at the port-a-potty because, as Tucker says, "I've never known her yet to let one go by."

Tucker was petting Maynard, the lucky goat, when his daughter, Amy, called to him.

"Mom's fallen!" she said.

Sure enough, Mary Helen had stepped in a hole.

Tucker's actual words to his wife at that moment?

"Better you than DeAngelo," he said.

Tucker would like to make it clear that at the time he didn't know the ankle would require eight screws and two metal plates to fix.

On the other hand, there's this: "The way the season turned out, we're going to have to break the other one next year," he said. "Someone's got to pay the price."

Tucker laughed. Truth is, there's no way to duplicate the emotions of the last few months.

There's only one first time. Or only one first-time-in-32-years.

"I've had a game-time stomach ever since the bowl was announced," he said. "It's been euphoric. I only wish my father could be here."

As for the extra seat, Tucker's plans didn't quite work out. It turns out somebody needed the ticket. Who was he to deprive a fellow Memphis fan of a place to sit?

He brought his father's cap to New Orleans but surrendered the ticket. His daughter, Amy, put it best.

"He doesn't need it anyway," she told her dad. "He's got the best seat in the house."

AT LONG LAST – NO LONGER A DREAM: TIGERS WIN A BOWL
DECEMBER 17, 2003

At half past nine in the Superdome a raucous band of Memphis Tigers assembled near midfield, some standing, some kneeling, some sprawling to the turf.

They posed for a picture. A historic picture, really.

First Memphis bowl champion in 32 years.

Funny how nobody had to be reminded to smile.

The Tigers put the perfect ending on a nearly perfect season Tuesday night, beating North Texas 27-17 to win the New Orleans Bowl.

They had waited three decades for this moment. Small wonder they hurried the celebration just a bit.

With 33 seconds left on the clock, Memphis players doused head coach Tommy West, then raised him on their shoulders.

It was only fair, really.

Lifting the man who had lifted them.

West and his team didn't just win a bowl game Tuesday. They changed the perception of what the Memphis football program might become.

"There are some guys here who bought into a dream," West said. "Not what it was, because it wasn't very good."

"What it could be."

The bowl performance was compelling, joyous evidence and it began well before the opening kick.

Tiger fans poured into town — by train, plane and automobile — splashing New Orleans with royal blue.

A local face-painter walked through the plaza outside the Superdome before the game, willing to paint faces for either team.

"I've painted a hundred Memphis faces," she said. "North Texas? Maybe five."

At a pregame pep rally the band leader asked for three volunteers from each side to come up and dance on stage.

Instantly, he had three Memphis dancers beside him. A North Texas dancer could not be found.

Of course, Memphis fans have been waiting a long time to be invited onto any kind of stage. Given the slightest bit of encouragement, they didn't hold back.

John Calipari jetted down for the game. Scott Scherer sat in the stands. The six Cheering Elvi showed up and did their thing.

"It's the first time I've worn polyester since the '70s," said one of them. "But it's worth it today."

He said this at halftime. Things were going well by then.

Danny Wimprine completed his first 10 passes for 162 yards. He threw for one touchdown and ran for another before getting knocked woozy.

Memphis led 17-3 at the half. North Texas could have used a pep talk from their famous alum, Dr. Phil.

But give the bad guys credit. It wasn't easy beating Green.

They pulled within a touchdown. Momentum seemed to be switching sides.

Which is when the Tigers did what they always seemed to do this year: Just enough to win.

"Remember when you learned to ride a bicycle for the first time?" said Mike White, a Memphis fan. "When you get it, you get it. That's what's happened here."

The Tigers didn't have their starting tailback. Their backup tailback went down in the first half. Their quarterback didn't know if there were three Cheering Elvi or six.

But they won.

Naturally.

Same ol' Tigers, you know?

When Coot Terry ended the final North Texas drive, the celebration began.

There were tears everywhere. And hugs and phone calls and high fives.

"Wow," said Memphis athletic director R. C. Johnson.

"It was worth the wait," said longtime assistant Murray Armstrong.

"Is everyone off the field?" said trainer Eddie Cantler.

No, Eddie, they were taking their sweet time. Thanking the fans. Drinking it in.

West ran over and stuck the cap he'd worn all game on the head of John T, the boy with Down syndrome who has set a new standard in collecting kicking tees.

"I wanted to give him something," West said.

Someone asked West how many times he'd been doused by Gatorade before. West said he couldn't recall.

"But it felt good," he said, before reconsidering.

"No, this time, after this year, it felt great."

TRUE BLUE – FAME, FORTUNE ARE NICE BUT FRIENDSHIPS TOP ON WILLIAMS'S LIST
JANUARY 15, 2005

DeAngelo Williams walked to the lectern and delivered the news. "I have decided to forgo..."

To forgo? To forgo his senior year?

Awww, darn.

"...my NFL career."

Ha!

Leave it to Williams. Faking left, then going right.

Right back to Memphis.

Right back to the coach, the teammates and the city he has come to love.

"It's the NFL vs. the city of Memphis," Williams said. "Hands down, the city of Memphis won."

Who says things like that?

Who means them when they do?

The best running back in the country, that's who.

A running back so elusive, so compelling, he can draw a packed house for an impromptu press conference.

Memphis fans came from everywhere, from law firms and doctors offices and ...

"Hooters," said Kevin Pembroke, a Memphis fan. "My buddy called me in the middle of lunch and told me about it. I left a hot wing on the plate."

Four Memphis students showed up in DeAngelo For Heisman T-shirts. They had their markers all ready to go.

"We're going to put an 'x' through 2004 and change it to 2005," said Brett Heinrich. "He's going to see us and change his mind."

That assumes Williams was going to go pro, of course. Before the press conference, nobody knew.

Not his teammates, not his mother, not his beloved head coach.

"I just wanted him to make the right decision for him," said West.

Well, sure. But how does a guy figure out what that is?

Maturely, as it turns out.

Painstakingly, too.

Williams and West spent hours together discussing the variables. The money. The risk of injury. The presence of so many gifted running backs in the draft.

"We weighed everything," said Williams.

"I'm sick of him," said West.

And if you believe that ...

But West left Williams alone to make the final decision. Williams made his mental lists.

Reasons for going:

1. He ran for 1,948 yards this year.

2. What are the chances he'll duplicate that?

3. The NFL scouts loved him.

4. He'd probably go at the end of the first round, and might have gone higher than that.

5. Mel Kiper Jr. said Williams could be the first or second running back taken.

6. If he came back, he could blow out a knee.

7. Money is nice.

9. So is fame.

10. Did we mention money is nice?

That was one list. The other wasn't nearly as long.

1. He loves everything about playing football in Memphis.

There. That's it.

How in the world did the second list win?

Because Williams is a rare kid, a kid who says things you want to frame and hang on your wall.

Someone asked him what his No. 1 goal would be for the new year. The Heisman? A championship? An even higher position in the draft?

"To keep developing friendships with the fans and the players on the team," Williams said.

That's it.

More friendships.

And he meant it, too.

The thought struck Williams the other day, when safety Scott Vogel happened to call. Vogel, a senior, was feeling a little low now that football is over for him.

They chatted. Talked about all sorts of things. When he hung up, Williams thought about how nice it is to have friends to confide in, to pick you up when you're down.

How many 21-year-olds you know would even have that thought? How many would let it stand between them and a big pile of cash?

"He's able to focus on what's real and what's not," said West.

What's real is the pleasure Williams takes in being a college student.

What's real is the affection he has for his head coach.

What's real is the palpable loves he feels from fans.

"There's nothing like running out of the Tiger head when it's inflated," he said.

When it's inflated.

Everyone laughed.

Memo to marketing: Make sure that for the opener, the dang head is blown up.

Williams deserves it. Deserves it and more.

First, he carried Memphis football to respectability. Then he carried it to two bowls.

Now he's reminded everyone that, yes, there's more to life than cashing a check.

Women cried at the press conference. Men, too.

"Coach West always said that athletes and coaches don't cry," corrected Williams. "Their eyes sweat."

So they were sweating Friday. Sweating with joy and surprise and more.

"It just boiled down to love," said Williams.

Right back at ya, kid.

MURPHY STILL FIGHTS, BUT IT'S A NEW BATTLE
SEPTEMBER 4, 2005

The old man sits in a wheelchair, a cookie and a cup of juice in front of him, but nobody has seen the piano player.

It is 4 p.m. on a Friday afternoon in the Alzheimer's section at Trezevant Manor. There's a social hour every week at this time. It is sweet and it is sad and it is not where the old man would have chosen to spend the last years of his life. But we don't get to choose, do we?

He lives down the hall in room 141. His roommate — they used to argue pretty good — is no longer conscious.

There's a picture on the wall above the old man's bed. It's from 1967.

A cluster of happy football players are lifting their coach in the air. The scoreboard reads Tigers 27, Rebels 17.

Billy 'Spook' Murphy is the coach in the picture. He is also the old man in the wheelchair, waiting for the piano player.

He sleeps under the picture every night. He may not even recognize it.

But it is a reminder of who he was and might still be.

"This would be his biggest nightmare," said Murphy's daughter, Libby Ladyman, nodding toward her dad. "But look at how he lived his life. He wasn't going to go easy."

• • •

On Monday at the Liberty Bowl, Memphis and Ole Miss will play a football game. It would be fitting if, sometime before kickoff, you spared a thought for the two men who forged the series out of fury and friendship.

Former Ole Miss coach Johnny Vaught won't be at the game. At 96, he's finally beginning to act his age.

As for Murphy, 84, he will doubtless be in front of a TV. But will he understand the game through the haze of Alzheimer's?

"I don't know," said his son, Mike. "I doubt it."

Mike and Libby weren't certain whether to talk about their father for this column. They want him to be remembered the way they remember him, hard on the outside, soft on the inside, a man's man back when that meant something.

He could whistle anything. He could whoop anyone. He had a pretty voice and a prettier wife and a weakness for helping people.

"He laughed from his toes," said Libby.

"He could remember every card in a bridge game," said Mike.

"You either like him or you don't," said former Memphis dean R.M. Robison, back when Spook was still coaching, "but you don't ignore Billy Murphy."

Except now you do. Or most do, anyway.

John Bramlett stops by nearly every week. He usually brings a milkshake. Bud Davis comes by Saturday mornings, and you can set your watch by it.

But they're the exceptions. Mike and Libby understand. Because Alzheimer's isn't easy to look at.

"It's no way to end a life," Mike said. "It scares me to death. Alzheimer's drains a whole family.

"But you can't pretend it doesn't happen. Presidents get Alzheimer's. If it can happen to my father, it can happen to anyone."

He was bigger than life, tougher than dirt, a coach, a Marine, a survivor.

His grandfather was a Texas lawman. His father died when Billy was 10. His mother ran a boarding house and didn't exactly coddle the kid.

Murphy grew into an All-SEC football player at Mississippi State. He met his lifetime sweetheart, Elizabeth.

When Memphis administrators decided in 1958 that they wanted a real football program, they realized they needed a fighter.

Which Murphy was. Ask anyone who knew him.

After one game at Starkville, Mississippi State fans started to rock the Memphis bus. Murphy told the players to stay seated. Then word came that the fans were rocking Elizabeth's car, too.

"Go get 'em boys," Murphy said.

He coached 14 years. His record was 91-44-1.

Everyone looks at this as the golden age of Memphis football, but doesn't 91-44-1 have a certain shine to it?

And then, in 1971, he resigned. Because fighters accumulate enemies.

He was 50, a year younger than Tommy West is today. The man born to coach football never coached another game.

His kids wonder about that. They're certain he had some games left in him. But Murphy stayed on as athletic director because he didn't want to move his family.

How rare is that for a coach? To put family over ambition?

"He said he came to stay and he meant it," said Libby.

At 65, he retired for good. At 69, he had a heart attack. Somewhere in the years after that, his mind started to wander.

He would lose track of his car. He figured a way around that one. He had this gizmo that flipped open the trunk from afar. He'd just look for the car with the trunk flying open.

He'd forget the password to the gate at his subdivision. Often, he'd have to wait to be let in.

"And of course he'd forget names, but he could fake it because he nicknamed everyone," Libby said. "He's the only person I've ever known who could call someone Fatso or Shorty and they'd consider it a compliment."

Alzheimer's moves at its own pace. Sometimes fast, sometimes slow. Nobody can predict it. But the last few years have been difficult for everyone.

Murphy doesn't recognize most people. He'll take an occasional poke at someone if he thinks they're trying to hurt him.

"He's fighting it, because he doesn't know what he's got," Mike said. "He's certainly not giving in to it."

This makes sense, really. Go back to Okinawa in 1945. Murphy's job was to slip up close to the line and direct artillery fire.

One day, the line moved. Murphy was caught on the wrong side of it. His mother got a telegram declaring him missing, presumed dead.

All the while, Murphy was lying on his stomach in a rice field, too close to an enemy machine gun nest.

He finally decided to take a chance. He had a grenade and maybe a second or two to throw it.

"He took them out," said Libby. "After that, the Marines would always say, 'Let Billy throw it.'"

A military newspaper wrote that "on four separate occasions he escaped with his life." The paper called Murphy "Lucky Looey."

But it wasn't luck, it was pure force of will. The same will he used to keep him alive in that rice paddy. The same will he used to build the Memphis athletic program from nothing.

That's why Libby and Mike aren't surprised at how this turned out. The old Murphy would hate to be living like he is today. But he's living like he is today because he's still the old Murphy.

No, it doesn't look particularly gallant. There's no hope of victory.

Elizabeth died of cancer in June. If her husband could have understood it, he would have doubtless chosen to go with her.

But there are warm moments nearly every day, moments of humor and humanity.

Jeffrey Jackson works in facilities at Trezevant Manor. He has a big heart and a big voice.

"COACH!" he'll holler, walking into the room.

Murphy and Jackson are buddies.

Friday, Libby dropped in to see her dad. She wanted to tell him about the Ole Miss game.

Three of Murphy's four grandchildren went to Ole Miss. He didn't mind a bit.

"He respected Ole Miss," Libby said. "And, of course, he and Coach Vaught were best of friends."

Libby sat in a chair and pulled it close to her dad. He patted her arm as she talked to him.

"Are you going to watch the game?" she asked. "You would have loved DeAngelo."

Libby ended the visit the way she always does. With a hug and a kiss and the words she hopes he remembers.

"You're my hero," she said. "You're the bravest man I've ever known."

MEMPHIS MAY HAVE FOUND ITSELF A QUARTERBACK
APRIL 7, 2013

Paxton Lynch took his first snap from center, turned to make the handoff and, well, nobody was there.

"He turned the wrong way!" said Memphis coach Justin Fuente. "You think he was nervous?"

I think he may well have been nervous. I think he will get over that in time. I think that if the Memphis football program emerges as a real threat to win the American Athletic Conference in the next few years — as many expect — it will be in part because Lynch makes a whole lot of plays that turn out better than his first one.

"Kids," said Fuente, still shaking his head over the botched handoff. "But he is going to be a really good player for this program."

Fuente said this in the wake of the Memphis spring game, at which — you will be shocked to hear this — optimism ran amok.

How amok?

"Just remember, if the planets align and we win the conference this year, it's still a BCS bowl," said Memphis fan Scott Forman.

Now that's amok.

But there's reason for the good feelings. The defense is going to be improved. Transfer receiver Joe Craig has injected some speed into the offense. A quartet of gifted running backs will be arriving with the freshman class.

And then there are the quarterbacks. Yes, with an "s."

You know that old saying, that when you have two quarterbacks you have no quarterbacks?

That's bunk.

When you've got two quarterbacks, you've got two quarterbacks, which is two more than the Memphis program often has.

This couldn't continue if the Tigers were going to change their identity. Just look at some other underdog schools that have flourished in recent years.

Boise State built its program around quarterback Kellen Moore. Utah went undefeated when led by quarterback Alex Smith. TCU rose to prominence with quarterback Andy Dalton. Anyone sensing a trend?

"These days, you can't play without a quarterback; you've got no shot," Fuente said. "He doesn't have to be an All-American. At TCU, we used to talk to Andy Dalton about being John Stockton. He has to be able to distribute the ball."

Memphis has two potential distributors. Jacob Karam returns after hitting his stride at the end of last year. In the Tigers' last three games — all wins — Karam completed 40 of 52 passes for 579 yards and seven touchdowns.

Normally, you'd think that would be enough to win him the job going into next season. But not with Lynch ready to go after a redshirt year.

"He's got a presence," said former Memphis quarterback Patrick Byrne, who stopped in on a practice earlier in the week. "He reminds me a little of Colin Kaepernick."

Which is crazy, of course. Lynch can't run like Kaepernick. But you know who Memphis offensive coordinator Darrell Dickey thought of when he first saw high school tape of Lynch?

"Tom Brady," said Dickey. "I said it, Coach Fuente said it and (quarterbacks coach) Brad Cornelsen said it. Now, this doesn't mean he's going to be the next Tom Brady ..."

Of course it doesn't. Nor does it mean that Lynch will beat out Karam and start this year.

But it's sure nice to dream, isn't it? Nice to be able to ponder the idea of a big, strong Memphis quarterback — Lynch is 6-6, 225 pounds — taking apart an opponent's secondary?

"He has some talent," is the kind of understated thing Fuente tends to say about Lynch, before quickly adding: "And he has a lot to learn."

Saturday, Lynch didn't do anything special. The same could be said for the entire team. Fuente — plainly a little paranoid about spies in the building — went with his most vanilla offense, and gave the walk-on quarterbacks as many snaps as the scholarship guys.

But even then, you could see the talent, see what all the excitement is all about. You know with some hitters in baseball, they say the ball sounds different coming off the bat? With Lynch, the ball looks different coming out of his hand.

So, yes, there was optimism at the spring game. And not all of it was because of the warmth of the sun.

"What is the ceiling for Paxton Lynch?" said Fuente. "I do not know."

AMERICAN ATHLETIC CONFERENCE CHAMPIONS/CAUSE FOR CONFETTI
NOVEMBER 30, 2014

It exploded over the heads of the celebrating players, in joyous clouds of blue and white.

Confetti.

When has the Memphis football program ever had occasion for confetti? When has it ever had occasion for that kind of extravagant, billowing happiness?

It has long been a program of tears and frustration. It has long been a program of shredded hopes and careers.

So it was almost surreal Saturday, as the Liberty Bowl sky turned a shimmering blue, as the commemorative T-shirts were handed to player after player, as the big gleaming trophy was carried to the stage.

Mike Aresco, commissioner of the American Athletic Conference, tried gamely to make the formal announcement.

"I want to congratulate the University of Memphis on winning," he said, and the rest was drowned out by cheers.

But the commemorative T-shirts said Memphis won a championship. The trophy, the hugs, and the crying said that, too.

"We told you to wait for this year," said Memphis linebacker Charles Harris.

New and updated Memphis football slogan: Wait until right now.

Memphis ended its 50th season of football at the Liberty Bowl by smashing the University of Connecticut, 41-10. With the victory, Memphis: 1) won its first conference championship since 1971, 2) won nine regular-season games for the first time since 1963, 3) won six games in a row for the first time since 1969, and 4) proved that, yes, indeed, it really is possible for this university to have a football program that is a source of joy, satisfaction and pride.

Until recently, people wondered about the last one. And not without considerable cause. From 2009-11 the Tigers were a staggering 5-31.

Small wonder the calls to abandon football altogether became a sort of civic cliché.

And then head coach Justin Fuente arrived, preaching old-fashioned verities like hard work, patience, discipline and unselfishness. Isn't it remarkable how far those old-fashioned verities can still carry a team?

"Just go 1-0," said Fuente, before the opener against Austin Peay. He then said it every single week.

So the Tigers went 1-0 against Austin Peay, and 1-0 against Middle Tennessee State, and 1-0 against Cincinnati and, before long, all those 1-0's started to pile up.

Saturday, the players all wore bracelets that said "Complete the Mission," which is what they ultimately did.

Paxton Lynch threw four touchdown passes. Lynch, you will recall, is the quarterback Fuente refused to bench last year.

Keiwone Malone caught two of those touchdown passes. Malone, you will recall, is the receiver Fuente declined to play until he shaped up off the field.

That is what effective coaching looks like, by the way. That's how a devastated program is slowly rebuilt.

A year after ending its season by losing to UConn by 35 points, Memphis won its first conference championship in more than four decades by beating that same UConn team by 31.

The fourth quarter was more celebration than anything, more of a countdown than a contest. Players hugged. Coaches grinned. It seemed like every fan in the stadium was recording the event on a cellphone.

"This is incredible," said Kenny Derryberry, in section 102, choking back tears. Kenny and his wife, Tammy, have been coming to the games since the 1980s. As it happens, they're retiring to Florida after this year. So this was their last game as season-ticket holders, and they were having a hard time letting go.

But then the Derryberrys pointed out another couple, Paul and Joyce Robinson, who have been coming to the Liberty Bowl for 50 consecutive years.

"This has been the greatest thing," said Paul Robinson, 82. "I never thought we'd see anything like this."

See anything like a championship, he meant. See a ceremony and a trophy and a celebration that could go on for a good long while.

"We finally have a football team," said Robinson.

Confetti all around!

ONCE AGAIN, TIGERS REWRITE SCRIPT TO FIT
DECEMBER 23, 2014

MIAMI — Bobby McCain stood on the stage at the 50-yard line, next to the big, shiny trophy, and led his teammates in a last, glorious cheer.

This was after the final interception to win the thing, and after the double-overtime touchdown pass, this was after the 54-yard field goal that could have been good from 75, this was after the improbable fourth-down touchdown pass to the wrong guy.

This was after Memphis and BYU combined for 103 points and 905 yards of offense, this was after the postgame helmet-swinging melee that ended up on TMZ. This was after quarterback Paxton Lynch — returning to his home state of Florida — won the game, then lost the game, then won the game again.

This was after all that glory and tumult and electricity. McCain climbed up on the stage and led his teammates once again.

"We're 1 and 0!

"We're 1 and 0!

"We're 1 and 0!

"We're 1 and 0!"

That cheer has now been repeated an astonishing, almost unbeliev-able, 10 times. But never with more gusto than it was on a Monday after-noon-turned-Monday-evening in Miami. Never with more emotion than after this double-overtime slugfest.

The Memphis Tigers earned their 10th win of the season by defeating Brigham Young in double overtime, 55-48.

"It means everything," said Memphis athletic director Tom Bowen. "It didn't matter what the odds were, it didn't matter what the challenges were, it didn't matter what the down was, our guys have been through so much."

Which just about sums up this year in Memphis football, doesn't it? A bunch of players who had been through so much — so much losing, so much turmoil, so much ridicule — found a way to rewrite the script.

Maybe that's why they didn't panic when BYU appeared to wrest this game away from them. Maybe that's why they didn't call it a season when BYU's Zac Stout picked off a Lynch pass and returned it 19 yards for a touchdown to put Memphis down 45-38.

It was Lynch's fourth turnover — and third interception — of the game. Memphis coach Justin Fuente decided to have a talk with his guy.

"Pax, we got your back, brother, we're going to go back out there and throw the ball," he said. "You're our guy. You're going to have to make plays."

So that's what Lynch proceeded to do. And those plays will be re-played over and over by Memphis fans, will become a part of Tiger lore.

Fourth-and-seven at the BYU 30. Just 1:34 left. Lynch fired the ball toward 155-pound Keiwone Malone, who flat outwrestled the BYU defensive back for the ball.

Fourth-and-four at the BYU 5. Just 53 seconds left. Lynch dropped back, stepped around one tackler, stepped around another tackler, waved to someone in the end zone, then fired a pass across the field to Malone to tie the game.

Who was Lynch actually throwing to?

"I didn't ask," Fuente said.

Lynch confessed after the game was over.

"Alan Cross," he said.

And so it was tied. And headed to overtime. And that's when Jake Elliott did his thing.

After BYU got a field goal, the Memphis offense threw it in reverse, leaving Elliott to hit a 54-yard field goal or lose the game.

"He'd hit from that long before," said Fuente, which would sound like wishful thinking if we didn't know how it turned out. But then BYU coach Bronco Mendenhall called a timeout to ice the kicker. Elliott was not impressed.

"It gave me a chance to get a little more focused up," he said.

Either that, or jacked. Because the kick would have been good from 75 yards. Or as they say in M-Town: Whoop that kick.

After that, it felt like destiny. How could Memphis possibly lose? Lynch found Roderick Proctor for his seventh touchdown of the game — four running, three passing — which used to be a season's worth for a Memphis quarterback.

Then DeShaughn Terry grabbed an interception to set off the celebration/brawl.

And, no, that was not the way anyone from Memphis wanted to end a classic game like that.

"I hope it doesn't take away from an incredible football effort," said Fuente, which should not be too much to ask.

This Memphis team won more games than anyone could have possibly imagined. This Memphis team resurrected a football program many thought was beyond hope. And then, on a national stage, against a storied program that has been to 10 straight bowls, this Memphis team showed the whole country the guts and determination that task required.

So here's to the first 10-win Tiger football team since 1938. Here's to a bunch of players who made Memphis football a thing. And here's to a head coach who summed it up as he was walking through the hallway, after the postgame news conference.

"I don't know about y'all," said Fuente, laughing. "But I'm tired."

MEMPHIS STUNS OLE MISS
OCTOBER 18, 2015

David Rudd, the president of the University of Memphis, held his iPhone high to capture the joy and the bedlam.

Paxton Lynch, the best quarterback the university has ever seen, ran over to his parents, to tell them he loves them.

Fans spilled over the walls and onto the field. Security guards laughed in happy futility.

Anthony Miller, the walk-on receiver, decided to do a lap around the entire inside of the Liberty Bowl, and never mind that he couldn't see clearly because of the tears.

"I just broke down," he said. "The nation should take notice of us now."

The nation will. The nation already has. A nationally televised 37-24 victory over No. 13 Ole Miss will do that for a city and a team.

"It's historic," said Rudd.

"It means everything," said Memphis athletic director Tom Bowen.

It means the Tigers will be ranked in both polls, will have a chance to stretch their winning streak to 14 games and beyond, and are one of the favorites to play in a New Year's Eve bowl game.

But that's getting ahead of ourselves. Let's begin at the beginning, which, for present purposes, shall be considered the ceremony early Saturday morning to take the wraps off the Liberty Bowl's new "John 'Bull' Bramlett Lane."

Bramlett loved playing against Ole Miss. He died six days shy of a year ago.

"We're going to win," said Nancy Bramlett, John's widow. "It's going to be icing on the cake. John is watching and we are going to win."

OK, but John may have gotten a little nervous when Memphis went down 14-zip, along with most of the 60,241 fans.

But the players?

The players left nervous behind somewhere between BYU, Bowling Green and Cincinnati.

"Coach (Rohrk) Cutchlow told us before the game 'Your best can ride with anyone,'" said Memphis tight end Alan Cross.

Let the record show their best is better than Ole Miss.

That's right, better. Just better. There was nothing fluky or accidental about this win.

Memphis out-gained Ole Miss, 491-480. Memphis had more first downs, 31-25. Memphis dominated the time of possession, 37:20-22:32.

And when the game was in the balance, it wasn't the upstart team from the American Athletic Conference that tried to get by on too-clever sleight of hand; it was the big, bad team from the SEC.

To wit: Early in the second quarter, leading 14-7, Ole Miss faced a third-and-one from the Memphis 10.

Ole Miss coach Hugh Freeze decided to hand the ball to Robert Nkemdiche, his five-star, all-world defensive lineman. Nkemdiche got stuffed and left the game for good.

Bramlett would have loved that moment. He would have reveled in what happened next. Because the Nkemdiche play was the clear turning point, the moment when his Memphis Tigers took charge.

On its next five possessions, Ole Miss ran a total of 14 plays for 11 yards.

On its next five possessions, Memphis scored three touchdowns and a field goal.

"Tigers are on an absolute tear," tweeted ESPN. Over on Twitter, the word "Memphis" started trending worldwide.

This was the day unfolding just as every Memphis fan had dreamed it might unfold. This was the perfect portrait of what Memphis football has become.

The previously maligned defense rose up to hold Ole Miss to 1.7 yards a carry. The lightly recruited quarterback looked like the best player — for either team — on the field. Someone asked Freeze how the Memphis receivers were able to get so open.

"A lot of that has to do with their quarterback," he said. "He's one of the best quarterbacks I've seen."

Lynch completed 39 of 53 passes for 384 yards and three touchdowns. Three former walk-ons — Miller, Alan Cross and Mose Frazier — caught 24 of those passes for 256 yards and all three scores.

Meanwhile, in the stands, the Vanilla Gorilla played his air guitar, longtime sufferers snapped photos as evidence that all this was really happening, and the massive crowd broke into an impromptu wave.

Who would have imagined that on the day Justin Timberlake was inducted into the Memphis Music Hall of Fame, he would be the second-most celebrated Justin in the city? Who would have believed that a party featuring Timberlake, Jimmy Fallon and Keith Richards would be the second-most joyous party of the night?

The game turned into a countdown. Rudd assured a reporter he had already found a booster to pay for new goal posts. Except, it turns out, Memphis won't even need new goal posts. Destroying Ole Miss was evidently enough.

Instead, it was all happiness. All selfies and tears and high-fives. Fuente doffed his cap as he walked off the field and into the tunnel. Lynch bounced and danced in a student mob.

"I got hit harder in the pile than I did in the game," said Lynch. "Like nothing I've experienced in my life."

So now come the updated polls and the updated expectations. Now comes the chance to turn this moment into something more. Indeed, that's what separates this memorable Tiger win from nearly all of the memorable Tiger wins that preceded it. This one is about more than the final score.

It's about a program that is changing its trajectory and maybe its destiny. It's about what has happened and what might happen still.

"The city's got our back and we've got their back," said Cross. "No telling where that can lead."

VI

MOMENTS

OUR DREAM, THEIR TEAM

Steve Ehrhart opens the top drawer of his desk, pulls out the check.

The check is old, fading, essentially worthless except as a small slice of history.

The NFL sent it to Ehrhart a few years ago. It's the payment for the antitrust verdict Ehrhart and the USFL won against the NFL in a previous decade. The check is for $3.76. Damages and interest. Not enough to buy a hot dog and a Coke at today's game between the Oilers and the Raiders.

Ehrhart keeps the check as a reminder. He looks at it every once in a while, says it helps him stay humble. And this week, when the NFL comes to town for real, he looks at it even more than usual.

"It's bittersweet," Ehrhart says. "That's a good word.

"On the one hand, I'm glad to have an NFL team here. I don't begrudge them anything.

"But you think about everything we went through to get a team of our own, all the effort ..."

Ehrhart trails off. He's not bitter, just pensive. He reflects the mood of his city.

The NFL is here. After three decades of frustration, the NFL has finally come to Memphis. But drive all over town, talk to anyone you'd like and you'll hear the same thing.

This is not a celebration; this is not what we expected; this is not the way this week was supposed to feel.

• • •

Pepper Rodgers is still trying to sell tickets. The guy has taken a lot of flak around town. But you try to do his job, just one day, and you see how hard it is.

The Oilers don't live here, don't practice here and have the public relations instincts of, oh, Marge Schott. Remember that travel disaster?

Remember when the Oilers tried to use Memphis tax dollars to finance their commute from Nashville? How is anyone supposed to sell tickets after THAT?

Rodgers does his best. He was born to be a salesman. He's been selling since he arrived in Memphis more than a decade ago. First, he tried to sell Memphis to the NFL. Now, he tries to sell the NFL to Memphis.

"At the time we had a CAUSE, see," says Rodgers. "That makes all the difference in the world. We filled that stadium every exhibition game, had a lot of fun.

"What I don't want is for people to see the crowds in Memphis and think we couldn't do better under different circumstances. If we had gotten an expansion team, it would have been a great success. We'd be like Jacksonville or Carolina."

Rodgers stops himself. He's not working for Memphis any longer. He's working for the Oilers.

"But I still think we can do OK this year," he says. "All we need is for the team to win some games. I mean, if we win Sunday..."

• • •

Roy Smith stands over the Liberty Bowl field holding a long, spattered paint gun.

"You start with the curves," he says, pulling the trigger, starting to move his hand in an arc. "Curves are the hardest."

Smith can paint anything. He says it's something you are born with, like the ability to hit a baseball. He can paint cars. He can paint buildings. He can also paint football fields.

Smith has painted a lot of names on this field over the years. Grizzlies. Showboats. Mad Dogs. You name it.

"The Mad Dogs were my best customer," he says. "They wanted that logo everywhere.

"But I don't care what they want me to paint. If they want me to paint the Gettysburg Address on this field, I'd paint the Gettysburg Address."

Today's orders are simpler. Paint the word "Oilers" in one end zone. Plain white, no border. It's cheaper without the border.

"This is an easy one," he says, "relatively speaking."

Smith stops, admires his work. He is just about finished with the "O." The whole word will take five or six more hours.

"I'm glad to have the work," he says. "But it doesn't mean anything special."

• • •

John Malmo is on something of a rant. Not at the Oilers, at Nashville.

Nashville will send a few thousand fans to Memphis for the game. That's it. Period. David Climer, a sports columnist with *The Tennessean*, explained Nashville's feelings about Memphis this way:

"Nashvillians view Memphis the same way New Yorkers think about Newark," Climer wrote. "There's a line of demarcation somewhere just the other side of Jackson that is best left uncrossed."

That sounds just like Nashville, when you come to think of it. Snooty. Self-important. Out of touch with reality. Nashville gets an NFL team and suddenly thinks it's Manhattan.

So Malmo, the head of the Memphis Park Commission, can't help taking a shot.

"What's amazing to me is that the Memphis media hasn't pummeled Nashville for not supporting their team during two exhibition games and for not buying tickets for a three-hour drive. To support their own damn team!

"No sour grapes and all. But I truly believe, if the roles were reversed, there would be 20,000 people from Memphis in Nashville."

• • •

John Koski will tell you that Memphians still care about the NFL.

Koski works for the local Fox affiliate. Last week, his secretary's phone started ringing and ringing and ringing.

"I've been asked all week long," he says. "What does the Oilers game mean for our telecast of Dallas vs. Pittsburgh?"

It's not surprising, actually. Let's say the NFL decided to stash a team in Los Angeles for two years. Then move it to Sacramento or something. Call it the California Gold Rush. You think Los Angeles would prefer to watch the Gold Rush than the Packers or the Cowboys?

So Koski got a lot of calls. After a while, he could guess what people were calling about.

"There was a lot of interest," he says. "At first, I thought we couldn't show our game. Now I'm told that if the Oilers don't sell out, we can go ahead and show it."

Koski tries to be diplomatic.

"Nothing against the Oilers," he says. "I support the Oilers.

"But some people are very relieved."

• • •

Dick Hackett, for one, has forgiven the NFL.

"The proof is in the pudding," he says. "I bought four season tickets."

Hackett was mayor of Memphis through part of the expansion drive. He was disappointed with the way it turned out. But he got over it a long time ago.

"I think everybody has to make their own decision," he says. "But this is what Dick Hackett and his family are doing."

Hackett has divvied his tickets up this way: His 15-year-old son gets one; his 10-year-old son gets another; his 80-year-old father gets the third; Hackett keeps the fourth for himself.

"My sons have never been to a game," he says. "Neither has my father. Sunday we'll have three generations going to an NFL football game in Memphis.

"What's so bad about that?"

• • •

Steve Ehrhart calls back. He has thought about the topic. He has one more story about the expansion days.

"Before the 1986 season, I talked to Al Davis about the Raiders coming here to play the Showboats.

"We really talked. Al was a renegade and he didn't care what the NFL would think. I had a vision of the Raiders playing in the Liberty Bowl.

"The league folded before we could play. But here we are, 12 years later, and the Raiders are going to be playing at the Liberty Bowl."

Ehrhart initially figured he'd sit this game out. But then he started thinking about the old times and remembered that conversation with Davis and started to reconsider.

"Come Sunday morning, I imagine I'll go," he says. "I think I'll want to see it.

"We put a lot of blood, sweat and tears into bringing the NFL to Memphis."

HEISMAN NOT THE MEASURE OF MANNING
DECEMBER 14, 1997

They finally met, not on a football field, not on a glorious Saturday afternoon in Knoxville or Ann Arbor, but in a plush, elegant boardroom in this town that is filled with them. Tennessee's Peyton Manning and Michigan's Charles Woodson. Face-to-face. Together at last. And you know what? Manning was the better man.

Woodson won the Heisman. He swept every region but the South. He is the most popular football player with sportswriters this year. But in defeat, Manning was as Manning always is. Gracious. Humble. A model of what we once thought a college football player should be.

Did Manning resent the process?

"No," he said. "I'm excited to be here as a candidate."

Did Manning regret his decision to return for his senior year?

"Absolutely not," he said. "I wouldn't change a thing."

Did Manning have any final thoughts he'd like to share?

"I feel bad for the people of Tennessee," he said. "I would have liked to have brought this home to them."

Some of you might be getting a little tired of the Manning-as-paragon stuff you continue to read in the paper. The guy isn't Mother Teresa, he isn't perfect. He watches a lot of game film. He knows his football history. This does not make him a saint.

Still, on this most disappointing of nights, Manning reaffirmed that he is a remarkable superstar. Even if you don't like Tennessee — and there are plenty who do not — it is awfully tough not to like Manning. In this overheated, overdone beauty contest that is the Heisman Trophy, Manning refused to join in. He conducted himself with dignity at the start. He conducted himself with dignity in the end.

And that's the sadness of this day, really. That's the reason to feel some regret. Not because Manning got ripped off. Not because the voters selected an inferior football player. But because in rejecting Manning, in selecting Woodson, the voters missed a chance to remind people what a college football player is supposed to be.

There was a column in a New York newspaper Saturday morning by some guy named Lenn Robbins, a Heisman voter who voted for Woodson. Robbins explained why he didn't consider Manning's decision to return for his senior year in casting his ballot.

"Manning is one of the lucky ones," he wrote. "And while I don't hold it against him, I don't give him bonus points for having the luxury of being able to play four years. Nor do I give this naive notion of the concept of the student-athlete any added weight."

Startling, isn't it? In three quick sentences, the guy gutted everything that is good about the college game. You read stuff like that, you no longer wonder why the sports world is coming apart, why a basketball player thinks it's fine to throttle his coach, why humility and honor have given way to self-promotion and greed.

Manning doesn't have time to dwell on all this, naturally. He's got the Orange Bowl to look forward to, then the NFL draft, then a career in Chicago or Indianapolis or some such place.

If he brings to those pursuits the same grace and dignity that he brought to this night, the guy will do just fine.

A MAGICAL DRIVE - HOMETOWN
GOLFER LIGHTS UP FESJC
JULY 31, 1998

He was finishing up another interview. He was answering another round of questions. When suddenly, the kid realized he didn't know the name of the guy who was asking them. So he smiled, stuck out his hand, introduced himself.

"Hi," he said. "I'm David Gossett."

As tag lines go, it may be hard to find a better one for the first day of the FedEx St. Jude Classic golf tournament. He is your neighbor. He is the boy next door. He also happens to be one shot off the lead after 18 holes. So it's high time you meet him.

Gossett, a 19-year-old amateur from Germantown, set this tournament ablaze Thursday. Nick Price may be tied for the lead. Paul Azinger may be a sentimental favorite. But Gossett had the kind of day — the kind of utterly magical day — that folks around here will remember for a long, long time.

He shot a 5-under-par 66. He played the course like he is 19 going on 40. Then, when it was over, he sounded exactly like you'd hope a kid in the summer between high school and college would sound.

"It was awesome," he said, his blue eyes sparkling. "It was a lot of fun out there."

Fun? It was more than that. It was dazzling. It was breathtaking. It was a grand coming-out party that nobody would have dared to script.

"I knew he could have a day like this," said Larry Gossett, his father. "But for him to have a day like this, at his home course, in his second professional tournament ... Yeah, it's special."

Gossett arrived at the first tee at 8:55, part of the final group of the morning. He wore a coral colored shirt, pleated khakis, a relaxed smile. He had played the course a thousand times. But this was the first time there was a guy in a straw hat waiting to introduce him.

Paul Sharpe, the announcer, boomed the words into his microphone.

"Completing this outstanding group, from Germantown, Tennessee, David Gossett!"

Gossett stepped to the tee box. He took a long look down the fairway. Then he smacked the ball high and hard and right down the middle.

"I hit a real solid drive, " said Gossett. "After that, I was fine."

And then they were off, off down the fairway, off into history. He missed a birdie putt on that first hole. He didn't miss his birdie putts on the second, third and fifth. When he birdied the eighth and ninth holes to finish the front nine at 5-under — his birdie putt on No. 8 was especially sweet, a 20-footer as true as anything you've ever seen — people figured they might be a part of something special.

"Nice playing!" said Jim Murphy, a fan from Memphis who happened to catch Gossett making the turn. "Now go out and break the course record!"

Gossett did not do that, of course. He had one more birdie, one more bogey, and wound up the back nine exactly where he started it. But by the time he headed down the final fairway, his gallery had swelled to thousands.

It was a grand sight, a special moment, the kind of event that reminds you why sports are better than fiction.

Three years ago, Gossett spent this week making some extra cash, lugging cameras for *Sports Illustrated*. Now he was carrying something else around with him.

Now he was carrying a tournament.

JUST HOLD ONTO THE FOOTBALL
NOVEMBER 15, 1998

Simplest play in football.
You lean over the center.
You take the snap.
You run around for a second.
You slide to the ground.

Arkansas quarterback Clint Stoerner has taken maybe 10,000 snaps in his lifetime. It is second nature to him. It is as natural as shaking hands.

So he leaned over the center.

He took the snap.

He ran around for a second.

And then he ...

"Dropped the ball," he said. "No reason. I can't explain it. I just dropped the ball."

Maybe you saw it, maybe you watched it on TV.

Arkansas had the ball at midfield. A minute and change left in the game. Garbage time, really. Tennessee fans were already heading for the exits.

Then Stoerner took the snap, ran a little sprintout to his left. And, untouched, he dropped the ball.

"This loss is on me," he said. "All I had to do was hold on.

"My teammates didn't lose this game, they won it.

"One man lost this game for this football team.

"Me."

• • •

Maybe we care too much about college sports. Maybe the pressure is too much.

When Bill Buckner makes a blunder, when he is forced to relive it again and again, well, that's OK. He's a professional. He gets paid.

But what does a college kid get out of these games except memories? And what if the memories become nightmares instead?

Tennessee and Arkansas hooked up to play an enormous football game Saturday. *Sports Illustrated* sent a reporter. So did *USA Today*. So did *The Los Angeles Times*.

They saw Tennessee win a thriller, 28-24. But they saw something else, too.

They saw a kid make the kind of mistake that could haunt him forever. They saw a kid make the kind of blunder he could take to his grave.

Tennessee was finished, see, as finished as a team can be. Arkansas had the ball at its 49-yard line. Just 1:43 left in the game. Even if Tennessee got the ball back, the offense wouldn't have time to do spit.

Tennessee took a timeout. Stoerner shrugged and went over to talk to his coach.

"Everyone is saying, 'Hold onto the ball, hold onto the ball,'" he said. "I'm like, 'What do you think I'm going to do?'"

The play was called "Right Deuce Pass 4 Sprint." It wasn't as complicated as it sounds. The idea was for Stoerner to roll to his left, kill some time, stay inbounds.

But after a couple steps, Stoerner started to slip. He tried to catch his balance with his hand. And when he did, the ball slipped away. Nobody touched him. Nothing but air.

Stoerner looked back behind him, tried to find the ball.

"It was sickening," he said. "Everything you worked for, slipping away."

• • •

Tennessee scored. Of course, Tennessee scored. Four plays after the fumble, Travis Henry plunged into the end zone.

As Stoerner walked off the field, a blond television reporter stuck her mike in his face.

"How do you feel?"

"Horrible."

"What happened?"

Here, Stoerner took his fist and pounded his chest hard.

"Right here," he said. "It's on me."

He kept this up for the next hour. No matter who happened to stop by. The beat reporter from Little Rock. The columnist from Nashville. The radio guy from ESPN.

It was remarkable, really, because everyone kept firing questions designed to let him off the hook.

"Was the ball wet?"

"No."

"Was it a bad play?"

"No."

"Did you trip over the center?"

"No," he said. "It's all on me."

He sat there for an hour, patient and composed, taking the blame all by himself.

He may have slipped, he may have fallen.

But he was a standup guy to the end.

MAR-VOL-OUS! – TENNESSEE WINS IT ALL
JANUARY 5, 1999

So this is how you toast a title.

So this is how you celebrate perfection.

So this is how you react when you have won your first national title in 47 years.

You sprint to the center of the field. You run that enormous Tennessee flag from end zone to end zone. You dance and leap and sing "Rocky Top" loud enough to wake the desert.

"Tennessee is No. 1," you shout.

And from everywhere in the country — from Ann Arbor to Gainesville, from Lincoln to Los Angeles — you hear nothing but joyous silence in reply.

Tennessee is No. 1. Tennessee proved it with a 23-16 win over Florida State at the Fiesta Bowl Monday night.

Can you blame the Vols for dancing?

Can you blame Vol fans for singing "Rocky Top" a thousand times?

Tennessee last won a title in 1951. So there had been 47 years of disappointment. Forty-seven years of frustration. Forty-seven years of watching the other guy take home the trophy.

Georgia won a title. Florida won a title. Alabama won more titles than you can count.

The Vols had the biggest stadium. Just not the biggest trophy case.

Well, all that has changed now. All that has changed because of a team that didn't do anything but win.

"It's been 47 years since Tennessee football had got one of these," UT coach Phillip Fulmer said, accepting the trophy. "And we have a special place for it.

"This football team is one that believes it could get it done. We worked hard tonight and we got it done."

They did it as they have done all season, by calling on a number of heroes and by calling on the defense in the end.

Tee Martin completed his first season as a starter — and he also completed some huge passes. There was the 79-yarder to Peerless Price in the fourth quarter, the big blow of the night.

Price, the latest in the long line of Vol receivers, caught four passes for 199 yards. He was the game's offensive MVP.

The defense starred, too, with big hits and bigger plays. Cornerback Dwayne Goodrich stepped in front of a Marcus Outzen pass meant for All-American Peter Warrick, picked it off and returned it 54 yards for a first-half touchdown.

The Vols held Warrick to one catch for 7 yards.

Goodrich was the defensive MVP.

The game wasn't decided until Tennessee made another huge defensive play. Florida State had the ball with Tennessee ahead by 7, in the final two minutes. But cornerback Steve Johnson intercepted an Outzen pass, ending the threat.

"We congratulate Tennessee for the national championship that they deserve," said FSU coach Bobby Bowden. "They did a good job of covering Warrick. We tried to get the ball to him, but they took him out of the game."

And so fireworks filled the cool desert night and Vols spilled onto the Sun Devil Stadium field, and the wait was over.

It was left to Price to put it all in perspective.

"Nobody believed but us," he said. "I bet you all didn't even believe in us.

"It just feels good.

"Real good."

IT'S ABOUT MORE THAN BASEBALL
APRIL 1, 2000

The day before the day before the opening of the grandest little ballpark that's ever been built, Patrick Tansey comes wheeling around the corner of S. Fourth and Madison, in a hurry to check out the progress.

He has been coming here every day for more than four months. To this very spot, a place beyond the centerfield wall, where you can look through the chain-link fence and watch a baseball diamond being cut and polished in the heart of a city.

Tansey, 34, isn't a huge baseball fan, mind you. He doesn't build his life around the Redbirds. But somehow, he's fallen in love with this building, hook, line and dugouts.

"I walk over here every day at lunch," he says. "I just like to see what's being done."

Tansey isn't alone in this devotion to this spot, to this one place where you can peer inside the construction site. For the last few months, it's been the modern equivalent of a knothole. In one hour the other day, more than 50 people stopped by to watch the painters and plumbers and the electricians. There were white people, black people, lawyers and bankers and truck drivers. Some hoisted themselves up on two concrete barriers for better viewing.

"There's a steady stream," says Keith Johnson, vice president of the nearby downtown YMCA. "Every day, they're out there."

Starting today, of course, we won't need to peer through chain link or stand on concrete barriers to see AutoZone Park. Starting today, we'll be able to walk right in the front gates or watch it on television.

But for putting things in perspective, it didn't get much better than standing next to Tansey the other day, as he marveled at the transformation.

"A year ago, this was a hole in the ground, nothing," he says. "And now, this. We did it right this time, didn't we?"

• • •

Good morning, Memphis. And welcome to your new ballpark. It has cypress trees in centerfield, a grassy bluff in left, and the ability to flat take your breath away.

Allie Prescott, the president of the team, has taken more than 100 people on tours the past few weeks. It's one of his duties. And his favorite part is walking them through the gate, to the field, and hearing that sharp, involuntary intake of breath when they first see the diamond.

"I don't say anything," he says. "I just let them stand and look at it."

It is something of a miracle, this ballpark, and not just because it looks and feels like a slice of heaven. It's a miracle because of how it was done, and when, and against what backdrop.

Do you remember the year 1996? Do you remember what a dismal time that was for sports in Memphis?

The Pharaohs had left town. The city had been abandoned by an Arena League team. The Oilers/Titans had settled on Nashville, putting an end to the city's NFL hopes forever. And after all that, Chicks owner David Hersh had announced that he was thinking of taking his Double-A franchise to Jackson, Tenn.

Nothing against Jackson, mind you. They make a fine potato chip, among other things. It's just not the size city that should be able to compete with Memphis for a sports franchise.

"It was pretty depressing," Prescott says, "to think of Memphis without baseball."

This, of course, is when Dean Jernigan stepped up, a homegrown kid who loved his city even more than he loved baseball. You know the story by now, don't you? Jernigan got a call asking for his help. He said, hey, why not?

"Someone had to do something," he says. "If we didn't, who was going to?"

Jernigan negotiated to buy the Chicks. When that failed, he applied for a Triple-A expansion franchise instead. He found land for a ballpark. He decided to run the team as a nonprofit enterprise. He hired the best architects to design the stadium. He sold local banks on financing the deal. He persuaded the Cardinals to come on board as the major-league affiliate.

In the end, Jernigan — along with his wife, Kristi, who has been a full partner the whole way, often more deeply immersed in the details than her husband — conceived, spearheaded and delivered an $80.5 million downtown ballpark for $8.5 million in public money.

Really, it was an astonishing lesson in leadership, in a city that needed one. For so long, Memphis sports fans have waited for someone to salvage their sports future — a sports authority, the NFL, anyone. Then along come the Jernigans to show that the way to do something is to, well, do something.

"We wanted to raise the standard," Kristi Jernigan says. "To show what can be done in Memphis."

Oh, there were still skeptics along the way, of course. Given the history, that's to be expected. Remember the hole in the ground? Remember the jokes about the downtown wave pool?

Even as of last week, people drove past the ballpark, took a look at all the trucks and the scaffolding, and wondered aloud whether the park would be ready.

So it was with great pleasure that Prescott led another brief tour the other day, three days before the opener. A few workers were replacing strips of sod on the bluff, because the sod that was in place didn't look quite right. The groundskeeper was mowing diagonal stripes into the emerald outfield. A painter was painting "Welcome to AutoZone Park" on the roof of the first-base dugout, putting the finishing touches on the "W."

"People ask me if it's going to be ready," Prescott said, opening his hands and gesturing toward the park, as if that were all the answer anyone needed. "Believe me, in every way that impacts the fan experience, it will be ready."

• • •

At bottom, AutoZone Park isn't just about baseball. It's about progress and downtown and changing, if only at the margin, the way that Memphians perceive themselves and their city.

"This ballpark is not about winning baseball games," Dean Jernigan says. "It's not even about supplying first-class entertainment. It's about bringing all the elements of our city together."

Is this too much to ask of a ballpark? Yeah, maybe. It's still just a ballpark, after all, a nice place to sit and watch the summer game. The Pyramid was a hit the day it first opened, too. And then look what happened.

Still, you see the way people have taken to this particular ballpark, and you can't help but think something special might be happening here.

The YMCA has built bleachers on its roof, and sold tickets to today's opener for $20 a pop. The bleachers will be available to members all year long. There's not a better view in the city.

A local advertising agency decided to distribute its tickets to today's game in an employee lottery. But in order to qualify for the lottery, employees had to have their time sheets in on time. For the first time in recent memory, every time sheet was finished.

And then there was the constant gathering at S. Fourth and Madison these past few months, as people stopped to peer through the chain link at the construction.

Wednesday afternoon, they were still trickling in after lunch hour, happily volunteering what they liked best about the new stadium. Gregg Shawen, of Cordova, said he liked the old-time look of the place. Margaret Ridolphi, of Memphis, said she liked the way it was "plopped right down in the middle of the city."

And then there was Kevin Elliott, of Memphis, who after admiring the park from foul pole to foul pole, offered up this answer.

"What I like best," he said, "is that I already have my ticket."

HERE! HERE! HERE! 15,000 CHEER PARK
APRIL 2, 2000

Rob Painter is a grown man. He is 26, for heaven's sake. A student of construction at the University of Memphis. A serious student of serious things.

But let the record show that a little after noon on Saturday, he stepped onto the soft, green turf in the left field bluff, dived into the grass, and rolled.

"It's finished!" he said, by way of explanation. "Opening day is finally here."

Well, yes. The opening of a ballpark, and the opening of an era, too.

After three years of planning, three years of digging and dust, they took the wraps off the stunning, brick-and-steel playground known as AutoZone Park. The Memphis Redbirds defeated the St. Louis Cardinals, 10-6, before 15,000 happy fans. And if they all had their own way of marking the occasion — Redbirds' infielder Stubby Clapp did a flip, Dean and Kristi Jernigan lifted glasses of champagne in their private box, Mark McGwire smiled, signed autographs and rested his ailing back — Painter's inaugural roll in the grass neatly captured the mood.

The weekend of April 1, 1975, the Peabody Hotel closed its doors, symbolizing the sorry state of downtown. Exactly 25 years later, AutoZone Park flung open its gates, symbolizing the new, heady mood of renewal.

"I think," said Jack Buck, the legendary announcer for the Cardinals, looking around the park, "that this is nicer than Wrigley Field."

Silly?

Of course. Nothing is nicer than Wrigley Field. But that's the thing about AutoZone Park. People see it, and tend to get carried away.

Walt Jocketty, the Cards GM, first saw it from the sky, flying in with the team Saturday morning. The pilot told him to look down to his left.

"It's incredible," he said. "It's so much more than I expected."

Tony LaRussa, the Cards manager, first saw it Saturday morning, when he walked onto the field for batting practice. He mouthed a quiet "Wow."

"I can see a lot of guys being called up by the majors," LaRussa said, "and saying they don't want to go."

The place was stunning, a small piece of paradise between green grass and splotchy blue skies. Rockey the Redbird parachuted in before the opening pitch. The Navy mustered a flyover. Forty-six people — 46! — combined to throw out a cloudburst of first balls.

And out on the Bluff, fans scrambled to avoid or catch incoming homers during batting practice.

"You know what?" said Anne Marie Porter, of Horn Lake, putting down a blanket, "We're going to get killed out here."

Oh, the day was not entirely perfect, of course. The sound system was hit-or-miss on the Bluff. The roof leaked in spots. There were lines to the beer tap and lines to the men's room, which seemed to make some internal sense.

And then there was the absence of McGwire, who stayed in the dugout with a bad back. But even McGwire seemed moved by the day, taking time to mention a video the team had been shown on the bus on the way to the game, explaining how the Redbirds turn all their profits back to charity. "A lot of guys went, 'You've got to be kidding me,'" McGwire said. "Why can't everybody do that?"

For the rest of the afternoon, McGwire made like the rest of Memphis and enjoyed the view. He saw Fernando Vina get the first hit, Darrell Whitmore commit the first error, Eli Marrero hit the first home run.

And after two hours and 44 minutes of baptism by baseball, the Cardinals' Mike Matheny lofted a ball into Whitmore's glove in left, ending a day that will be savored in this town for a very long time.

"It's like expecting a new baby," is how Buck put it. "You know it will be beautiful, but you don't know how beautiful until it's here."

CITY'S RECRUITING MESS HITS A NEW LOW
JANUARY 10, 2001

He sits in a plain school chair, hands folded, the periodic table of the elements over his left shoulder, and unspools a story that — if it's true — takes us lower than we've ever been before.

A story about how he and another high school coach combined to sell the services of a talented defensive lineman.

A story about how they'd sit down with college recruiters and, very calmly, ask for two cars and a hundred grand.

A story about how they changed the request to $200,000 cash because, you know, that would be harder to trace.

A story about how they bought a new safe to hold it all.

A story about how now, finally, after watching the other coach keep all the money, after watching the player get nothing at all, he decided to tell everyone.

You, me, the NCAA.

"I couldn't lie," says Milton Kirk, leaning forward in that simple school chair. "Why would I sit here and lie to y'all? People say don't do this, don't say this. But the kids knew I was doing it, the people in the community knew I was doing it, I knew I was doing it. So why am I going to sit up here and lie?"

Albert Means, the defensive lineman from Trezevant High School, indicated through Kirk Tuesday he's planning to drive to Tuscaloosa today, withdraw from the University of Alabama and come home.

According to Kirk, Means is thinking about leaving because he's just now learned his services were bartered away by his high school coaches, and he's displeased with the news.

"He's unhappy and he wants to be closer to his mother and family," Kirk said. "Right now, the boy's just frustrated and unhappy now that he's found out the way this happened."

Not everyone agrees with Kirk's version of events. Lynn Lang, the head coach at Trezevant, the man Kirk says made hundreds of thousands brokering Means's signing, says Kirk is making it all up.

"What he's saying is totally false," Lang says. "He's not credible. He's always had a wild imagination, that's all."

But if it is true, if the recruitment of Albert Means played out the way Kirk describes, we have a new winner in the fun game of Memphis recruiting limbo we've been playing for the past few weeks.

Never mind the allegations that Melrose coach Tim Thompson might have kept some Kentucky jackets during a recruiting visit.

Never mind the news that ousted Kentucky recruiting coordinator Claude Bassett sent Thompson $1,400 in money orders.

This is the easy winner; this is how low we can go.

"It was $200,000, cash," says Kirk. "That was the number."

The astonishing thing is how casually Kirk talks about all this, how easily he relates the tale.

Kirk — who now teaches science and coaches football at Sheffield High — was the offensive coordinator at Trezevant the past six years. Lang was the head coach. Before Means's senior year, in 1999, Kirk says Lang asked him to "coordinate" the sale of the player.

"It was like, 'Coach, how do you want it, what do you want to do?'" Kirk said. "He said, 'Well, I want me this. And I want you to get something for helping me.'

"He said, well, he wanted an Expedition. And I said, 'That's what we'll go for.' So he presented it as a truck for him and a truck for me. And $100,000 cash."

And, according to Kirk, that's the deal the two presented to college recruiters throughout the fall of '99. Kirk said he personally sat in on meetings during which the deal was presented to coaches from Georgia, Alabama, Mississippi State, Arkansas and Michigan State. An assistant coach from one of those schools confirmed Tuesday he was offered the deal. Kirk said there were other meetings he heard about, but did not attend.

Oh, yeah, and if recruiters wanted to come watch a tape of Means in action, there was sometimes a price for that, too.

"When they came by the school at Trezevant, and they wanted to see him, and they wanted a tape, they would tell them, $100," Kirk said. "After they left him, then they would come to me and tell me what happened.

"I guess he just got greedy. I guess whatever way he saw he could make a buck, he was trying to make it."

The most startling part of the whole story — besides the staggering sums involved — is the notion that Means not only didn't profit from the auction, he didn't even know about it.

How, then, could the coaches sell Means? If the kid wasn't in on the action?

"(Lang) had the kid's and the mom's 100 percent confidence," Kirk said. "He had him wrapped in the palm of his hand."

And how then did Lang explain to Means that Alabama was the place for him?

"He said, 'You're going to Alabama,'" Kirk said. "This is where you go."

Kirk knows he's not an unbiased witness to any of this. He's moved from Trezevant to Sheffield, for starters, after a falling out with Lang. And then there's the small story he tells about what happened when Kirk went to Lang in June, to ask for his share.

"He told me he was going in another direction," Kirk said.

But Kirk insists he's motivated by more than bitterness, more than a desire to get his.

"Here's a kid that did what we asked him to do. Here's a kid that needs help. I'm talking about, right now, this kid doesn't have the basic clothes for a college student. Here's a kid that doesn't have a suit and tie.

"I just don't think, as coaches, we can continue to fabricate to young men to be the best they can be, and do the best they can, and then, we don't live up to our part.

"That's the big thing. And it's a personal thing, more than anything else."

IT'S TIME AGAIN FOR FOOTBALL
SEPTEMBER 21, 2001

Molly Jenkins, 12, decided she'd make a big sign to tell the entire country just how she felt. She spent hours doing it. She cut out letters from magazines. Pasted them on a large piece of construction paper. And Thursday night, when it was done, she held her sign up for everyone to see.

"MSU loves America," the sign said.

Then she flipped it over.

"But we hate Ole Miss."

Ahhhh, college football. Isn't it grand?

Terrorism can shake the country to its very core.

The stock market can tumble and tumble and tumble again.

But college football, in all its abundant, brassy, Southern-fried, over-the-top glory surges on.

South Carolina 16, Mississippi State 14. Because you can't stop forever. Because it seemed like it was time.

That's a question that has been troubling all of us, isn't it? When is it time?

When is it time for ESPN to stop playing that mournful version of its theme song? When is it time for David Letterman to be a wise guy? When is it time for Dave Barry to be funny? When is it time for Howard Stern to be crude?

When is it time to whistle? Or gossip? Or sing in the shower? Or dance?

When is it time to answer the question "how are you" with something other than "as good as can be expected?"

And, yeah, when is it time to care if the home team can run the ball or catch a pass or stop the quarterback draw?

Nobody can answer any of this, of course. It's all horribly new. But as for the last question, anyway, Thursday night seemed to work OK.

Some 43,579 fans showed up for the game. And if it was quieter than usual, if 30,000 American flags replaced 30,000 cowbells as the accessory of choice, it was still — we might as well just go ahead and confess — fun.

And it was. Truly. Fun to see guys run into each other. To hear a marching band. To watch Lou Holtz beat another Top 25 team on the road.

Sure, it was more fun for South Carolina than Mississippi State — the Gamecocks had a whopping 238 rushing yards — but you get the point.

"This is America's sport," Holtz said. "And it was good to be playing it again."

None of this means that the horrors in New York and Washington have been pushed out of anyone's thoughts. Just talk to Jackie Sherrill. His son, Justin, recently completed his training as an Air Force fuel specialist. The Mideast could be his next stop.

Or better yet, talk to Mississippi State corner Richard Ball.

His stepsister recently moved to New York to start a new job. She happened to be sitting in a car outside the World Trade Center on Sept. 11. She hasn't been heard from since.

Ball played anyway. He walked into the field before the game holding a corner of an enormous flag.

He accepted some hugs from teammates.

Then he went out, lined up at defensive back, and knocked down a pass.

And while nobody can know what it is about college football that made Ball play Thursday night — he declined to be interviewed afterward — maybe the kid had it figured out better than most.

It wasn't a matter of life and death out there.

Just life.

LEWIS MAKES SHORT WORK OF TYSON
JUNE 9, 2002

Mike Tyson lay on the canvas, deposited there by a gentle shove, which followed a hard right that Lennox Lewis later said he felt right through his hand to his shoulder.

Tyson was bleeding over both eyes. He was bleeding from his nose. He held his glove up to his face, as if he might stem the damage.

Then he lifted his head. Once. Briefly. Before falling back to the canvas for good this time.

And that's how it ended.

Decisively.

Brutally.

Even — we told you weird things could happen at a Tyson fight — gallantly.

Lewis retained the heavyweight championship of the world Saturday night with a knockout of Tyson at 2:25 of the eighth round.

It was a measure of how one-sided the fight was that all anyone could talk about afterward was how darn well Tyson took his beating.

He did, too. He was here just a week, but the guy has plainly learned something about Southern hospitality.

Tyson wiped blood from Lewis's cheek when it was done. He talked about his profound affection for Lewis and his mum.

"He's a magnificent, prolific fighter," Tyson said. "If he thinks I don't love him and his mother, he's crazy."

Then Tyson asked for a rematch. Pleaded, really.

And while it may have seemed like the right thing to say at the time, it's hard to know why anyone needs one.

So Lewis can have another eight rounds of target practice?

So Tyson can lose another fight to a real fighter?

So we can all gather at The Pyramid for another of these celebrity wing-dings?

OK, that part would be fun. It may be a while before Samuel L. Jackson, Denzel Washington and Leonardo DiCaprio converge in Memphis to watch the Grizzlies.

But, even then, would fans be so easily fooled into thinking the fight would be compelling?

That's what happened this time. That's why more than a million sensible people forked over $54.95 to see this one. They hoped that, somehow, the Tyson of 1988 might show up again.

It was a silly notion, of course. Like going to the 2002 Masters and hoping that the Arnold Palmer of 1962 might come walking up to the first tee.

Tyson looked fabulous when he entered the ring. The music pulsed and everyone rose and roared and it could have been a decade ago.

A line of security guards moved to the center of the ring. The idea was to keep the two fighters off each other. Or, maybe, to keep Lewis off Tyson?

Lewis was bitten by Tyson at the press conference in January. He had plainly never forgotten.

"Biting was first blood," Lewis said. "Tonight I got second and third."

And fourth. And fifth. And sixth. And right up to 193rd, really.

That's how many punches Lewis landed. Tyson landed just 49.

After the first round — the only round won by Tyson — it was hardly even competitive.

Lewis kept Tyson away with his jab. He rocked him with uppercuts. He opened a cut over Tyson's right eye in the third, opened a cut over his left eye in the fifth, and generally made him look small and helpless.

In the eighth, Lewis finished him. Knocked him into a crouch with a right-left-right combination, then down for good with a right to the jaw.

"I caught him good," Lewis said. "He took it like a man."

Well, yeah. And maybe that's a start for Tyson the person.

But for Tyson the fighter, it sounded a lot like a finish.

ON TOP OF THE WORLD – OH, BABY, WHAT A DAY FOR MICHEEL
AUGUST 18, 2003

After the triumph, after the tap in, Shaun Micheel ran to his wife Stephanie, hugged her, then leaned down and kissed her belly.

They are expecting their first child, a son, on Nov. 28.

The stories they'll be able to tell that kid!

About the day Daddy won his first PGA tournament.

About how it happened to be his first major, too.

About how he clinched it with one of the greatest shots anyone can recall.

It was a 7-iron to the 18th green. It flew, bounced three times, and stopped 2 inches from the pin.

When Shaun saw it, he pumped his fist in the air.

When Stephanie saw it, she started to cry.

"It was the perfect ending," she said.

No, the kiss was the perfect ending.

Because, oh, baby, what a day it was.

Micheel won the 85th PGA Championship Sunday on the same Oak Hill course where another Christian Brothers High graduate, Cary Middlecoff, won his second U.S. Open 47 years before.

Micheel did it with a gutty, wrenching performance — he shot 70 to finish 4-under for the week — that left him both thrilled and dazed.

"I really can't believe that this happened to me," he said. "It's kind of scary, really.

"Even up till maybe a month or two ago, I was trying to keep my card. To have my name on that trophy ... "

All the newspaper stories today will talk about Micheel's historic shot on 18. And it was a stunning shot.

Bob Tway has nothing on Micheel. Neither do Gene Sarazan or Tom Watson or any of the other architects of famous shots past.

But when Stephanie and Shaun saw this particular shot, they weren't just thinking about how close it was to the hole. They were thinking about how far they'd come.

From a subdivision in Memphis. From Colonial Country Club. His family lived on the 4th green, hers lived on the 16th.

"I think I first met him in my driveway, playing basketball," she said. "He was 12 and I was 10."

He went to Mt. Pisgah; she went to St. Benedict.

He switched to Christian Brothers; she switched to Germantown.

He played basketball and golf; she played soccer and cheered.

Then, after college, they got married, and lived happily ever after.

Except, well, two days after the wedding he had to go to a tournament in Hong Kong.

"Some people come out of college and go on the tour and have it easy," Stephanie said. "It wasn't like that for us."

They struggled. They kept at it. She kicked him in the rear when he was down.

The rap against Micheel has always been that he didn't quite know how to handle pressure, or weekends, or crowds.

He only made four cuts his first year on Tour.

Last year, he went into the final round of the B.C. Open with a three-stroke lead and shot a 74.

So Sunday, as Micheel and co-leader Chad Campbell walked to the first tee, Stephanie was cheerily open about her mood.

"I feel sick to my stomach," she said. "I hope I'm more nervous than he is."

Maybe, maybe not.

One of the charming things about Micheel is that he's not afraid to admit to human frailty. He doesn't put up a false front.

"It was a pretty difficult morning, actually," he said. "I had some oatmeal for breakfast and it got about three bites taken out of it."

Thus fueled, Micheel went out and played exactly well enough to win. He birdied No. 1.

"Great start!" said Stephanie.

He bogeyed No. 2.

"That's OK," said Stephanie.

Did we mention she walked the entire 72 holes?

After 22 years of waiting for this moment, why let a little thing like pregnancy keep her away?

And Shaun rewarded her — and everyone — with a demonstration of clutch golf.

No, he wasn't perfect. But every time Micheel needed a big shot, he pulled one out of his bag.

He set the tone with that birdie on No. 1. He hit a ridiculous driver to the green on No. 14. After Campbell sank a wildly breaking putt to cut Micheel's lead to one stroke on No. 15, Micheel responded with a birdie on the next hole.

But the one everyone will remember is No. 18, and Stephanie has a small story here.

You know that tale about Micheel pulling two elderly drivers to safety in 1993 after their car ran into a creek? Stephanie and Shaun laugh about how, this week, it's taken on a life of its own.

"Now it's a raging river, a torrent," she said, laughing. "It's because he's never won, people have nothing else to write about him."

But the thing is, the story is true. And it's typical Shaun.

"He did it without thinking," Stephanie said. "His instincts are so good."

Sunday, Shaun didn't waste time fretting about his 7-iron on 18. He led Campbell by one thin stroke, but didn't let his thoughts get in the way.

He asked his caddie the distance. He had 161 yards to the front of the green.

"I was just concerned with hitting the ball solid," he said. "I certainly had a direction that I wanted the ball to go and where I wanted to end up, but it was not next to the hole, I can assure you of that."

It rolled next to the hole. Micheel literally ran up to the green.

The rest was all merriment and glory. A 2-inch birdie putt. A hug. A kiss.

"Your name is on that trophy forever," said CBS announcer Bill Macatee, handing him the silver cup.

The new champion grinned.

"I just hope they spell it right."

MANNING RETURNED FOR A YEAR LIKE THIS
NOVEMBER 22, 2003

The ball is on the 50,
the down is third-and-10.
He runs it down the sideline,
yes, Archie takes it in.
He plays for the Ole Miss Rebels,
Archie Manning is his name.
The best dad-burn quarterback,
who ever played the game.
The ball is snapped to Archie,
the down it is the last,
he throws it to the end zone,
another touchdown pass.
He puts points on that scoreboard,
for that big Rebel crew.
That's All-American Archie.
You know, Archie Who.

Langston Rogers, the long-time impresario of information at Ole Miss, apologizes if the punctuation isn't quite right. He didn't have the lyrics written down. He listened to an old tape, scribbling down the words, backing up the tape enough times until he got them all.

"That's it," he said. "'The Ballad of Archie Who.'"

Which is another reason Eli Manning could have run screaming from Ole Miss.

Forget the hate mail the Mannings received when brother Peyton picked Tennessee.

Forget that Ole Miss hadn't won anything in years.

They wrote ballads to his father.

Ballads! And everyone knew the words!

"I remember at the Sugar Bowl," said Randy Reed, who played with Archie at Ole Miss. "We walked onto the field — it was at old Tulane Stadium — two or three hours before the game. And in one end zone, there was a lady with a record player playing that song."

Small wonder Peyton went somewhere else. Any sane person would.

Small wonder Archie had butterflies — and not the good kind — when Eli told him he was going to play football in Oxford.

"The day he committed, I had all these calls, everybody saying I must be the happiest guy in the world," Archie said. "And I had to act like I was.

"But I had big worries. Big worries. Not so much of him, but of the expectations. He was a little skinny 17-year-old going up there into that."

It was too big. It was too much. It was ballads, by dang, and who could bear up under that?

Eli could.

Eli has.

That's All-American Eli.

You know, Eli Who.

• • •

Do you have your tickets yet?

They're still available, you know. On eBay. Where you can buy two seats on the Ole Miss 45-yard line for a mere $1,600.

Plus, you get an Ole Miss cap. Or a mouse pad. Or a keychain, or a pen, or a sticker, or a stadium cup or — this is the best one — a personalized white envelope.

The knickknacks are designed to circumvent Mississippi scalping laws. They're not charging extra for a ticket to the biggest game in the state of Mississippi in three decades, see, they're charging extra for the snappy pencil.

And it may be worth it. To see an Ole Miss team at this place again. To see an Ole Miss team play LSU for the chance to go to the SEC Championship in Atlanta.

And to witness the stunning ending to a family saga so steeped in tradition, glory, sadness, redemption and triumph that it could only be set in the South.

"It's surreal," Rogers said. "You couldn't have scripted it."

Archie? Your thoughts?

"Olivia and I would rather focus on the team," he said.

Yeah, yeah, yeah.

"But who would have thought it?" he conceded at last.

Nobody of sound mind, that's for certain.

Which is why the elder Manning really did have a queasy feeling about Eli going to Ole Miss, despite the family's profound love for the school.

Everyone knew Archie's story or, at the very least, could hum a few bars.

He came to Ole Miss from Drew, Miss., all red hair, talent and charm.

His sophomore year, he went home to find his father had committed suicide.

He married Olivia, the homecoming queen. He got fan mail from Richard Nixon. His appeared on the cover of *Sports Illustrated* under the following headline: "Archie Manning, Idol of Ole Miss."

But he was more than an idol. He was a folk hero, a rallying point, a salve. Not long before, Ole Miss had been known as the place that tried to keep out James Meredith. Sixteen thousand troops were sent to keep the peace.

That's how the nation perceived Ole Miss or, anyway, how Ole Miss folks thought they were perceived.

Until Archie.

Freckled, swashbuckling Archie.

How bad could a place be that produced a wonder like that?

"I don't think I could describe how big he was," Reed said. "I'm not sure I would have wanted to follow him."

So Peyton wisely went to Tennessee, where he had a splendid career under David Cutcliffe, the quarterback coach.

Eli knew he didn't want to follow Peyton to Knoxville. He told Cutcliffe, right up front.

But when Cutcliffe got the Ole Miss job, he figured he'd try again.

"It was the first phone call I made," Cutcliffe said. "I said, 'All bets are off now.'"

Said Eli: "I couldn't say no to him twice."

The next four years — Eli redshirted his first year — were dazzling, impressive and, truth is, disappointing too.

It sounds ridiculous. Eli threw for five touchdowns in his first start. He set records every other day. Season tickets jumped from roughly 32,000 the year before his arrival to 42,000 before this year.

But Ole Miss didn't win. Enough, anyway.

There was grumbling from Ole Miss fans that Cutcliffe had "wasted" the Manning years.

When Eli pondered whether to turn pro after last season, both his father and brother figured he'd go.

Not that Eli told them or anything.

At one point, Archie — who had invested serious time collecting information on the topic — asked Eli if he had any questions.

Eli shrugged.

"No," he said.

And then he decided to return. For every good reason you care to list.

He wanted to go out with the other fifth-year seniors.

He wanted to stick with his coaches.

He wanted to play better, to learn.

Besides — you ready for this one? — college was fun.

"If I didn't play a down of football Ole Miss is where I'd have wanted to be," Eli said. "I wasn't ready to give that up yet."

That's why Eli didn't regret his decision after the early losses to Memphis and Texas Tech. He didn't come back for the glory. He came back for the trip.

And the trip has gotten better, and better, and look where it's headed now.

To Vaught-Hemingway Stadium for a chance to win the SEC West in his last home game.

Go figure that.

Eli will walk through the Grove to the stadium for the final time. He will be joined on the field for senior day festivities by his mom and dad.

(Ever see 62,000 cameras popping pictures all at once?)

"It's going to be something," Reed said, "And I think we have a real chance."

Which is true. Ole Miss has a real chance. The Rebels haven't won six straight SEC games by dumb luck.

But at some level the outcome doesn't matter as much as the mere fact of this game.

That's the gift, the promise of Eli fulfilled.

The feeling Ole Miss fans have this morning. The giddy anticipation. The pride.

As for what will happen, we've drawn up a little ditty about that. With apologies to the original — hit it, boys:

The ball is on the 50,
the down is third-and-10.
Some 30 years have slipped away,
we don't know how or when.
A Manning still under center,
what other could it be?
The best dad-burn quarterbacks,
Ole Miss will ever see.
The ball is snapped to Eli,
the down it is the last,
he throws it to the end zone
and what shall come to pass?

A glorious win? Atlanta bound?
Or a loss to LSU?
Either way, they're father-son,
Two legends, cast in blue.

OLE MISS MISSES ITS PERFECT ENDING
NOVEMBER 23, 2003

T*he ball is on the 32,*
The down is fourth-and-10.
With Eli under center,
to save the day again.
He sizes up the defense,
barks out hut, hut, hut,
he steps back in the pocket,
then falls down on his ...

Hey! What kind of no-good, purple-wearing, vowel-flaunting LSU fan came up with this ridiculous ending?

He falls?

Eli Manning falls?

In his last home game, with a trip to the SEC Championship on the line, trailing by just a field goal, down to his last play, Manning has an offensive lineman step on his foot?

And that's how Ole Miss loses to LSU?

With Manning on his keister?

Nuh-uh.

Don't believe it.

Might as well say that Jonathan Nichols, Mr. Automatic, missed two field goals. One of them a chip shot.

What?

That happened too?

"We had chances," said Manning. "That's the way football goes."

Or geaux, as the case may be.

LSU ruined what may have been the best party this town has ever seen by beating Ole Miss Saturday, 17-14.

A record 62,552 fans showed up. The Grove spilled over with revelers.

Bill Brown, from Olive Branch, brought a yellowed newspaper along with him. It was from 1968. The headline read: "Super Manning Lifts Rebels Over LSU."

"You can use the headline tomorrow if you want," Brown said. "Just photocopy it."

Yeah, well. Maybe next generation.

Manning wasn't super. Although, he said this so often and openly after the game that it feels like piling on to repeat it.

Manning completed just 16-of-36 passes for 200 yards. He threw one pick and one touchdown.

"I wish I could answer why," he said. "That's the thing that's bothering me."

Even then, the defense played well enough to give Ole Miss a chance to win the thing. Which is when two things happened that, well, just don't happen.

Nichols missed a kick.

Understand, the guy never misses. He had attempted 24 field goals this year. He had made 23 of them. The one he missed was from 52 yards.

This time, he missed two. Including one from 36 yards in the waning minutes.

"Everything was perfect," Nichols said. "The snap, the hold, everything but the kick."

But Ole Miss got the ball back. One more chance for Manning! Which is when the other thing that never happens happened.

It was fourth-and-10. Ball on the Ole Miss 32.

"We had a good play called," Manning said. "They were blitzing, and we had made an adjustment to cover it. I was going to get it to Chris Collins on the dig route."

He might have, too. We'll never know. Ole Miss guard Doug Buckles stepped on Manning's left foot and toppled him.

This had not happened all year. It happened just once last year.

"If it had been my right foot, I could have regained my balance," Manning said. "But my left foot ..."

Manning plainly struggled with the loss. At one point, talking about his last walk through the Grove, he misted up, then caught himself.

"I wanted to play the best game of my life," he said. "Everyone was trying their best. I was trying my best."

Which is the bittersweet part of this, isn't it? Of course he was trying his best. Of course Nichols was trying his best. They were trying just as hard as they were when they took this town on a six-game magic-carpet ride.

This time, it didn't work out. If it were easy, Ole Miss wouldn't have taken three decades to get back to this point.

But they did get back to this point. Remember that, too. They created a day that will be remembered forever.

Barry Wicktom is one of the thousands of Ole Miss fans who crowded into the Grove before the game. At one point, he found himself sitting on a picnic table, overcome by pure, dopey gratitude.

He looked toward the Heavens. He said a small prayer of thanks.

"It doesn't get any better than this," he told himself.

Well, maybe a little.

VII

FAVORITES

OLYMPICS "MIRACLE" HAS WHOLE NEW SPIN

Cammi Granato looked out over the ice, watched the flags waving and the sticks soaring and the whole star-spangled celebration, and she realized she had seen this scene once before.

She had seen the gloves and sticks flying in the air. She had seen the hockey player draped in the enormous American flag. She had seen the growing pile of players, joining in one big victory flop at the end of the ice.

But in 1980, when Granato and the rest of America first witnessed that scene, it was a pile of American men celebrating a gold medal. Now, 18 years later, it was a pile of American women.

Granato thought about this as she skated toward her teammates. She thought about the words that defined that moment, too.

"Now I believe in miracles," she thought.

Then she dived on the top of the pile.

• • •

Did you see that incredible game? Did you see the American women win the first women's hockey gold medal? And did you think about Lake Placid, too?

Karyn Bye did. She plays for the American team. Growing up in Wisconsin, she would play floor hockey in her basement. She would always pretend she was Bill Baker, one of the American men who won the gold medal in 1980.

"Bill Baker is at the point," she would say. "Bill Baker gets the puck. Bill Baker shoots. Bill Baker scores!"

It was silly, she knew. A girl named Bill. A girl named Bill playing hockey in the basement.

"It was unrealistic to think I'd ever play in the Olympics," she said. "They didn't let girls play."

And that's the first miracle, really. That this team ever existed in the first place.

250 | AFTER THE JUMP

"Everyone on this team is an incredible story," said Ben Smith, the coach. "It's an entire team of pioneers."

Granato is a forward. When she was 15, a boy asked her on a date over a faceoff. She swiped the puck and skated away.

Bye is a forward, too. She had always played on boys' teams growing up. The coaches would list her "K.L. Bye" in the program so the opposition wouldn't know the difference.

And on and on it went. They all were different, they all were the same. Girls who had started skating when they were small, who didn't realize they weren't supposed to tag along with their brothers to the rink.

"When we came together, it was like, 'I know you,'" said Bye. "'I did that, too.'"

They traveled together all year long, playing all comers, trying to drum up interest in women's hockey.

Evidently, they won some fans along the way. Just before the gold-medal game, Bye received an urgent telegram from the United States.

"Good luck," the telegram read. "I'll be watching."

It was signed by a Dr. Bill Baker.

• • •

The Olympic hockey stadium was packed. Every big sports columnist was there. The guy from Chicago. The guy from New York. The guy from Los Angeles. Dave Barry was there, too.

And why not? It was for the gold medal. Canada and the United States had played 14 times before, each team winning seven. If you needed a subplot, there was the controversy that had sprung up during their last game, when Canadian forward Danielle Goyette went after American forward Sandra Whyte. Canada's coach, Shannon Miller, said Whyte had made a nasty crack about Goyette's father, who died of Alzheimer's disease two weeks ago.

Somehow, the game lived up to every expectation. It was taut, thrilling, spellbinding. The American team was held together by goalie Sarah

Tueting, a classical cellist from Dartmouth. Tueting was this year's Jim Craig, although she might not understand the reference.

A year or so ago, when Tueting showed up for practice, Smith asked her to work with a special goalie coach for a day.

"He was working with her," Smith said. "After a while, she was muttering under her breath to the guy, 'Who the (bleep) are you?'

"When she went home, she called her father and told him that some guy had coached her that day, Ed Craig or Jack Craig or something. He said, 'Jim Craig, the goalie who won the 1980 gold medal at Lake Placid?' She said, 'Ooops.'"

So Tueting might not have a great sense of history. But she made up for it with a spectacular sense of timing. In the most important women's hockey game ever, she was nearly perfect, not allowing a goal until late in the third.

In the meantime, Whyte was exacting her revenge. Whyte has insisted all along that she didn't say anything about Goyette's father. She says Miller, the Canadian coach, simply made it up.

"It was upsetting," said Whyte. "It's too bad a coach would use a player's grief as a motivational tool."

Shannon may have motivated Whyte, instead. In the U.S. team's media guide, Whyte describes her hockey fantasy as follows: "Gold medal game of the 1998 Olympics, USA crushes Canada, 5-0, and of course No. 9 scores two goals and adds a few assists."

Well, this was close. Whyte assisted on two goals as the U.S. team built a 2-0 lead. After Canada scored to draw within one, Whyte skimmed the puck into the empty net with eight seconds left to clinch the win and the medal.

"I put my hands up," Whyte said. "I was waiting for my teammates to come and get me."

And so they did. They spilled over the boards, they went and got her, they fell into that happy pile.

• • •

A last word here about the Canadians: Wow.

As much as Americans might savor this win, hockey means more in Canada. Maybe that's why the entire Canadian men's team showed up for the game. Wayne Gretzky was there. Eric Lindros was there. By contrast, a few members of the American men's team straggled in toward the end.

The medal ceremony was heartbreaking. It went on forever. The Americans were thrilled to get their gold medals. The Finnish players were thrilled to get their bronze medals. And there were the Canadians, bowing their heads to accept their silver medals, like so many glittering millstones around their necks.

But then it was time for the teams to shake hands. And the very first Canadian player in line was Goyette, who scored the only Canadian goal, who will now take her medal home to grieve for her father.

"They won," she said, simply. "I wanted to congratulate them."

Miller was even more gracious. Unlike Smith, the American coach, Miller has worked with the women's game forever. Leave it to her to put the whole thing in perspective.

"There's a feeling of emptiness," she said. "But interestingly enough, when they showed Cammi Granato's face on the big screen and showed an Olympic gold medal going around her neck, my feelings changed. I had an incredible feeling of joy going through my body. Because an Olympic gold medal was being hung around the neck of a female hockey player."

• • •

And now they go home.

That's it for the women hockey players. They have no place to go, no place to play. Unlike their male counterparts, they won't go back to high-paying professional jobs. They'll go back to mothers and fathers and boyfriends and careers.

Maybe that helps explain why they were so popular here, and why they became so popular at home, too. They are a perfect successor to that 1980 team. Jim Craig sent a telegram to the women after the game, congratulating them. Can you imagine Craig sending a telegram to the pros?

"Women's hockey has grown up in the dark," said A. J. Mleczko, a forward. "I hope we shined a light on it while we were here. Now we all have to go back to our lives."

Whyte is going to try to find a job. Her three roommates from Harvard are already doctors and lawyers. She feels like she's a bit behind.

Lisa Brown-Miller is going home to her husband. She got married two years ago but left for training camp in Lake Placid one day later. She thinks it might be time for a honeymoon.

Tueting, the goalie, is going back to Dartmouth. There's a cello there that has her name on it. She already has decided that she won't play hockey in college, that she'll concentrate on her classical music instead. As of March 30, she'll be sitting in class, learning organic chemistry. She has no plans to play hockey again.

"I know it might sound sad," she says, "but it's really not. I have this."

Tueting takes the gold medal in her hand, holds it up to the light.

"Isn't this a great way for it to end?"

HE'LL BE MISSED HERE, TOO
JUNE 21, 2000

Usually, at this point in the week, Vicki Hopkins would go out shopping for her golf guests.

They came every year at this time, just to be in Memphis for the FedEx St. Jude Classic. They always stayed in Mark and Vicki Hopkins's spare bedroom.

So Vicki would go out and buy raspberries because, oh, how her guests liked raspberries.

And she'd buy some cabbage to cook on the grill because that had become something of a golf-week tradition.

And sometimes, she'd even get a new ironing-board cover because, with all the ironing that went on during the week, you never knew when the old one would wear out.

This year, though, Hopkins isn't going shopping. She's skipping on the raspberries, the cabbage, the ironing-board cover.

See, the Hopkins annual guests weren't your usual golf fans. They were Payne and Tracey Stewart.

Maybe you've read enough words about Payne Stewart. Maybe you figure that last week's achingly beautiful 21-tee salute into the Pacific was the right time and place to end a season of mourning.

But here's the thing about Stewart people seem to forget, sometimes. As much as he's missed at the big, splashy tournaments like the Open, he's missed maybe even more at the smaller ones.

It's just the kind of guy he was, pink knickers, but blue collar. It didn't matter what other players came to a tournament. Didn't matter if Tiger Woods took a pass or Greg Norman stayed home. You could look at the pairings sheet, see when Stewart was teeing off, and say, hey, let's go walk a few holes with the guy in the funny pants.

"He loved Memphis," said Vicki Hopkins, from her home in Cordova. "We talked about it all the time. He was in awe of the way Memphians were drawn to him."

Stewart came to Memphis 14 times between 1982 and 1999. Every time, he stayed with the Hopkinses.

They knew each other from Springfield, Mo., which all three called home. And if they weren't fast friends then, that changed soon enough.

"He called and asked if we'd have a room for he and Tracey," Vicki said. "We just hit it off."

Stewart called Mark "Hop." He called Vicki "Miss Vicki." When the foursome wasn't talking about golf or kids, they were playing spades or laughing.

There was the time Mark caddied for Stewart in the pro-am and Stewart missed a key putt.

"If I could only get a good caddie," Stewart muttered.

"If I could only get a pro that can play golf," responded Hopkins.

Or there was the time Stewart ducked into the porta-john in the middle of a round. Lingered so long people began to wonder. Finally, he emerged with a big wave for Vicki.

"Hey, Vicki," he hollered. "Must have been the pasta you cooked me."

Crude? Yeah, maybe. Or at the very least, irreverent. But that was life with Stewart. Funny, open, spontaneous.

The foursome vacationed together in Anguilla one year. They were together for last year's Ryder Cup triumph. When Stewart came to Memphis a few years ago, they all went down to the FedEx facility and flew a simulator.

"He loved life, he loved his family," Vicki said. "One time, he asked me, seriously, what I'd say about him if someone asked. I said, 'You have to be the most devoted father I've ever known.'

"He told me, 'That would be OK, Vic.'"

And then came last year, the best and worst year the Hopkinses can remember. Stewart came to the FedEx St. Jude but missed the cut. He planned to stay the weekend anyway, until Tracey prevailed on him to leave early for Pinehurst.

"She said he should start preparing for the Open," Vicki said. "He agreed to stay Friday night, then fly out Saturday morning."

A week later, Stewart won the thing, of course. Sank a 15-foot putt to clinch the title. Back at their house in Cordova, you might have heard Mark and Vicki screaming.

"I waited and waited to call him, because I knew he'd be tied up," Vicki said. "I finally called him on his cell phone at 9 p.m. The first thing he said was, 'Now we know why I missed the cut in Memphis.'"

The rest of the story, you know. The rest is so heartbreaking that Vicki still can't listen to music on the radio, for fear she'll hear a song that starts her crying.

Not long after the Open, Stewart caught a chartered flight from Florida to Dallas. Something went desperately wrong. A simple business trip became an eerie tragedy, a silent, aerial funeral procession.

For the Hopkinses, it was excruciating. They watched it on television like everyone else. Thought about calling Stewart's cell phone number, but decided to leave that to Tracey.

"It was a nightmare," Mark said. "At first, we didn't know if it was Payne. And then we didn't know if he was up there with the children."

These days, Mark and Vicki can at least talk about the day, even as they still struggle to make sense of it. They were supposed to fly to Pebble Beach to watch Stewart defend his title. Instead, they watched a ceremony on television.

"It's hard to have closure when it's out there all the time," Mark said. "We half expect him to call and tell us when he'll be getting here."

Sometimes, when things get especially melancholy, Vicki thinks back to last year, to as sweet and humble a Payne Stewart story as you'll come across.

It was early one morning, before the tournament. Stewart's door was half-open. Vicki could tell he was reading a book of spiritual verses.

Ten years earlier, Stewart wouldn't have come near such a book. Even now, he was a little abashed about it, for fear people might realize there was a good guy under those knickers.

"Is it good?" asked Vicki, nodding at the book.

Stewart looked up and grinned.

"Yeah, it is," he said. "But you don't need to go around telling everybody."

GREEN JACKETS AND MA'AM
APRIL 9, 2003

Perhaps you haven't been following the Masters saga as closely as some. Perhaps you're not entirely clear where Martha Burk, Hootie Johnson, Jesse Jackson, Tiger Woods and a splinter group of the KKK stand on the topic of admitting a woman member to Augusta National.

Well, this is your lucky day. We have tried to summarize the issues in a way that is easy to digest and reflects the maturity and decorum of the participants.

Lucky for us, we are big fans of Dr. Seuss.

Hootie:

I do not like that Martha, she
is one who really bothers me.

I do not like her on a tee,

I do not like her close to me.

I do not like her, can't you see?

I do not like her — Love, Hootie.

Martha:

But don't you want a golfing gal?

A putting, driving distaff pal?

You've got a Warren, Bill and Al,

Don't you want to add a Sal?

Hootie:

No! I want no golfing Sal!

Unless she comes with husband, Hal!

Martha:

Then you and yours will rue the day,

you sent me and the girls away.

We'll raise a fuss and have our say,

we'll make those in green jackets pay!

Hootie:

Go ahead! Just try! You'll see!

You silly girls can't bully me!

We'll put the Masters on TV,

and just for kicks, we'll make it free!

Martha:

Then we'll hold a rally, too,

to shame the piggish likes of you.

We'll carry signs, the whole day through.

Great golf for all! Both Bob and Sue!

Jesse:

Hey! Over here! Guys, look at me!

It's Jesse! Want some company?

Can I play, too? Can I make three?

If TV's there, that's where I'll be!

KKK:

And how about us, we'll lend our might,

'cause we think Hootie boy is right!
We'll fight all day, we'll fight all night!
To keep girls out — and golf balls white!

Hootie:

I'll not relent! I'm duty bound!
(Except on keeping champs around,
that ban was dumb, not wise or sound).
But on the girls, I'll hold my ground!

Tiger:

Hey guys, about your little spat,
I really won't get into that.
I hit it long. I hit it phat.
Do you like my Nike hat?

Hootie:

So join us here in spring '03
with Tiger, Martha and Jesse
It ain't the same, but thanks to me
it's guaranteed to be girl-free!

ONE YEAR LATER, TRAGEDY IN TRIATHLON INSPIRES
MAY 23, 2004

From *the journal of Eric Singer, 5/18/03: You called from your cell phone around 10:30 to excitedly tell me that the race was delayed because of weather and cars were parked in the race course. You didn't know when it would get going. You were speaking loud and fast and I could tell that you were excited. I said that I was sure you'd do well and that I loved you. We told you to call us from the finish line.*

The last time anyone saw the real Donna Singer, she was honking her bicycle horn. The horn was shaped like a little pig. She reached down, honked it a couple times and smiled.

Of course she did. Donna Singer smiled her way through life. She painted her toenails in a rainbow of colors, led the cheeriest exercise class in suburban Chicago, and celebrated Passover with the help of a giant rubber locust.

So when Singer saw Donna Carter and her family standing along Pleasant Ridge Road in Millington, she wasn't just going to pedal on past. It's not like she was going to catch the main pack of racers anyway.

She honked her little piggy horn. She smiled.

"She was looking back, just smiling at us and she fell," Carter said. "It was very sudden. We ran to her. She was unconscious and bleeding, badly, from her nose."

"It still blows me away. She was wearing a helmet, doing everything right. It's a sad, sad story. She was just being friendly."

From the journal of Eric Singer, 5/18/03: Noon. Almost at the exit at Lorenzo Road, speeding so that we wouldn't be late (to a birthday party). My cell phone rang. It was Sgt. Peterson from the Sheriff's office. I first thought that I had been spotted speeding by some air patrol, but I didn't make the connection. "Are y'all in Memphis?" No, we're in Chicago. "Do you know Donna Singer?" Yes. "Is she in Memphis?" The accented syllables were so exaggerated that I had a hard time understanding. There had been an accident and they were taking you by helicopter to the hospital. You fell off your bike. You were being taken to the "Mayuhd." At least that's what it sounded like.

In Millington this morning, 1,600 athletes will compete in the 22nd Memphis in May Triathlon.

In suburban Chicago, a 39-year-old father of two will wake up and drive a few miles to an assisted-living facility to visit his 39-year-old wife.

He will brush her teeth. He will sit her up in her chair. He will listen hard to the sounds she makes, straining to find words and hope.

"Occasionally, I get glimpses that maybe she's back there," Eric Singer says. "Right now, I think she's gone. Whether she'll be back or not, even the doctors can't tell me."

This is not an easy story of triumph. This is not a story of a woman falling and getting back up.

That's what you're supposed to do, right? That's what we tell our kids. Fall down. Get up. Off you go, then.

But what if someone can't get up? What to tell our kids about that?

What to tell them about a fall that steals a life, that devastates a family, that leaves a father to raise two children alone?

"What do I make of it?" Singer says. "It's amazing what you can do when you have no other choice."

One moment, Singer was driving his kids to a birthday party. The next moment, he was frantically booking a flight to Memphis, calling directory assistance and finding no listing for any "Mayuhd."

Ahhh, he finally discovered. Not the Mayuhd, the Med.

Donna was unconscious, in critical condition and bleeding in the brain.

From the journal of Eric Singer, 5/18/03: I am on the phone with the Med asking them to put a phone to your ear so that I can tell you I love you before surgery. You need a craniotomy to relieve pressure, bleeding and swelling on your brain. They want my verbal consent to surgery. They tell me that you can't talk and are not conscious. I don't care. Get the phone to your ear. But you won't be able to hear because the respirator will be loud. Do it anyway!

They met when they were 17, working together in a movie theater. He was an usher. She sold popcorn.

"I was a '70s-looking guy with hair parted in the middle," Eric says. "Even then, she was thin, mature and beautiful."

They made each other laugh. For the life of him, he can't recall what they did on their first date.

"The funny thing is that she would remember it precisely," Eric says. "She'd remember where we went and what we were wearing."

He became a lawyer, trained at the University of Chicago, a guy who would routinely work 80-hour weeks.

She drove carpool, taught fitness classes — spinning, anyone? — and had a license plate that read "DFWDMS."

"It stood for 'Don't Fool With Donna Marie Singer,'" Eric says. "Only the 'F' didn't really stand for fool."

That was Donna. Full speed ahead. She helped everyone, too. Dived right in.

How did she start doing triathlons?

A boy in her son's class had leukemia. An organization called Team in Training raised money for the Leukemia & Lymphoma Society.

Hello, triathlons.

Hello, Memphis.

"The kids wonder about that sometimes," Eric says. "Why would she go? And why would something bad happen to someone doing something good?"

By the time Donna was out of surgery, Eric had arrived in Memphis. They would not leave the city for five weeks. Eric would not leave the hospital for days.

"I had never been to Memphis and I didn't know anything about Memphis," he says. "I was in a fog.

"At some point, I went for a walk. Until then, it hadn't even clicked that it was on the Mississippi River."

From the journal of Eric Singer, 5/18/03: Rabbi Dan Rabishaw came to see me. Turns out that he is one of four rabbis at one of the oldest and largest Reform congregations in the country. Here in Memphis. Incredible. I didn't even know there were Jews in the South.

Kate Baser had a plan: She would go to services at Temple Israel, find the family of the woman injured in the triathlon, and invite them for a meal.

Baser had been taught all her life to do mitzvahs — acts of grace — and this seemed the right time for one.

"I had heard he was going to be at services," Baser says. "It turns out, he was right behind me."

Singer was sitting with his sister and father.

"Have you eaten dinner?" Baser asked. "Have you even slept?"

Eric's beleaguered look was answer enough.

"We live literally a quarter mile from the temple," Baser said. "Come and eat, just eat and go. You don't even have to talk to us."

In this way, a friendship was born. Baser spent the next five weeks trying to make the Singers feel at home. She had the family over for Memorial Day. She brought Corky's to the Med.

"It makes you feel good to do something for someone and expect nothing in return," she says. "And, in return, we now have the love of a family we never would have had."

Eric has a list of people he calls his "Memphis heroes." It's too long to print.

There are doctors and nurses, rabbis and runners.

"We were greeted and adopted in a way I can't imagine happening in any other city in the world," Eric says.

But Memphis is still the place where Donna fell. It represents kindness, generosity and mind-numbing grief.

"I have always said that if Donna gets better, I want to bring her back to meet the people who helped her get through it," Eric says. "If she doesn't, I think it would be too hard."

From the journal of Eric Singer, 9/23/03: Over the last 12 weeks, I have learned a great deal about traumatic brain injury, neurosurgery, coma and recovery. As I fumbled through the fog of emotion and medical explanation, I learned that all of these topics share one element in common — time. ... Unlike the TV depictions of coma recovery, Donna will not just "wake up."

Eric ends every day by writing in his journal. He began it his second day in Memphis. He wanted to tell Donna all the things she missed and realized he'd never be able to keep track.

The journal is written to Donna. It's sweet, funny and enough to break a heart.

"After some ice cream, you started making some noise of jumbled syllables, but Sarah and I heard 'I want' among the jumbles. I have no idea what you wanted, but you were trying to tell me. Your eyes opened wide, with that wrinkled brow, turning your head sharply left and right, once right to Sarah after she called for you. You rubbed your nose and later wiped your ice cream into your mouth. You'd fade, close your eyes, and have another momentary awakening, before fading again. I can't tell if these are sleepwalking states or whether you are conscious. I suspect the former."

Eric reads his words to Donna the morning after he writes them. Because she just might hear.

"We don't know if she can see or understand what she's hearing," he says. "She responds to sounds, sometimes she smiles. But sometimes that's just her. She can be in the room, alone, smiling."

Donna started showing some improvement in October. She began moving a little, mostly her left hand, then her left arm.

The doctors say that the parts of her brain that suffered the most damage control memory and speech. Every visit, Eric starts by reminding Donna who he is, what happened, and why she's not at home.

"I tease her about that," he says. "I mean, if she can remember, she's probably annoyed as hell that I'm repeating myself every time."

Eric then chats with his wife, the same way he would if she could respond. He kisses her cheek. Teaches her to drink through a straw.

They listen to books on tape together. Or watch movies. Sometimes, they dance.

It's not a conventional dance. Donna can't move from her chair. Eric leans over, hugs her and rocks.

"When I'm putting her to bed, I think about what the two of us used to do with the kids," he says. "It's the same thing. We'd put on Billy Joel or James Taylor and literally dance them to sleep."

From the journal of Eric Singer, 12/19/03: Fund-raiser was the annual pie in the face. This time to benefit your fund. Volunteered again this year to take a pie to the face. Before I got in the hot seat, Jane told me Adam was in the hall by himself. I found him walking around, asked him what was wrong and hugged him. He cried that he missed you. We just hugged and cried there in the hall until the pain passed. I told him to come humiliate me with a pie to the face. Adam hit my head ... Saw stars for a minute. Probably getting out his anger about all of this.

Not so long ago, Eric moved a television into the living room. Even though Donna would have hated it. Because Donna would have hated it, actually.

"It would have sent her into orbit," Eric says. "I did it anyway because I want them to know it's just us now."

Adam turned 10 two days after the accident. He had another birthday last week.

Sarah has eighth-grade graduation coming up. She's 14.

"They both have feelings in common," Eric says. "They wonder why she went on the trip. Mostly, they miss her. A teenage girl needs a mom to fight with. An 11-year-old boy needs a mom to cuddle."

Adam still cuddles. He takes off his shoes and crawls into his mother's bed.

He's learning about computers at school. Sometimes, he gives her PowerPoint presentations about his day.

"He's very good at sort of ignoring the disaster," Eric says. "He talks to her about anything at all."

Eric has cut back to half time at his law firm. He survives on four hours sleep.

"He's a great Dad," says Kate Baser, the friend from Memphis. "And a great Mom."

But then there are moments, impossible moments, and you wonder how he bears it all.

A couple months ago, Eric went to Adam's parent-teacher conference. A temporary teacher who didn't know much about Adam had asked the class to write about their biggest challenge this year.

Adam's biggest challenge?

"To wake up my mom."

From the journal of Eric Singer, 1/6/04: As I walked briskly to my meeting, all along LaSalle Street were cones, signs and safety tape, saying 'Caution,' or 'Warning,' and 'Falling Ice.' Like there is anything that you can do if a brick of ice falls on you and kills you, like that poor shopper on Michigan Avenue a few years ago. Walking along, minding his own business, and BAM, he's dead. Not all that different from your accident. Signs really should say, 'Caution, Vengeful God,' or 'Warning, Life May Suck,' or 'Caution, Unfair Things Happen to People All Of The Time.' What the hell are you supposed to do to avoid it? Stay inside?

In February, Eric took the kids on a trip out of town for the first time. They went to Wisconsin, where Eric and Donna had gone on their honeymoon.

At the end of the trip, the kids asked if they could buy a vacation place.

"Maybe someday," Eric said, then caught himself.

It's the same thing Eric and Donna used to say to each other.

"Maybe someday."

Now someday is gone. It's hard not to feel bleak about that.

"I don't miss what we had," Eric says. "I miss what we should have had.

"I'm disappointed that my kids don't have their Mom to rely on. I'm disappointed that my wife and I don't have this time to watch our kids grow up."

Not long ago, Donna was included in a function that brought together infants and elderly patients, the very young and the very infirm.

Eric started thinking about babies. About how they grow and progress.

"You were left there like furniture, unobserved and unaware," Eric wrote. "Will you still be there in 20 years, with gray hair, still entirely dependent and still unaware? Will anyone there know who you used to be?

"Each month, it becomes less likely that you will ever come home. You will never recover. But the babies will become children and the children will grow, develop and mature. Their progress leaves me both happy and at the same time sad. But I don't and can't cry."

From the journal of Eric Singer, 5/17/04: It is not an anniversary to either celebrate or mourn. Just another day since the accident. The kids and I are going to escape the day and privately let it pass.

In the wake of the tragedy, Mike Palm, the coach of Team in Training, decided to retire. He said he didn't have the stomach to continue. He sold his bike.

A few months passed. He missed the sport. He bought another bike.

Today, Palm and some two dozen athletes from Chicago will compete in the Memphis in May Triathlon.

"It's not about us, it's about Donna," Palm says. "We wanted to be here for her."

The race will be formally dedicated to Donna Singer. Saturday, organizers and friends laid a wreath at the spot where she fell.

"There's still some hesitation," Palm says. "Her training partner didn't come down. She said it was just too much for her.

"But the two people she drove down with last year will be here. There will be a lot of people competing with Donna in their hearts."

Eric is grateful for the support, but he's not planning to mark the day.

Wednesday, the actual anniversary of the fall, he took Adam and Sarah to a water park.

"We talked about the year," he says. "I can't say I've made sense of it. The only way I'm able to survive is to rely on the help of a lot of people. I don't make sense of it other than to just keep going, because you don't really have a choice."

There is hard inspiration in this, in Eric's ability and resolve to find the strength.

You do what you have to do. You brush teeth, make cupcakes, love your kids enough for two.

"There have been some good things," Eric says. "The friendships. The incredible outpouring of support we've received. The fact that I'm spending more time with my children.

"There are even factions in my family — I wouldn't say they were warring, but they weren't the warmest — and they've come together over this."

Eric will write another entry in his journal tonight. He'll read it to Donna in the morning.

He'll do the same thing the next day.

And the next day.

And ...

People sometimes ask Eric if he's going to try to publish his journal as a book.

He tells them he isn't sure.

"I wanted to know what the ending is," he says. "Now I realize it's probably not going to have an end."

From the journal of Eric Singer, 1/20/04: As I was working, Adam sleep-walked out to the living room, looked right at me, looked around the room and said 'Dad, where's Mom?' I winced and walked him back to his room to dream about finding you.

A HEAVY HEART SKATES

TURIN, Italy — Kimberly Derrick's mother sat in the stands at the Olympic short track, holding a wallet.

It was like any other wallet, brown and worn.

Holly Derrick, Kimberly's mother, turned it over in her hands.

"It was his," she said.

Of course.

They had retrieved it from his pocket, after he died.

Darrell Edwards, 74, was in Turin to watch his granddaughter, Kimberly, race for the United States.

Gosh, he was proud of that girl. So proud, he said he'd like to burst.

"He told everyone on the plane over about her," Holly said. "Then he told every Italian he met on the street."

They had a long day of sightseeing Friday, then went to the Bank of America House to relax. The Bank of America House is a refuge for Olympic athletes and their families. Edwards leaned into a soft, red couch.

Minutes later, he started to convulse. Someone screamed for a doctor.

One showed up, almost instantly, but there was nothing to be done.

Edwards was gone. A heart attack. Before the ambulance carried his body away, Holly and her husband, Kenny, were given the wallet.

"It fell open, and here's the first thing we saw," Holly said.

She opened the wallet, to reveal an old picture of Kimberly, from maybe eight years before.

Kimberly was smiling like crazy in the photo.

And she was wearing red, white and blue.

• • •

At 7:50 p.m., a slight 20-year-old skated in the 1,000-meter short track race as a tribute to her grandfather. If it's not too late to submit memorable Olympic moments, how about that?

Kimberly Derrick didn't win a medal. She didn't have a chance.

"She wasn't herself out there," said Holly. "She was skating for her granddaddy."

That's what she always called him, too. Granddaddy, though he was sometimes more of a dad.

When 2-day-old Kimberly first came home from the hospital in Blytheville, Ark., she came home to Granddaddy's house.

"We lived with him for her first three years," Holly said. "He did everything for her. He walked her to sleep, he sang to her, he taught her how to ride a bike."

They had this game, the two of them. They played it all the time.

"I love you more than you love me," Kimberly would say.

"No, I love you more than you love me," Edwards would say back.

"No, I love you more than you love me," Kimberly would say again.

They could carry on like this for a good long while.

They wrote it in every birthday card. They said it instead of goodbye.

When the Derricks moved to Ohio, then Michigan, it didn't change a thing.

"Daddy loved all his grandchildren," Holly said. "But it's a little different when you've lived under the same roof."

Kimberly grew up to be an in-line skater, then switched to ice. Edwards — who didn't understand any of this stuff, at first — became her biggest fan.

When Kimberly stunned everyone and won a spot on the Winter Olympics team, Edwards asked his employers at Burns Hardware to find someone else to take his spot for a week.

He flew over Sunday, along with the rest of the family. They got lost trying to meet up with Kimberly in the athletes' village.

"Of course, nobody spoke English," Holly said. "So Daddy went up to a volunteer, and he did like this ..."

Holly moved her legs in exaggerated fashion, like a skater.

"We thought he was crazy," she said. "But the volunteer took us to the right place."

The whole trip was like that, a hoot, a celebration, an adventure in sign language.

At Wednesday's qualifying races, Edwards made friends with the Japanese fans in front of him.

"They couldn't speak English and he couldn't speak Japanese," said Patty Edwards, another of his daughters. "But they somehow figured it all out."

So then came Friday, and disaster, and the family can't help but wonder if they should have taken it easier.

But how often do you go to the Olympics? How can you take it easy then?

The plan was for Kimberly to meet up with the family at the Bank of America House. She called to update them from the train.

"I'm almost there!" she said.

Holly and Kenny, her parents, went to meet her at the train station.

"We told her, just standing there, in the street," Holly said. "It was bad."

Kimberly dissolved. And yet, she never thought about skipping the race.

Anytime someone dies, and the survivors press on with their schedules, people say the deceased would have wanted it that way.

But if there's anything that was clear in the gray blur that was Friday night, it's that this particular deceased would have wanted it that way.

"No question," said Kenny. "She had to race. She had to race for him."

How's that for added pressure? On top of everything else?

The family had to figure out how to get the body home. It turns out they don't embalm people in Italy. So they had to ship the body to an American military base. And meet with the people at the Embassy. And how can anyone prepare for a race during all that?

The United States Olympic Committee pitched in with a hotel room.

"She slept for nine solid hours," Holly said. "She was emotionally spent."

And at 7:50 in the evening, Kimberly skated onto the ice for the 1,000-meter quarterfinals. Four women would race against each other for eight laps. The first two to cross the line advanced to the semis.

"From the United States, Kimberly Derrick!" the announcer said.

Folks in Blytheville might have heard the cheers.

Kimberly looked small, even vulnerable in her sleek blue suit. She started out strong.

"Let's go Kimberly!" yelled Kenny.

By the third lap, she started to fade. She fell to second, then third, then crossed the line in fourth. She was subsequently disqualified for impeding one of the other skaters around the rink.

In the locker room afterward, Kimberly collapsed, too distraught to speak.

"She can't even talk," said Amanda Baska, one of the race officials, "she's basically falling apart."

The USOC later released a written statement.

"This was the most emotional day of my life," it said. "I'm proud to be at the Olympics and at the same time my heart hurts so much. I had to race because that's what my grandfather would want me to do. He was my biggest fan, the one who held my hand while chasing my dream."

She will chase it without him now, and that will be hard. But she will carry his memory wherever she skates. She will doubtless hear him, too.

Like after Saturday's race. Holly knew exactly what Edwards would have told Kimberly.

"He would have said that she skated awesome, and that he was proud of her ... and that he loved her more than she loved him."

THIS DALY DEAL LEAVES A SAD TASTE
MAY 25, 2006

So John Daly was at this bookstore ...

No, really! He was.

Wednesday night, on the eve of the FedEx St. Jude Classic, Daly appeared at Barnes & Noble to sign books.

That's right, to sign books. Not breasts, or behinds, but books.

Which is easier than the other things, because they're not as curved and stuff.

Also, books don't giggle when you sign them. And they can't marry you and divorce you and take what's left of your fortune after you've already lost $50-$60 million at casinos.

So book signing is the way to go! Especially when you wrote the book yourself.

My Life In & Out of the Rough is the title of Daly's book, and who ever figured the guy for an author?

"Shakespeare sucked," Daly wrote, and it's about time somebody said it. Compare these two romantic passages:

A. "For where thou art, there is the world itself, and where thou art not, desolation."

B. "All told, we did it 10 times that day."

Shakespeare wrote A, Daly wrote B.

Who does a better job of getting to the essence?

But the point is, we may be seeing a new Daly, a cultured Daly, a man of letters (the book) and music (he sings!) and theater (he stars in his own reality show) and wine (uh, you better be sitting down for this one).

Today, Daly is releasing his own line of wines.

Uh-huh, it's true. And weird. And a lot like Rush Limbaugh endorsing a pharmacy.

A John Daly wine? Doesn't the world already have Boone's Farm?

The wine must come in a box. A really big box.

Possible advertising slogan: "The one bottle to have when you're having more than one."

Fredric Koeppel, who has reviewed wines for this paper, once described a wine as "a rich, ripe, meaty and fleshy wine, gushing with black and red fruit flavors."

Daly wines are meaty and fleshy, anyway. Gushing with M&M and Diet Pepsi flavors?

But they definitely have a smoky taste. With just a hint of stripper's perfume.

You've heard how wines have tannins?

These wines have farmer tannins.

"Created to reflect the character of one of the world's most thrilling and big-hearted golfers," said the press release.

OK, so the wines are wildly erratic. But if you stick Daly's name on the bottle, maybe people will drink the stuff.

Which is the only sad part about all this. By now, there's not much point weighing in on the highs and lows of Daly's life.

He's self-destructive. He raises a lot of money for sick kids. Everyone knows the good and the bad of the man.

Endorsing wines, though? When Daly has struggled so mightily with alcohol? There's something pathetic about that, like Art Schlichter endorsing a bookie.

The same goes for the book, which outlines Daly's new strategy for dealing with alcohol and gambling.

Alcohol: He's going to drink beer instead of Jack Daniel's.

Gambling: He's going to switch to $25 slots.

"If I make a little bit, then maybe I move up to the $100 slots or the $500s," he wrote. "It's their money. Why not give it a shot and try to double it?"

So even there, he left himself a loophole, just like any good addict.

But he sure was a hit Wednesday night. Fans lined up an hour before Daly arrived. They applauded when he went to the rest room. The line wound through the Science Fiction section, through Mystery, through Biography, all the way to Bargain Books.

"Why do I like him?" said Bill Taylor, 32. "Because he doesn't put up with bullbleep."

Daly signed golf balls and T-shirts and never mind the bum back that threatens to knock him out of this week's tournament.

He started at 7 p.m. He signed some 300 books. And today, there are 18 holes and a wine launch.

"Perfect Round," is what they call the Bordeaux, and when is the last time Daly had one of those?

It's a bittersweet wine, robust but sad, warm but also insidious.

"I'd buy it," said Taylor. "I bet it's strong."

Yeah.

Grip it and sip it.

BURGERS AND FRIES? TRY PIG LUNG AND FLIES
AUGUST 15, 2008

B EIJING — After careful consideration, I ordered the sheep penis.

It was either that or the fried cicadas and I try to stay away from fried food.

"Fried cicadas, fried crickets!" called the guy behind the counter.

What? Haven't they ever heard of broiled?

I could have had the dog, I guess. You can order it by the pound.

Maybe I could have gone on to write a best-selling book about the experience: *Marley in Me.*

The finless eel sounded tasty. Except I prefer my eel with the fin.

A buddy suggested the pig lung with vegetables. I've never been big on vegetables.

So, I went for the sheep penis.

There's a sentence I never thought I'd type.

"Chinese people eat anything with legs except the table," said Justine Chiu, a native, so she should know.

It makes sense at some level. When 1.3 billion people want lunch, they can't all get the chicken fingers. Although, come to think of it, I wonder what the Chinese make of that particular phrase.

"Chicken finger? What is chicken finger?"

It's better than fried chicken stomach, that's what it is.

The Chinese eat everything. A menu over here offers fried chrysanthemum.

You know that children's book, "The Very Hungry Caterpillar?" The Chinese call it, "Very Hungry for a Caterpillar. Or Maybe a Centipede."

So of course I had to try. When in China, and all that.

I took a cab to the Donghuamen Market which, loosely translated, means "Mid-South Fair."

Just like the fair, they serve everything on a stick. Only instead of a Pronto Pup, it's an actual pup.

"Seahorse! Centipede!"

Can you imagine eating a centipede? What an impressive feet!

Now, it's possible that you, like me, wonder if this whole thing is a big, Chinese practical joke.

"Let's set up carts where we sell the most disgusting things in the whole world!" they may say.

"Like crickets."

"And silk worms."

"And we will watch the American journalists eat these things!"

"Will American journalists really eat silk worms?"

"Yes! They will eat worse!"

"What is worse than silk worms?"

"Sheep penis!"

"Ha ha ha."

After more than a week in China, this seemed like a reasonable scenario to me. The Chinese are legendary practical jokers. Ask Joey Cheek.

I consulted Chiu, the native, who was down at the Donghuamen Market.

"Do the Chinese really eat this stuff?"

"Of course," she said. "We eat everything that flies except airplanes, everything in the water except a boat."

So that was that. I had to do it. But, with so many delicious choices, what to try?

Fried fish skin or fried sheep kidney? Sea snake or starfish? Donkey or pigeon?

My friend, Dave, had a question about price.

"How much is that doggy in the window?" he said.

I went with scorpion as the appetizer. Three scorpions, impaled on a stick, then dunked in boiling oil.

Crunch.

Crunch, crunch, crunch.

They tasted like nothing, like salted peanut shells.

So then it was the sheep. What could possibly go wrong?

I ordered. I ate. I will regret it until my dying breath. However awful you might imagine the experience to be, I assure you, it was worse. There are garbage cans in Donghuamen Market. Defeated, I availed myself of one. But still, the memory was there. I knew only one thing that would rid me of it.

Back to the Media Center we flew. Back to the place that held the key.

"Can I help you?" said the woman behind the counter.

"Yes," I said. "I'd like a Big Mac."

FINDING SOME HOPE AMONG THE HOPELESS
MAY 19, 2009

It was one of those days for Peter Gathje, one of those days of utter hopelessness.

He had to wake up and plug in the coffee pots. Usually, he found joy in that.

Gathje helped found Manna House, on Jefferson, a bungalow that supplies coffee, showers and a change of clothes to the homeless. He is passionate about the place.

But on this day, he was grumpy. Just because he was grumpy.

"I was just down," he said.

The problems are so big. The solutions are so slow.

He had been plugging in coffee pots for nearly three years at this point.

"It was September 29," he said and, yes, he remembers the date.

Because on September 29, something happened to Gathje that sustains him to this day.

• • •

Where do you find hope in this city? Do you even bother to look anymore?

The bosses asked me to write one Metro column a week starting today. My first thought was, "Where to begin?"

There's a new corruption scandal every day. It seems like every issue still boils down to race. The mayor's solution was to — ready for it? — launch a possible run for Congress.

It's depressing, isn't it? It's almost impossible not to feel angry and bitter and down.

Which only compounds the problems, at some level. Because now people have lost hope.

So I begin with hope.

With one man, and one morning, and a small story even he can't quite believe.

"It was just one of those days," said Gathje, 51. "I was peeved. I didn't want to be there."

Who among us hasn't had one of those days? You may be embarking on one now.

Drivers are rude. Neighbors get robbed. The economy stinks, which is obvious to everybody but the person who reappraised your house.

Gathje turned to his prayer book and, don't worry, this is not a prescription to pray.

Manna House is not a place that forces people to have religion with their coffee. Volunteers didn't even invite the homeless to join their morning prayer — they kept them waiting outside until it was over — until they got a complaint.

"HOW ABOUT US?" someone hollered, from the streets.

After that, the volunteers invited them in.

Anyway, Gathje turned to the daily entry in his prayer book. It said something about archangels, which got Gathje thinking about angels and a passage in the Bible that goes like this: "Do not neglect to offer help to strangers for, in doing so, some have entertained angels unawares."

Hmmmm. Angels unawares.

That might work, Gathje thought. He would bolster himself with the notion that he might be serving angels unawares.

Or not.

"Honestly, I was still gloomy," he said.

And then the day began. And the guests — that's what they call them at Manna House — started to pour in. These are the people the rest of us cross the street to avoid. The homeless and the hopeless and the severely disturbed.

"It's controlled chaos," said Gathje, who was working out back when a volunteer said that a guest — we'll call him "Ron" — wanted to see him right away.

This was not good news. People tended to ask for Gathje after another volunteer had already declined a request.

"What do you want?" Gathje asked Ron, exasperated.

Ron shook his head.

"I don't want anything," he said.

Ron is mentally ill, mind you. He wanders into Manna House every few months. You would call him crazy. Gathje waited to see what this was all about.

"I have something for you," Ron said, and he pressed it into Gathje's hand.

It was a tiny purse. Like, really tiny. The sort that might have been made for a doll.

"An elf purse," Gathje thought to himself, but what he actually said was, "Well, thank you, Ron."

"No, you idiot," Ron said. "Open it."

So Gathje opened it. And he pulled out a small silver pin.

It was an angel. The pin of an angel.

Honest.

"It nearly knocked me to my knees," Gathje said. "On that day? An angel? How did he know? I started to tear up."

Now, it's possible you don't believe in angels. That's certainly OK. But do you believe in goodness? Do you believe there are moments of clarity that — even in the most hopeless of times — remind us what the enterprise is supposed to be about?

This was one of those moments for Gathje. Hearing him tell the story was one of those moments for me.

It's easy to be beaten down by the problems that face this city. That's true if you are a cop or a stay-at-home parent or a columnist.

But is it a reason to stop chipping away at the problems? To stop waking up and plugging in the coffee pots?

Speaking of which, Gathje spent last Friday morning at Manna House, spreading gravel out back.

The yard is remarkably peaceful, cool and canopied by trees. The gravel helps stave off the mud in spots. Gathje went at it with shovel and sweat and wheelbarrow.

"I'm not naïve," he said. "I expect people to act as people do. Let's be realistic. We're all broken. But when we understand we're all in this together, when we act consistent with our better natures, there is joy in that."

Gathje keeps his angel pin by his bedside, for the dark times. He thinks about how his exchange with Ron ended on that day.

"You have no idea what this means to me," Gathje said.

Ron — the crazy one — beamed back at him.

"Oh," he said, "but I do."

ZEN AND THE ART OF LIVING IN MEMPHIS
SEPTEMBER 23, 2009

He did it. Mayor Pro Tem Myron Lowery really did it. He stood there Tuesday, with the Mississippi River as backdrop, with the television cameras rolling, with the Dalai Lama waiting for his official welcome to Memphis, and he said ...

Hello, Dalai!

Yes, really.

Hello, Dalai.

Then Lowery gave the Dalai Lama a fist bump.

The Dalai Lama paused for a moment, as if pondering how to respond to this curious gesture. Then he cheerfully bumped back.

So welcome to Memphis, Dalai!

You're looking swell, Dalai!

It's so nice to see you here where you belong!

And, absolutely, Dalai, I could go on typing the lyrics to that song, but then I wouldn't get to tell you how thrilled we are to have you in town.

Do not be put off by Lowery's informality.

Do not read anything but joy into that fist bump.

Do not be surprised if a panhandler approaches you while you're walking around downtown today and asks you for some change.

You, of all people, should be able to tell him, "Change comes from within."

Ha!

Another Dalai Lama joke. I'm surprised Lowery didn't use that one, too.

But we really are glad you're here, Dalai. I think, when you look beneath some of the surface differences, you'll find that Memphis is your kind of place.

You eat meat every other day; we eat barbecue every other day.

You sit quietly and meditate four hours a day; we sit quietly and watch football for at least that long.

You come from Tibet, the land of Mt. Makalu; we come from Memphis, the land of Mt. Moriah.

Oh, and you should see the views from Mt. Moriah, Dalai. They were even more astounding before Platinum Plus was shut down.

But enough about mere physical beauty. Memphians share your sense of Zen.

On "$5 Cover," the Web TV show about Memphis music, the singer/philosopher Muck Sticky was quoted as saying: "Before enlightenment, chop wood, carry water. After enlightenment, chop wood, carry water."

Pretty deep, eh, Dalai?

Of course, Muck Sticky also said, "All you ladies out there know by now that Muck Sticky gets freaky-deaky."

Baby steps, Dalai. Baby steps.

But the point is, we get you. We might even need you right about now.

For all our strengths as a community — did I mention barbecue? — peace and harmony have been in short supply.

There's too much us against them around here, Dalai. We're split a dozen different ways.

City vs. county.

Black vs. white.

Private vs. public.

Rich vs. poor.

Republican vs. Democrat.

And that doesn't even include our impossibly wacky mayoral race.

Or religion. It doesn't include religion. We're one of the most religious cities around.

You'd think that might make us more humble, more compassionate, more understanding as a community, wouldn't you, Dalai?

Hahahaha.

It's all: My truth against your truth. My Father can take your Father. My path to Heaven is truer than yours.

Don't just take my word for it, either, Dalai. Ask Steve Montgomery, the senior pastor at Idlewild Presbyterian Church.

"Part of the problem with religion in Memphis is that it reinforces our prejudices," Montgomery said. "I would hope that having the Dalai Lama here, and listening to what he has to say, might teach us that we're all in this together."

So good luck with today's talk, Dalai. No pressure or anything.

Usually, we count on the Memphis Tiger basketball team to bring us together. But it's expected to have a down year.

Which means it's up to you. Well, you and Allen Iverson. There's another guy who's living in exile.

Help us be a more generous community. Open a heart or two. Maybe your words and your presence will remind us of our common humanity.

Or, maybe not.

It shouldn't be that hard, should it? You once put it better than Muck Sticky himself:

Be kind whenever possible.

It's always possible.

GIFT OF LIFE BONDS TWO NEAR-STRANGERS FOREVER
MAY 16, 2010

The idea arrived gently, out of nowhere. "Like a feather falling in my lap," Molly said. She was at a meeting that Saturday in early January, a 12-step recovery meeting. The moderator rang a small bell and "one of the women in the meeting happened to mention that she had seen on Facebook that Alex needed a kidney and that she really wanted to help him," Molly said.

Alex was another member of the recovery group; Molly turned this over in her head.

"I had just gone and donated blood two days before," she said. "I thought, 'I'll just call them Monday and find out what my blood type is.'"

It was O positive. It was a match. But, then, sitting in that room on that Saturday, Molly somehow already knew it would be.

"I just felt like it was something I was supposed to do," she said.

• • •

This story is about one person helping another person. Because — how did she put it? — she thought it was something she was supposed to do.

What a concept, eh? One person is supposed to help another person? For no reason other than their shared humanity?

Many of us are too distracted and self-involved to bother checking the box on our driver's license so that our organs can be used after we're dead. Molly is 100-percent, emphatically alive.

She plays guitar. She works at a local PR firm. She has a boyfriend and a whole mess of other friends.

Alex wasn't one of them.

"We'd say 'Hi' in the room," Molly said.

They were just different, more than anything else, in nearly every way.

She's 33; he's 54. She grew up in Memphis; he grew up in Mexico. She lived inside the loop; he lived on a small farm in Eads. She's single; he's married with a 12-year-old daughter. She's Jewish; he calls himself agnostic.

"I don't like people," he said. "I think they're out to get me."

So Alex was appropriately floored when Molly approached him before a meeting and told him she was thinking about giving him a kidney.

"Better watch out," he said. "I might come after you with a knife."

OK, so maybe it wasn't the best way to encourage a potential donor. But you'd have to meet Alex. He's warmer than he'd like you to think.

The man owns an alarm company. His profession involves anticipating the worst.

Also, he was dying. His kidneys were shutting down. It didn't have anything to do with past excesses. Alex had the same hereditary kidney disease that killed his father and his father's two sisters in their 30s.

So Alex was gratified when Molly approached him but he was mystified, too. He told her as much when they bumped into each other in the Methodist Hospital parking lot before their first big round of tests.

"I don't know why you're doing this," he said. "But thank you."

It became the central question, of course. Why was Molly doing this? She didn't have anything to gain by it. Alex wasn't family or anything.

"I had one friend I'm close to hang up on me," Molly said. "She said, 'Molly, we talk all the time, and you've never even mentioned this person. I'm sorry, but that's just weird.'"

The transplant team was even more skeptical. As professionals, they're paid to be.

"They interviewed me like the CIA," Molly said. "They had a social worker interview me, a chaplain interview me, two doctors interview me and they all asked similar questions. 'Are you doing this for money? Have you been forced?' One of them insinuated that I might be doing it for inappropriate reasons. I thought, 'Does she really think I'm trying to woo him by giving him my kidney?'"

Molly told all of them what she knew from that moment in January.

"I felt like I had to step up," she said. "Alex needed something, and I had it. I just kept following the little signs forward and I kept saying, 'You know what? I'm going to keep going until somebody tells me 'No.' And nobody ever told me 'No.'"

Said Alex: "I was paying them off."

They laughed at that one. They tend to laugh a lot.

"We love to make jokes about this," said Molly. "It's one of our favorite things in the world."

Maybe that's because the reality is almost too big to contemplate. How do you thank someone for saving your life? And not with a sudden burst of instinct and adrenaline, either. With a thoughtful act of self-sacrifice.

For the longest time, Molly didn't dare tell her parents. When she did, it did not go well.

"My mom was hysterical," Molly said. "They called me later and my father said, 'Here's what your mother and I think. We love that you want to do this. We want you to want to do things like this, and think about doing things like this.'"

Pause.

"We just don't want you do it."

Said Molly: "That makes me sad."

She explained that she was just following their example, that she had seen her mother drive to the West Clinic to hold the hands of those undergoing chemotherapy.

"There were months of crying and trying to talk me out of it," said Molly.

Surgery was set for Tuesday, March 30.

Alex and his wife, Kristy, drove to Methodist University Hospital that morning with their 12-year-old daughter, Abigail.

Alex felt lousy. He had been feeling lousy for months. Beyond that, he was wary.

"Until the last minute, I thought there was a good chance she was going to turn around and say, 'Listen, there's been a big mistake.'"

Alex wasn't used to this kind of generosity, among other things. He's an alarm guy, if you recall.

"There's a part of me that just isn't comfortable receiving," he said. "I've never been comfortable receiving anything from anybody. It's always, 'Let me earn it.' There was no way to earn this."

Molly was at the hospital with her parents when Alex arrived. Talk about an awkward moment.

"I had never met them," Alex said.

Er, hello. I'm Alex. You've heard of asking for your daughter's hand? I'm asking for her kidney instead.

Which is when a series of small miracles began to happen. Or, if not miracles, you pick the word.

Molly: "When Kristy and my mother met, it was like — what did you call it, Alex?"

Alex: "A Vulcan mind meld."

Molly: "They're the same person. I think Kristy, being a mother, understood in a deeper way than I could understand what my mother was going through."

Molly and Alex were readied for surgery. When Alex was wheeled away, Abigail, his daughter, started to cry.

Molly: "I learned later that my father — who, when we were children, was a harder man than he is now — went over and hugged her and said everything was going to be OK. He could not have done that before."

Back in surgery, Molly heard Alex on a gurney somewhere behind her.

"I'll arm wrestle you for the bigger kidney!" she said.

The doctors decided to take the left one, leaving Molly with the larger right one. They opened Molly, located the kidney, then opened Alex and made the transfer.

Molly's first words upon waking: "How's Alex?"

Alex's first words upon waking: "How's Molly?"

"For me, that was big," Alex said. "I may not be much, but I'm all I think about."

Meanwhile, the kidney was adjusting to its new owner just fine.

"As soon as they put it in, I peed all over them," said Alex.

"We don't know whose urine it was," Molly said.

More laughter. Always more laughter. See how this all works?

A few days later, Molly's parents drove her home.

"I get it now," said Molly's mother. "You were right."

This is not to say it was all wrapped up and easy at that point. Molly, in particular, had some hard days ahead. The recipient of an organ transfer is on the better end of the transaction. He suddenly has a functioning body. The donor has to heal from having a chunk of her sliced out.

At one point, Molly wondered aloud when she'd start to feel better.

"This is what you gave Alex," said a friend. "This was part of the gift."

It makes it even more humbling, when you think about it. Who gives a near-stranger something like that?

We're all out for ourselves. It's a dog-eat-dog world. Except, maybe, when someone decides that it doesn't have to be.

Molly heard about a need. She decided there was something she could do. At its purest, this story is less about a kidney than it is about the heart.

What if all of us listened for what we're meant to do? What if we let our feathers fall into our laps?

Molly will tell you that the day she gave Alex her kidney was the greatest day of her life. She has a deeper relationship with her mother than she's had in years. She has a friend in Alex that she'll have for life. She goes riding on his horses with Abigail. He's throwing a "kidney shower" for them on his farm in Eads.

What do you bring to a kidney shower?

"Kidney beans," she said, "anything kidney shaped."

Yes, it should be a hoot.

About the only thing that makes Molly uncomfortable now is the attention. She didn't do it for the compliments.

She did it because she thought she was supposed to, because she saw an opportunity to help.

"I just wanted to do something nice," she said. "It's not as complicated as people think."

FEDEX VP KNEW BEST WAY TO THE TOP
DECEMBER 16, 2011

Be like Burnetta.

Yes, Burnetta. Never mind Mike.

How many kids can follow Michael Jordan's path to success, anyway?

It's a ruse, a trap.

Burnetta Burns Williams is the one to emulate.

What, you've never heard of her?

That may be our problem, right there.

Williams died Tuesday morning of pancreatic cancer. She was just 57 years old. But the story of those 57 years should be celebrated in every Memphis schoolhouse, held up as an example of what one person can accomplish if they put their mind — and I really do mean mind — to the task at hand.

We all know Jordan was cut from his high school team. Better we should know that Williams started off in Cleaborn Homes.

Jordan went on to star for the Chicago Bulls. Williams went on to become corporate vice president and treasurer of FedEx Corp.

Yes, treasurer. As in, she handled the finances.

"It's a big, big job," said Alan Graf, the chief financial officer of FedEx Corp.

Williams was named one of the 100 most influential people in finance in 2008. She was recently named one of the 100 most influential African-Americans in corporate America.

When she died, I got an e-mail about it from an acquaintance. My reaction: Who?

This is my failing. This is our failing. This does not escape our kids.

Which success stories do they hear most often? What does the path to the top look like to them?

It should look like a young girl going from hardest Memphis to highest Wall Street. It should look like that girl asking for extra help in math.

"I guess she sort of adopted me," said Ruby Fentress, who was Williams's math teacher at Hamilton High School. "She had an internal drive."

The drive took her from Hamilton to Yale. Then from Yale to a graduate degree in finance at MIT. After a few years with Equitable in New York, she returned to Memphis to work for FedEx.

"Burnetta was a trail blazer," said Vicki Palmer, who recruited Williams to FedEx. "Not only did she go to Yale, she majored in mathematics at Yale. Then she went into finance. There were only a handful of African-American women who were corporate executives back then."

Up the ladder Williams ascended. She was known to be smart and gracious and tough.

"She was brilliant," said Graf. "I worked with her for 30 years. She was a big part of our company."

The moral?

It's not hard to figure out. But let's ask Williams's sister, Joyce McKee.

Fifty years ago, the two girls shared a bed in the family apartment in Cleaborn Homes. There were five kids in the family, three boys and the two girls.

"We had two bedrooms," said McKee. "Our parents slept in one and the kids slept in the other. We thought we had it good."

Their father hadn't made it past 10th grade. Their mother made it to maybe eighth. But both parents were smart, and understood how the world works.

"We were taught that education is what matters," said McKee. "Education is the only way."

Williams took the lesson to heart. She studied her way to the top. When she got there, she took every opportunity to pass the message along.

"I remember her making a speech about it," said McKee. "It's not where you come from, or where you lived. It's the choices you make in life."

And, no, this doesn't mean that everyone has an equal shot at the American dream. It's easier if you get a head start. It's easier if you grow up in privilege and are educated at the finest private schools. But that's certainly not the only way.

We should tell our kids, this, shouldn't we? We should be teaching it in all our schools.

Forget Mike.

Be like Burnetta.

There's no telling how high you'll soar.

SAVING GRACES – HORN LAKE MAN ON ROAD TO RECOVERY
JUNE 3, 2012

She decided to crank up the music. The doctors didn't have any better suggestions to cut through the coma.

"If anything was going to revive him, Rush and Wilco were going to do it," said Amanda Killen. "I didn't know what else to do."

The neurologist had given her the bad news not long before. Her husband, Jay, was utterly unresponsive.

"It doesn't look good," he said.

"Are you telling me he's dying?" she asked.

"It doesn't look good," he said again.

Just a few days earlier they had been putting up Christmas lights at their house in Horn Lake. The Friday after Thanksgiving. Jay, 43, said he wasn't feeling real hot.

But how did that turn into her husband, lying in a hospital bed, staring at nothing at all, breathing only with the aid of a ventilator? How did that turn into a neurologist taking her into the hallway and gently breaking the grim news?

"Their best guess was that an infection from pneumonia was having an effect on the brain stem," said Amanda. "The nurse told me that when the pupils fix like that, it's not going to get better."

So she cranked the music up high. And she had a nice long chat with her husband in that room at Baptist Memorial Hospital-DeSoto.

"I yelled at him," she said. "I told him I wasn't ready for him to go. I had a very frank conversation with his mama, who is deceased. I said, 'You can't have him yet.'"

Amanda can't explain exactly what happened next. It gives her shivers, even now, thinking about it.

"His leg moved," she said. "The nurse told me it was just a reflex, not to put any stock in it. But his leg moved. I could see it. He was in there, shaking his leg."

• • •

This is a story about grace. I know this because Jay says it is, the only way he can.

He spells it. Or we spelled it together. One painstaking letter at a time.

Jay Killen can't speak because he's still on a ventilator. He can't move his hands to write. But he can nod, slightly, when you recite the alphabet and get to the letter he has in mind. So this is how the communication goes.

Me: "What's your story about?"

Jay nods to indicate he wants to spell something.

Amanda: "A, B, C, D, E, F, G ... "

Jay nods.

Amanda: "G?"

Jay nods again, to indicate that's correct.

Amanda: "A, B, C, D, E, F, G, H, I, J, K, L, M, N, O, P, Q, R ..."

Jay nods.

So that's a "G" and an "R."

Amanda starts the alphabet again: "A ... "

Jay nods quickly.

So it's G-R-A ...

Amanda guesses: "Grace."

Jay nods, correct. Because what other word is there, really? How else to explain what happened in that hospital room that night? Or what has happened in the more than six months since?

The morning after Amanda noticed Jay's leg move, she showed it to Dr. Rahul Sonone, the neurologist.

"Jay, shake your leg," she commanded. Whereupon, Jay's leg moved.

"Well, this is something totally different," said Sonone, both thrilled and stumped.

What followed is the kind of thing that restores your belief in the practice of medicine. It was medicine, the way we believe it should be. Three doctors, all specialists, got together to brainstorm the possibilities.

"They worked all day to try and diagnose him," Amanda said. "They went through everything. Could it be rabies? Guillain-Barré syndrome? Then Dr. Sonone came up with the idea of botulism."

This was preposterous, of course. There are fewer than 200 reported cases of botulism a year in the United States, and the vast majority of those are infant botulism.

"I had never seen it," said Dr. Manoj Jain, who is supervising the case now that Jay has been moved to Baptist Memorial Hospital-Memphis. "Dr. Sonone thought of it because he had seen a case when he was a resident."

It made sense, given the symptoms. Botulism is a bacterium that releases a toxin, and that toxin, in turn, binds to the nerves and depletes its receptors. The result: paralysis.

It wasn't clear where Jay could have gotten the botulism. It's often caused by poorly canned foods. But Amanda's mother had helpfully cleaned out everything in the fridge, so that was the end of that.

The doctors called the Centers for Disease Control, in Atlanta. An antitoxin arrived by FedEx at 2 a.m. and was administered immediately.

"I was thrilled," said Amanda. "I'm like, 'Whoohooo, an antitoxin, he's cured!'"

Well, no.

All the nerve receptors would have to grow back. Jay would have to learn to do everything again. The antitoxin stopped the damage, but Jay was still on a ventilator, still unable to breathe, to move his lips, even to blink.

"They said it could take 12 months," said Amanda. "You can't even wrap your head around a conversation like that. 'The good news is that he's going to be fine. The bad news is that it's going to take forever.' And so our journey began."

Yes, that's what she said. And so our journey began. After the possible coma, after the music, after the leg moving, after the diagnosis, after the antitoxin. That's where their journey began. Or the best parts, at least.

Amanda realized Jay couldn't be left alone in his hospital room. He couldn't speak, couldn't move his fingers, couldn't summon help if something went awry. She would need to stay with him 24 hours a day. Except, she couldn't possibly do that. She worked as an administrator at Hutchison School. She and Jay would need her insurance, at the very least.

She mentioned this dilemma to a friend, Janet Zimmerman. Where would she ever find people willing to sit with Jay? Would you believe, Facebook?

Zimmerman posted a note about Jay's situation. People started signing up to help.

"It was incredible," said Amanda. "A lot of them never knew me and never knew Jay."

They signed up for weekly slots, maybe for two hours, maybe for three.

"I honestly can't tell you why I did it," said Billy Reed. "But I'm glad I did."

Reed took 2:30-5:50 on Monday afternoons. Mac Edwards took Wednesday mornings, 9-noon. Alex Mautz took Thursdays from noon until 2 p.m. And so on and so forth.

"I won't lie to you, I felt awkward at first," said Mautz. "There was this guy I'd never met, lying there. He couldn't do anything. But then I said to myself, 'Aww, what the hell. I am who I am. Let's fumble through this.'"

And this is how it has gone for months now, people coming in and fumbling through. Only, the fumbling stops nearly instantly. Replaced by laughter or prayer or contemplation or long conversations, one letter at a time.

There are now 29 members of Team Jay. More, if you count the incredible nurses and the wonderful doctors, which are the adjectives Amanda uses to describe them all. To which, Jay nods, wanting to spell.

Amanda: "A ..."

Jay nods.

Amanda: "A, B, C, D, E, F, G, H, I, J, K, L, M, N ... "

Jay nods again.

Amanda: "A, B, C, D, E, F, G ... "

Jay nods again.

A-N-G

Amanda: "Angels?"

Jay nods in assent.

Jim Page likes to read Jay The New Yorker. Gretchen Winbigler, a masseuse, stops by to give Jay a weekly massage. Father Patrick, Jay's priest, comes by every week to watch a guy movie. As for Amanda, well, "Jay had never read the Harry Potter novels. Since I had him captured in a bed ... "

Miraculous things have happened since Thanksgiving. Some of them are physical. Jay can move his thumb now. He can sit up and go stretches of time off the ventilator. Once, his eyes were sewn shut, because he couldn't blink. Now he can roll his eyes at a particularly bad joke.

But the members of Team Jay will tell you that the more remarkable part of the story is what's happened to them.

"Janet is always saying that we're the greatest people to do what we're doing," said Mautz. "But believe me, we're getting a lot more out of it than he is."

There is something intensely humbling about the process. About having to measure progress in individual blinks or breaths.

"It's sort of a lesson in humility when you have to slow your ass down enough to say the alphabet," said Billy Reed.

Another lesson comes when Jay — paralyzed for more than six months — seems most interested in talking about how you've been.

He gives advice, too.

"Pearls from Jay," said Amanda, laughing at the thought. "People fight to keep their spots in the rotation. When he says something, they write it down."

The rest of us blather and tweet and text and update our Facebook statuses and generally unleash a torrent of words on the world. Jay —

who has to measure every letter — has people rapt, waiting for his next thought.

Which, of course, can strike Amanda and Jay as hilarious.

"The nurses think he's so sweet," she said.

Jay adds, spelling it out: "Wait until I can talk."

Nobody knows when that will happen. But the man will have a story to tell. About what it was like to be trapped inside himself, to hear the doctors talking about him as if he were brain-dead. Mention this to Jay and he spells out: "I was freaking terrified."

Once Julia, another member of Team Jay, asked him if he was lonely in there. Jay shook his head, then spelled.

Julia: "A, B, C, D, E, F, G ... "

Jay nodded.

Julia: "A, B, C, D, E, F, G, H, I, J, K, L, M, N, O ... "

Jay nodded.

Julia: "A, B, C, D ..."

G-O-D.

Jay nodded, yes, that's it.

It has been an impossibly long journey. There are miles yet to go. They were hoping to be out of the hospital by the Wilco concert at Mud Island a few weeks ago. Now Amanda has set a deadline of Christmas to be home.

They laugh together a lot, these days. About life and what it brings.

"Jay has always been one of those survivalists," she said. "He wants to bury a boxcar in the backyard with supplies and guns for when the s- hits the fan. Now we kind of feel like the s- has hit the fan and we didn't even need a boxcar.

"But it hasn't been a negative at all. That's the incredible thing. It sucks, but it hasn't been a negative at all. There are so many people who have helped us, so many people we have gotten to know."

So Jay's story is not about botulism, they insist. It really is about grace.

Me: "The grace of God?"

Yes, Jay nods. And then he wants to spell.

Amanda: "A, B, C, D, E, F, G, H, I, J, K, L, M ..."

Jay nods.

Amanda: "A ... "

Jay nods.

Amanda: "A, B, C, D, E, F, G, H, I, J, K, L, M, N ..."

Jay nods.

Amanda: "A, B, C, D, E, F, G, H, I, J, K ... "

Jay nods.

M-A-N-K

Amanda: "Mankind?"

Jay nods.

And the grace of mankind.

JOY AND GRIEF
AUGUST 14, 2013

They gathered as a family and decided to go through with it. Not because she would have wanted them to but because it seemed right, somehow.

This is what life looks like. This is what love looks like too. It is hard, and it is beautiful. It is glorious and heartbreaking and impossibly sweet.

So Sunday morning, the Fleming family dressed up for a christening. They joined hundreds of friends at Independent Presbyterian Church to see 7-month old Ann Fisher, Camille and Rob — yes, triplets — baptized.

"They were angels," said their mother, Nell Womack. "It was beautiful."

The family celebrated back at the big house on Pecan Grove. Then, a few hours later, they returned to Independent Presbyterian Church for the visitation for their mother, the triplets' grandmother, 54-year-old Liz Fleming, who died Friday of bladder cancer.

They were joined by thousands this time around.

"They had to cut it off after 2½ hours," said Scott Fleming, Liz's husband.

"We should have held it at FedExForum," one of the three Fleming daughters said.

When Liz died Friday morning, they thought about postponing the christening. But they finally concluded this was how it was supposed to be.

They would have the christening and the visitation Sunday. They would have the memorial service Monday. It would be a celebration of God and family and everything that really mattered to them.

"To me, the connection felt really special," said Nell Womack, after it was all over. "It was like God ordained it that way. I walked down the aisle with the babies on Sunday, and I walked down the same aisle behind my mother today."

• • •

Scott Fleming remembers getting the phone call from Nell last July, after the ultrasound. Nell and her husband, Joseph, hadn't had an easy time getting pregnant and had turned to in vitro fertilization. The doctor had implanted two eggs, so they were expecting twins.

"It's not twins," Nell told her father.

"Ah, well," said Scott. "One little baby will be nice ..."

"It's triplets," said Nell.

Whereupon, Scott Fleming screamed.

"Like John Goodman in Raising Arizona," he said. "It was a scream of pure joy."

And so begins this love story. But it is a real love story, and real love stories are not just candy and flowers. They are also diapers and CT scans and hospital beds.

The triplets arrived on Jan. 5, 10 weeks early, after more than two months of bed rest for Nell. They were tiny — 3 pounds each — but they were going to be fine.

Around about then, Liz Fleming told Scott she had a doctor's appointment. Casually, she said it. Because that's the way she was.

Two years ago, Liz sent her daughters a quote from George Bernard Shaw that goes like this: "This is true joy in life, this being used up for a purpose recognized by yourself as a mighty one, the being a force of nature instead of a feverish, selfish little clod of ailments and grievances complaining that the world will not devote itself to make you happy."

That was Liz Fleming. It's not that she was all seriousness. Far from it. She was funny and warm and generous to a fault. But complain? Who had time to complain? Liz was too busy embracing life.

"She put poems in our lunch boxes every day," said Ruthie, now 26.

"Our friends used to ask us what she wrote," said Caroline, 28.

"Roses are red, birds build a nest, I hope you do well on your chemistry test," said Nell, 30, reciting from memory. "They were always topical. They were wonderful."

Liz's trip to the doctor led to a second trip, this time for a CT scan. The CT scan led to another phone call Scott Fleming will never forget.

"It was January 17," he said. "Liz called and said, 'They found a mass on my bladder and two suspicious spots on my lung.'"

Stage 4 cancer.

"Liz and I never talked about it, but all the reading I did said she had about 13 months," Scott said.

It wouldn't be that long.

Two rounds of chemotherapy didn't do much of anything. Radiation only helped a little bit. So the Fleming family was faced with seven months that words can't begin to describe.

There were the triplets, bringing joy and chaos. Growing and making tiny fists and learning to smile. And there was Liz, in a hospital bed in the couple's bedroom, undertaking a fight she could not win.

There were miracles too. That's how the family thinks of them.

Like Ruthie and her husband, Andy, who had been trying to move back to Memphis, getting a bid on their house in Austin, Texas, a week after Liz was diagnosed.

Like the cool evenings of July — the coolest July in recent memory — when the whole family would head out around the neighborhood.

"Let's go on a walk," Liz would say, and off they'd go, Scott pushing Liz in a wheelchair, Nell pushing the babies in a triple stroller.

"People would walk with us," said Nell. "The whole neighborhood would join in. One night, I looked and there were 40 people walking with us. It was like a parade."

Scott and Liz — who began dating when they were 17 and 15 — set a goal of making it to a July vacation in Florida. When it became clear that wouldn't be possible, the three girls surprised them by decorating their screened porch to look just like their favorite Florida restaurant, the Red Bar in Grayton Beach.

"Complete with jazz, Christmas lights and our favorite entree, the penne chicken," said Scott. "It was a night we'll never forget."

So this is how the seven months passed. They brimmed with agony, and sweetness too. One day, on the way to a doctor's appointment, Liz turned to her husband and — for the first time, really — spoke about the end.

"Scott, I know this is the end," she said. "But I'm OK. I've seen my girls grow up, I've seen the men they are going to marry, and I've met my grandbabies."

• • •

Adrienne Hillyer delivered a eulogy at Monday's memorial service for Liz Fleming. She said that ever since January, people had been praying for a miracle. But somewhere along the way, Hillyer had a realization.

"She was the miracle," Hillyer said, referring to Liz. "God had answered our prayer even before we prayed it."

And maybe that is the best way to make sense of this story, which is — in many ways — the story of all our lives.

Life is sadness and it is hilarity, it is grief and kindness and joy. Life is three babies, arriving headlong into this world. It is their vibrant, 54-year-old grandmother, leaving it much too soon.

The Fleming family is unusual because all this was packed into a weekend. And because they handled it with unwavering faith and grace.

"I honestly loved the symbolism," said Scott. "There was grief but there was also new life."

"I sat in the same seat, in the same pew," Nell said. "It was like she was there the whole time."

So now the Fleming family is finally off on that Florida vacation. They are walking the beach, and listening to the ocean, and watching three babies play and grow.

"I just hope they all have a little bit of my mother in them," Nell said. "I'm pretty sure they do."

ATTITUDE OF GRATITUDE
NOVEMBER 27, 2014

He decided to paint one of the hearts like a Grizzlies logo. That's how it all began.

"We do a project for the neighborhood for Valentine's Day," said Erin Harris, the grown-up who started the Carpenter Art Garden in Binghamton. "We make yard hearts, and the kids paint them however they want, and we put them in yards all over the neighborhood."

So Donte Davis decided to paint a Grizzlies logo.

People really liked it.

"Other neighbors started asking for one of their own," said Harris.

So Donte painted more of them.

"They became really popular," said Harris.

Donte painted even more of them.

Then one day, Donte had an idea. It was when the grown-ups were brainstorming how to raise money to pay for a house — a real building — to go along with the art garden.

The art garden was lovely, to be sure. Kids who didn't have anywhere else to go were flocking to the after-school programs. But there was nowhere to take shelter when it snowed or it rained. The garden really needed four walls and a roof.

"Maybe I could paint more of these Grizzlies yard hearts and we could sell them," Donte suggested. "We could use the money I raise for the building."

...

Happy Thanksgiving, Memphis. May we all try to be as grateful and as generous as Donte Davis.

He's 13, by the way. Talk about humbling. When you consider his life from the outside, it's easy to wonder what he's so grateful about.

"His mother was a drug addict," said Harris. "She left when he was itty-bitty. He doesn't know where she is."

And his father?

"He died of a heart attack when Donte was 5," said Harris. "His aunt now raises him. Everyone calls her 'Grandma Caine.'"

Grandma Caine does her best, she really does. She raises Donte, and Donte's older sister, and Donte's younger brother.

"Grandma Caine's two daughters live with us, too," said Donte. "They're grown. They each have three children."

So there are a lot of people in the house. Or, I should say, houses.

"I don't know how many places I've stayed," said Donte, who stops counting when he reaches nine on his fingers.

There was the apartment just down the way from the Carpenter Art Garden, not far from the drug house.

"It didn't have any furniture," said Harris. "The kids all slept in one room. There weren't any beds, just ratty blankets laid out for each of them."

There was the house from last winter.

"It didn't have any heat," said Harris. "The landlord was a local slum lord and wouldn't fix the furnace."

None of this is atypical for the kids who come to the art garden, by the way. The atypical part is, well, Donte.

"He started coming more than a year ago, in June of 2013," said Harris. "We were doing print making, and he did it in a snap, and you could just tell immediately he was gifted. He has been to every single thing that we have had since. And then, of course, there's the Griz hearts."

The Griz hearts have gone crazy. The Carpenter Art Garden has sold more than 300. They recently raised the price to $25 a heart. The demand is not easing.

"He has spent hundreds of hours painting the hearts, and I'm not exaggerating," said Harris. "We opened this house last September and he is a very big part of it."

Not all the money went straight into the art garden's new structure. Harris put $5 from every heart into a savings account for Donte. Every now and then, Donte asks Harris if he can have some "Griz money."

"The very first thing he asked for was some money to buy some things for Grandma Caine's mother," said Harris. "She was having an 80th birthday celebration at the church, and she loved the color purple. Donte asked for $50 so he could take his family to the dollar store and buy everything that was purple."

A few months later, Donte asked for some Griz money to take his family roller-skating. He needed $50 for the skating and snacks and $20 for half a tank of gas.

"Then he decided to save up for a bike," said Harris. "We finally found one he liked at Target. This was early last summer. He let every single person he knows ride it, and in two weeks it was ruined."

So now Donte is once again bike-less. But when everyone in his math class at Lester Middle School did well on a recent test, he asked Harris if she could use some of the Griz money to buy the class hot wings.

"That's just who he is," said Harris. "He doesn't always think of himself."

Imagine if grown-ups in Memphis were so consistently selfless. Imagine if we were as grateful for what we have.

"He has the gift of joy, is how I think of it," said Harris. "I asked him the other day if his life was difficult and he said, 'Honestly, Miss Erin, I can't think of any way my life is hard.'"

So let the spirit of Donte Davis be with us this Thanksgiving Day. Let us aim to do as well as this 13-year-old kid.

"Honestly, he's been an inspiration," said Harris.

May we all be as generous with our hearts.

VIII

THE
MEMPHIS
GRIZZLIES
(2010-2015)

A GLORIOUS DAY FOR CITY THAT KNOWS BLUES

APRIL 18, 2011

San ANTONIO — The Grizzlies trailed by two and Mike Conley found Shane Battier and this is the day to break out the late, great Don Poier, isn't it?

Only in the movies and in Memphis. Only after a decade of frustrations and angst.

Only with longtime assistant Lionel Hollins at the helm, only in this Texas town where another Memphis team once collapsed, only with the ball in the hands of the most beloved of the original Grizzlies, the prodigal Battier.

"If I had one guy to shoot, it would be Shane," said Grizzlies owner Mike Heisley. "He won so many games for us."

But never a playoff game. Until now, that is.

"I was just trying to get it up on the rim and give Zach and Marc a chance to go get it," said Battier.

The best laid plans, and all that. The ball dropped through. The San Antonio fans stood, dumbstruck. If you have lived in Memphis for any length of time — if you have followed the fortunes and misfortunes of the Grizzlies franchise — you know exactly how they felt.

Better them than you, eh? Exactly 23.9 seconds later, it was gloriously done. Marc Gasol hugged Heisley by the side of the court. Zach Randolph — who agreed to a new contract with the team the day before — punched his fist into the sky.

Oh, and Battier changed and drove three hours to Houston, where his wife delivered the newest Battier, a girl.

"Single CRAZIEST day of my life," he tweeted.

Anybody want a cigar?

For the win. For the baby. For both Battiers delivering.

The final score was Memphis 101, San Antonio 98. Can you name a girl Trey?

"I know Beale Street will be a fun place tonight," said Battier. "Most of these guys don't understand the history and the heartache that the city has gone through."

It's not just the Griz-induced heartache, either. It's the NFL drive, it's the Tigers, it's everything.

Admit it: When the Grizzlies went up 7 with 4:03 left, and when they proceeded to miss four straight foul shots, and when San Antonio's Matt Bonner hit his only two bleeping 3s of the day, and when that 7-point lead somehow became a 4-point deficit with 1:06 left, you were thinking, "Arrrrgh, here we go again."

This was Dirk Nowitzki dropping in a 3-pointer to steal a win from the Grizzlies in the playoffs in '06. This was Mike Miller missing a 3-pointer that would have beaten the Spurs in the playoffs in '04.

This was three years ago, just down the road at the Alamodome, where the Tigers blew a similar lead because of — you guessed it — missed free throws.

This was exactly what Memphis teams do in these situations. This was why they invented the blues.

Except, over on the Grizzlies bench, the players were blissfully unaware of the coming calamity.

"Guys were even calmer," said Tony Allen. "We were like, 'Let's play.'"

So they did. Amazing, the difference it can make. The ending was different, too.

Allen fed Gasol for a layup. That drew the Grizzlies back within 2. One defensive stop later, Conley found Battier standing outside the arc for a chance to reclaim the lead.

It has been a curious return to Memphis for Battier. He'd be the first to tell you he hasn't been at his best. He knew he was expected to be the missing piece for this playoff team. When he didn't play up to his own expectations, he started to press.

"I felt like the walk-on at the end of the bench," he said. "I'm not used to being Rudy."

He meant Ruettiger, not Gay.

But somehow, it all came together in that moment, that merging of Grizzlies teams present and past. This was for the Gasol brothers and for the Cates brothers, for Hubie and Lorenzen and Zach. It was for the people who planted those "NBA Now" signs in their yards a decade ago. It was for every beleaguered Memphis fan.

It was for Arnold Perl and Andy Dolich, for Morris Fair's arena vote and for Jerry West's fruitless lottery trips. It was for Heisley, who has taken a pummeling in this city. It was for Poier, who really would have loved this game.

The Grizzlies have not exactly been on a magic carpet ride since they arrived in Memphis. It's been a long and tortured road. But when the ball found Battier and then the bucket, all things suddenly seemed possible.

They could steal another game Wednesday! They could win the series outright!

"There's no monkey off our backs," said Heisley. "We want to win a series now."

Meanwhile, back in the locker room, Battier quietly put ice on his knees. He's not the kid fresh out of Duke any longer. He wasn't certain this moment would ever come.

But it had. And he was a part of it. On the same day he became a father once again.

"I'm really happy for the city," he said.

Right back at you, Shane.

DESTINY CALLS, AND GRIZZLIES RESPOND
APRIL 24, 2011

Zach Randolph got the ball and the shot clock was winding down to zero and so he did the natural thing.

"I just shot the shot," he said.

From 26 feet away.

With the Grizzlies up by just a bucket, with an entire city on the precipice.

"I think there was a collective holding of breath," said Shane Battier.

Maybe some cursing under the breath, too.

"I was like, 'No, no, no,'" said Grizzlies owner Mike Heisley. "Then it was, 'YES!'"

Yes, the ball dropped through. Yes, the Grizzlies would win this game.

Yes, the most important, most meaningful, most thrilling day in the history of the Memphis NBA franchise would end the way it was supposed to end.

With 18,119 fans spilling out onto Beale Street, exhausted but jubilant. With Randolph, on the court, doing a merry jig.

"It's a win-win dance," he said.

Nice to see it, after all these years.

The Grizzlies took a 2-1 series lead over the San Antonio Spurs on Saturday, riding a wave of sound and emotion to a 91-88 victory.

As recently as two weeks ago, Heisley said that he still considered the first 2004 playoff game against the Spurs as the high point in franchise history.

Not anymore.

"This is what I hoped would happen in Memphis," he said. "If you didn't enjoy this game, you must be a zombie."

Or a Spur.

It was craziness from well before the tip, and where to even begin?

Jerry Lawler appeared in a basketball jersey, holding up his mythical crown. He said it was time to "pile-drive" the Spurs.

In the stands, Adam Groveman and Ryan Baum settled into their seats. They had walked — ready? — 11 miles to see the game.

Groveman and Baum are Orthodox Jews. They can't use cars on Saturdays.

So they walked. What, you think they were going to miss a game like this?

"We left at 1:35," said Groveman. "We got here at 5."

By the time the introductions began, the crowd was at a fever pitch. A massive picture of Eva Longoria — Tony Parker's ex — bobbed merrily in section 116 along with a sign that read, "She wit us."

Other signs: "Zeebo is my hero," "Welcome to the Grind House," and "Go Flop Yourself."

"It was everything I expected," said Battier.

Said Mike Conley: "I got shivers. The hair stood up on the back of my neck."

Conley and his teammates have waited a long time to see this town this cranked about the NBA. Heisley — and all those involved in bringing the franchise to Memphis — have waited longer than that.

"I didn't know if I'd get it, but I know I love it," said Heisley. "The crowd gets credit for this win."

Which is nice of him to say, of course. But O.J. Mayo and Randolph might deserve special mention, too.

After leading all game long — by as many as 15 points — the Grizzlies suddenly found themselves all tied up with 5:14 left. Those growl towels the fans had been twirling over their heads all game long? They were peeking out from behind them now.

Whereupon, the Grizzlies did what these Grizzlies always seem to do. In the words of Tim Duncan: "They made some great plays."

Mayo waited for Manu Ginobili to go flying past, then calmly potted a 3-pointer to put the Grizzlies up again. Then Randolph knocked down a couple foul shots. Then Marc Gasol hit a big jumper. Then came the play that defined this game.

"Exactly like we drew it up," said Mayo, laughing.

"It was a busted play," said Battier.

The play was designed to go to Gasol. When that broke down, Battier found Randolph standing outside the arc.

Duncan was covering Randolph. He decided to guard against the pass.

"I didn't assume that was in his arsenal at that point of the game," said Duncan.

Whoopsie.

"It felt good when it left my hands," Randolph said.

Bedlam followed. Then minutes later, Zach's dance.

"He earned his money today," Heisley said.

In the stands, a couple of weary fans stood and soaked it all in. It had been a long trip to this moment, whether measured in miles or years.

"I'd do it again," said Groveman.

"Tomorrow," said Baum.

Tipoff is 7 p.m.

RANDOLPH HELPS CITY REDEEM OLD PAINS
APRIL 30, 2011

Antonio McDyess hit the jumper and the Spurs took the lead for the first time since the opening bucket and FedExForum fell mournfully silent.

This was not happening.

This was not slipping away.

Rick Trotter, the PA guy, tweeted: "We can't panic!!! WE GOTTA KEEP OUR COMPOSURE!!"

Owner Mike Heisley couldn't bear to watch. It was exquisite agony. All the past failures, all the demoralizing collapses, came rushing back again.

And then Zach Randolph banished them. Just drove them the %#$*$#* out.

"I told Mike to get me the ball," he said.

Mike Conley complied. The rest will go down in glorious civic history.

The Grizzlies vanquished the Spurs.

The Grizzlies vanquished the demons, too.

They became just the second No.8 seed to defeat a No. 1 seed in a seven-game series, defeating San Antonio 99-91 at FedExForum.

"It's incredible," said Randolph. "I'm so happy for the city of Memphis."

Memphis is pretty darn happy for Zach, too. And for his formerly misbegotten franchise.

Yes, formerly.

Time to retire all those adjectives for good. The ones that seemed to be permanently affixed to the name of the team.

The laughable Grizzlies. The lowly Grizzlies. The inept Grizzlies. None of those fit any longer.

Make it the magnificent Grizzlies. Or the astonishing Grizzlies. Or the gritty, grimy, and impossibly big-hearted Grizzlies.

Friday night was all you needed to see. Friday night was this team, wrapped in one night. What exactly didn't happen Friday at FedExForum?

Jerry Lawler made a second appearance. He pulled his strap down for all the country to see. There was a monkey riding on a border collie at one point, for no obvious reason.

The crowd was bonkers. But nervous, too. It didn't help when Conley went out with two early fouls.

And then in came Greivis Vasquez, a rookie, and didn't I tell you this team was resilient? Rudy Gay can go down, O.J. Mayo can be suspended, Conley can be sent to the sidelines by the officials.

"I was mostly ticked," said Conley, talking about the fouls. "But then when I saw what Greivis was doing, I was like, 'Keep it up, young fella.'"

The Grizzlies rode Vasquez (11 points, 0 turnovers) and their defense to a 14-point lead. Spurs coach Gregg Popovich couldn't even get a timeout, the place was so deafening. But you knew it couldn't be that easy, didn't you?

Sure enough, the Spurs hung in. Manu Ginobili threw in a shot from 75 feet. Tony Parker hit just about everything. And Tony Allen lost his mind, briefly. He turned it over twice. Just Tony being Tony. McDyess hit the jumper to put the Spurs up, 80-79, with 4:40 left, and the crowd fell silent.

It was as if the Grizzlies had to pass one final test. As if they had to prove themselves to the basketball gods one more time.

You want to change your reputation? OK, then find a way to win this one.

The way was Randolph. The way has been Randolph all along. On a team of relentless workers, he has been the most relentless.

He had a reputation to change, too. Change comes slow in the world of sports. On the eve of this series, Rick Reilly wrote that the Grizzlies couldn't win because Randolph has an "extra punk chromosome."

Or maybe he meant an extra funk chromosome? An extra crunk chromosome? Whatever extra chromosome Randolph has, can the rest of us order one of them?

"He carried us on his back," said Marc Gasol. "He hit some shots that almost hit the Jumbotron."

The Grizzlies went on a 12-2 run. Randolph had 10 of the 12 and 31 on the night.

"Say hello to Mr. Reilly," he said, laughing.

But he wasn't angry at all. He knows how these things go. People start thinking of you one way, it's hard to change that.

You have to do something extraordinary. Something like the Grizzlies and Randolph did Friday night. Something irrefutably, emphatically wonderful.

"I feel like I'm from Memphis," he said. "It's never been like this anywhere else."

It's never been like this before here, either.

GUTSY GRIZZLIES WIN HEARTS IN TRIPLE OT
MAY 11, 2011

At 12:40 a.m., it finally ended.

Everyone was standing. But, then, they'd been standing for the better part of an hour. They'd been standing and gasping and cheering and groaning and screaming and pinching themselves.

Now it was done. Now the epic was over. The Oklahoma City Thunder had defeated the Memphis Grizzlies in three overtimes, 133-123. So the fans stood and watched and cheered.

Yes, cheered. You couldn't help but cheer. Cheer for the effort. Cheer for this game of games. Cheer for the privilege of being a witness and a part of it all.

The Grizzlies may or may not figure out a way to win Game 5 in Oklahoma City. They may or may not find a way to win this playoff series and advance to play Dallas in the Western Conference Finals.

But in a season of can-you-believe-this moments, this may be the one that lingers longest in our memories. This night of drama and of history. This night when the game was as full and as wild and as brimming with peril and possibilities as the river that has been making some history of its own.

"This is what it's all about," said Grizzlies general manager Chris Wallace, who was wandering around the Memphis locker room well after 1 a.m., shaking hands with his guys. "Except for getting the win, it doesn't get any better than this. This is why you get a team."

Which is exactly right, of course, and you'll have to pardon the people of Memphis for still thinking about things in this larger way. Memphians don't take their place in the national sports landscape for granted. They lived through too many disappointments, endured too many failed dreams.

So it was fitting that the Pursuit Team was recognized at mid-court before Monday's game began. That collection of local citizens believed before anyone else did.

They believed in the city and they believed in the power of sports, too. Not to cure every civic ill, but to inspire and forge a sense of civic pride.

Some said it was all terribly naive. Those people should have been there Monday night.

It was as grand a night as this city has seen in a long while, a celebration of basketball and community and everything that makes us who we are.

Gov. Bill Haslam was courtside, with his Memphian wife. Penny Hardaway cheered along with Gene Bartow and David Porter and Willie Herenton and Leigh Anne Tuohy and Josh Pastner and Houston Nutt and you get the general idea.

It was jubilant defiance in the face of a rising river. It was Memphis at its absolute best.

And then the game started and the Grizzlies bolted to the lead and, yes, it seems like it happened at least a week ago.

The Grizzlies went up by 18 and then fell behind by 10. They had a lead they couldn't possibly relinquish and then faced a deficit they couldn't possibly make up.

So they did both. Naturally. And then things really went nuts.

"The only thing I was waiting for was for Elvis to rise out of center court," said Shane Battier. "Even that, I don't think it would have surprised me at this point."

Marc Gasol, Zach Randolph and Kevin Durant all played more than 55 minutes. Gasol and Randolph combined for 60 points and 37 rebounds. The teams shots 90 free throws, 50 by the Thunder. Mike Conley and O.J. Mayo both fouled out and missed the last two overtimes.

But the Grizzlies hung in, and hung in, and hung in. Conley hit a ridiculous 3-pointer to send the game into the first overtime. Then, after Conley fouled out, Greivis Vasquez hit an even more ridiculous 3 to send it into the second overtime.

"When Greivis hit that shot, I just started laughing," said Battier. "What else could you do? At that point, it went from the ridiculous to the sublime."

In the third overtime, the Grizzlies finally fizzled, making just 1-of-9 from the field.

"It became a matter of just not having enough bullets," said coach Lionel Hollins. "Nobody wanted to go home."

In the locker room, afterward, the players dressed in relative peace and quiet. Print reporters had long since blown past their deadlines and TV wouldn't air fresh tape at 2 a.m.

Battier said he'd never been a part of anything remotely like this game. Wallace compared it to Game 5 of the 1976 championship series between the Celtics and the Suns.

"To be a part of something like this is special," he said. "I know it doesn't feel like that now."

And yet, oddly, it did. Even in that locker room. Even given that result.

The Grizzlies aren't so jaundiced that they aren't aware of the impact they're having in this city and beyond. They're just aren't ready to concede it's over yet.

So they dressed and they answered questions and they tipped their metaphorical caps to the Thunder. But as far as conceding that this epic game somehow clinched things for their opponents?

"No, Sir," Mayo said. "I don't believe that at all."

Even in exhaustion, the Grizzlies were resolute. It was time to go home. It was time to go to bed. Someone asked Conley if that 3-pointer was the biggest shot he'd ever hit.

Conley thought about it for barely a second.

"So far," he said.

THUNDER 105, GRIZZLIES 90 – GRIZ GIVE MEMPHIS SOMETHING TO BELIEVE IN
MAY 11, 2011

OKLAHOMA CITY — I believe that was an absolute blast.

I believe you will remember this Memphis Grizzlies team for the rest of your days.

I believe a whole bunch of you will save your growl towels, maybe even have them framed.

I believe that we will never again have to hear that the Grizzlies have never won a playoff game.

I believe the Grindhouse is a nickname that will stick around for a while.

I believe that Shane Battier's 3-pointer to win the first playoff game is as perfect a moment as I have ever seen in sports.

I believe the community needed a run like this.

I believe it's about more than basketball.

I believe in Memphis, in its people, and in its ability to surmount its problems with faith, joy and hard work.

I believe that spirit was perfectly reflected in this Grizzlies basketball team.

I believe that nothing that happened in Oklahoma City on Sunday afternoon changes any of that.

And yes, it's over. The Thunder defeated the Grizzlies in Game 7, 105-90.

"They made shots, we missed shots," said Battier, which is about all the analysis you need. This isn't a day for analysis. This is a day to bask in the kind of season that comes along once or twice in a lifetime.

Battier hit a winning shot and had a baby. Jerry Lawler pulled the strap down, twice. Giant celebrity heads bounced in the stands, wearing Grizzlies headbands. Every ticket sold out within minutes of going on sale.

FedExForum brimmed with Memphis in all its diversity, black, white, yellow and brown. The place rocked. Never mind the rising Mississippi. Come hell or high water has never had quite the same ring.

That's why Grizzlies owner Mike Heisley went to church Sunday morning and gave thanks to the Big Guy. No, not Z-Bo, although he might have mentioned him, too.

"This is all great," Heisley said before Game 7. "But it's nothing compared to what I've already seen. To walk into FedExForum and see all those happy people, to walk out onto Beale Street and see the reaction of Memphians, that was my dream."

So, yes, it would have been nice for the Grizzlies to win Sunday's game. But losing was OK, too. The most celebrated team in Memphis basketball history didn't win its last game, you know. Sometimes, it's about bigger things.

Like hope. And community. And the power of pride in a place. Nobody is pretending that all Memphians are now going to lock arms and join together to build an urban utopia, but let me ask you this: When's the last time you felt this good about this city? When's the last time you got all worked up about the consolidation mess?

Who had the time to be ticked at David Pickler or Martavius Jones when Manu Ginobili and Russell Westbrook were around? Who had the energy to be cynical about Memphis when everyone was so furiously believing in the place?

My own favorite moment came during Game 3 of the Thunder series. The Grizzlies trailed by a zillion. All of a sudden, 18,119 fans were silently, defiantly, holding up their "Believe Memphis" towels. They weren't told to do it. It was an organic expression of faith. In their players. In their city. In the power of faith itself.

How often have you heard it said that nobody is harder on Memphis than the people who live here? How often have you wished that people would just believe in its possibilities?

At that moment, they believed. And the belief actually helped. The Griz rallied to win the darn thing. There's got to be a lesson in that.

I believe that Tony Allen is an example of what can be done through hard work.

I believe Zach Randolph is living proof that you can overcome past mistakes.

I believe Al Green really rocks the national anthem.

I believe Lionel Hollins was the perfect coach for this team.

I believe in grit and I believe in grind.

I believe that 1,200 people met the team at Wilson Air after the game.

I believe that would have been a good Monday night crowd not long ago.

I believe the Grizzlies have already sold 2,000 new season tickets for next year.

I believe the Pursuit Team was absolutely right.

I believe the Grizzlies won more playoff games than any No. 8 seed in history.

I believe they might have won even more with a healthy Rudy Gay.

"I believe we did some amazing things," said Allen.

I believe what that man believes.

MEMPHIS, GRIZ PRIMER FOR NEW OWNER PERA
NOVEMBER 4, 2012

Welcome to Memphis, Robert Pera! Big day Monday, isn't it? But don't be nervous. I'm here for you. Herewith, 50 things you should know about your new basketball team and city:

1. The guy with the blonde wife on the front row is the Cracker Rapper. He made a video. I don't know whether to tell you to watch it.

2. Elvis jokes in Memphis are like Toto jokes in Kansas. Best to skip 'em entirely.

3. No need to ever say Walking in Memphis, either.

4. If you're going to follow one Memphian on Twitter, you can't go wrong with Tony Allen.

5. If you're 34, like your bio says, you should probably be on a barbecue team.

6. But you can actually be a wildly popular Memphian without eating barbecue. Shane Battier did it.

7. Yes, there are two mayors, and two Kings, and more than two Parkways. Just go with it, OK?

8. People will want you to draft players from the University of Memphis. Don't listen. It's pandering and it's ridiculous.

9. We're already up to No. 9? Then somebody has surely asked you if you have found a church home by now. Do not be offended.

10. There is no correct answer to the wet vs. dry debate. There is a correct answer to Motown vs. Stax.

11. Don't mess with the MLK Day symposia. They're important.

12. Don't mess with the Griz Grannies and Grandpas, either. I have no idea why, but people go nuts for them.

13. Memphis is more Marc Gasol than Pau Gasol.

14. Memphis is even more Z-Bo.

15. Keep Chris Wallace (but I already said that).

16. Keep Lionel Hollins (but you were going to do that anyway).

17. Let Tony Allen walk after this year at your peril. He invented grit and grind. Memphians truly love him.

18. After you've been here a while, you'll learn you can get anywhere on Poplar.

19. After you've been here a while longer, you'll learn you can get anywhere without having to go on Poplar.

20. You will hear that we have an inferiority complex, but that is so last decade. We actually think we're pretty cool.

21. Also, we believe.

22. If you continue to have that Twitter account, you will hear from a lot of people telling you to trade Rudy Gay. This is not necessarily fair to Gay, by the way. People used to want to trade Mike Conley.

23. Perkins Extended is a continuation of Perkins and runs parallel to Perkins. It's mind-bending.

24. The Griz aren't nearly as bad at drafting as people say. They miss up high, where ownership tends to get involved. But later picks have produced players like Darrell Arthur, Greivis Vasquez (don't ask) and Sam Young.

25. Rick Trotter really rocks the anthem.

26. People will wave at you. Go ahead and wave back at them.

27. Buy a house inside the loop. It worked for John Calipari.

28. Listen to Fred.

29. Set up a program at the University of Memphis Fogelman College of Business and Economics. Place is on the way up, just like you are.

30. Go to Jerry's Sno Cones and get a supreme, go to Brother Juniper's and get the San Diegan, go to Gibson's and get a warm glazed, go to Iris and get anything.

31. Oh, and that sandwich at Republic Coffee? It's called the Calkins, not the Ahab.

32. Read the letters to the editor whenever you're in town, if only for the chuckles.

33. DO NOT READ THE ONLINE COMMENTS.

34. Nobody likes to say this out loud, but the Memphis Tigers don't make your job any easier. They're just like a pro team. They're covered like a pro team. People have wondered why Oklahoma City drew more fans than the Grizzlies right off the bat. There are a lot of reasons, including Kevin Durant and local ownership. But the biggest reason: Memphis already had a civic basketball franchise.

35. Having said that, you should wrap your arms around the Tigers. The vibe between the two programs is authentic. The Grizzlies showed up at Memphis Madness to support the Tigers. Frank the Life Changer, the Tigers' trainer, works with Z-Bo during the offseason. Memphis might just be the best little basketball city on the planet.

36. Yes, people still call the Hernando DeSoto Bridge which opened in 1973 the new bridge.

37. If the airline fares get you down, you can always drive to Little Rock.

38. Wednesday night is church night.

39. Bless your heart is not a compliment.

40. Memphis fans hate the Heat as much for Mario Chalmers as for LeBron James.

41. Hamed Haddadi sends Memphians into paroxysms of unbridled, shrieking joy. Nobody has ever determined the reason for this.

42. How can you tell when Jerry Lawler is serious? When he pulls the strap down, of course.

43. Go easy on the Griz staff. They have worked hard to create momentum for the franchise. It hasn't always been simple, either. The team has been for sale ever since it arrived. There was the nasty ownership schism. For the longest time, the record was lousy. But now, there's some good stuff happening. Ticket sales are going up every year. The team wins international awards for the good it does in the community. You have to have employees you're comfortable with, ultimately, but this group has earned a long look at the very least.

44. The very large man who shakes it for the Dance Cam is named Rex. He is excellent.

45. The man wearing outlandish suits is Mark Goodfellow. He can get you auto financing, no matter your credit rating!

46. Cool places in Memphis: The Shell, the Greenline, the zoo (including five actual Grizzlies) and the Civil Rights Museum.

47. St. Jude Children's Research Hospital will change your life. But there are other worthy causes in Memphis. The Church Health Center. Bridges. If I wanted to list them all, I'd have to take out a full-page ad. Which, I understand, are available. But the point is this: Memphis has a heart as big and unceasing as the river that defines it.

48. Relax. You don't really have to memorize all this stuff. There won't be a test Monday morning. Memphis is a simple place. If you want to

pitch in, we'll have you. And if you're open to becoming a part of the community and you don't build walls around yourself and your organization then Memphians will fall in love with you. People like to talk about all our racial divisions. And they are real, no question. But Memphis loved the fast-talking Catholic snark from up North (Calipari) and Memphis loves the gee-whiz Jewish kid from Houston by way of Arizona (Josh Pastner) and Memphis loves the in-his-own-world black guy from Chicago (Allen). You know what those three men all have in common? They embraced Memphis. In their own ways, they became one of us. Do that, and the rest is just details.

49. Last thing: The Grizzlies matter. I mean, they really matter to this city. Memphis is a much more vibrant, interesting place than it was even a decade ago. The Grizzlies are both a part of and an expression of that. There was a moment, two years ago, during the playoff series against the Thunder, when Grizzlies fans held their towels aloft in joyous defiance of the odds. Believe Memphis, the towels said. It wasn't just about basketball. It was about belief in the place and in one another. And I don't really care if it sounds sappy. The fable this town treasures more than any other is the one involving a young man named Larry Finch, and a young team of Memphis Tigers, and what that team did to heal a troubled city. That's what basketball can mean in Memphis. That's what it has meant.

50. So truly, welcome to Memphis. You want a pickup game? Call Penny or Elliot. And, remember, Grindhouse is one word. Please be a wise custodian.

EVERYBODY'S HERO
MAY 17, 2013

OKLAHOMA CITY — When Zach Randolph missed those two free throws, it all came back, didn't it?

Blown free throws. A squandered lead. All that was missing was Mario Chalmers. And in his place was Kevin Durant, one of the most lethal basketball scorers on the planet, with 10.9 seconds to win the thing.

It was going to happen again. It might well have happened again. Except for the intercession of a crazy, wonderful basketball hellion named Tony Allen.

Leave it to Allen to make it all right. Leave it to the Grindfather to rewrite that tired old civic story.

Who said the team from Memphis always has to lose in the end? Who said that growing up on the banks of the Mississippi means having your basketball hearts broken?

Allen went after Durant with a fury. He wouldn't let him go right, then hung with him when Durant turned back left and — yes, indeed, this really happened — misfired.

Then Allen grabbed the rebound. Of course. And then he was fouled. Of course. And then he walked to the line and showed everyone exactly what you do with clutch free throws.

He dropped in the first. He dropped in the second.

"Tony's my hero," said Zach Randolph.

Today, in Memphis, he's everybody's hero.

The Grizzlies are going to the Western Conference finals. Go ahead, read that last sentence again. The team that was once the laughingstock of the NBA will play San Antonio or Golden State for the right to go to the NBA finals.

The Grizzlies won that privilege by defeating the Oklahoma City Thunder 88-84 on Wednesday, sweeping the top-seeded Thunder out of the playoffs in just five games.

"It's surreal," said Mike Conley. "It's crazy to see it all come together."

Start with a point guard who was supposed to be a bust. Add a power forward who was supposed to be a problem child. Mix in a chunky younger brother, and a coach who couldn't get a break and, c'mon, who would believe this stuff?

Oh, and add a wild man from the Boston Celtics. A guy who lives for defense. A man who makes two great plays for every bad one, but, boy, he sure makes the bad ones.

Allen did it again Wednesday night. He wasn't even in the game at the time. It was late in the third quarter, the Griz up by 11. Derek Fisher missed a 3-pointer except, wait, what was that blue thing on the court?

It was Allen's warm-up shirt. It slipped out of his hands as he was swinging it around the way he does. The officials called Fisher's missed 3-pointer good — interference, they said — and tacked on a technical.

Suddenly, that 11-point lead was down to seven. The Thunder had been jolted right back into the game. Allen's teammates reacted exactly the way you'd expect they would.

"I was ready to grab him by his throat," said Randolph.

This was a common theme.

"I almost strangled him," said Conley. "If I wasn't tired, I would have."

But Conley also knew this about Allen: Somehow, the guy would get it back.

"I told him, 'I know you just messed up big time, but you're going to make up for it,'" Conley said.

The game careened to the end. Quincy Pondexter hit a big 3. Allen converted a critical and-1. Marc Gasol hit one of those exquisite flat-footed jumpers.

That put the Griz up by six with 27.1 seconds left. It should have been over. But then came the collapse and the flashbacks and Randolph's missed foul shots.

They weren't bad shots, actually.

"They were good!" said Randolph. "They were in and out. I was like, 'Please, basketball gods, please.'"

When that didn't work, Randolph turned to Allen.

"He called on me to get the stop," said Allen. "He said, 'It's on you.'"

Few sentiments could make Allen happier. He loves it when it's on him. He craves the challenge of guarding someone like Durant. Allen was still ticked that he let Durant score on him at the end of Game 3 to send that one into overtime.

"I was just thinking of the last game, how he went right," said Allen. "I jumped on his right hand and was able to recover when he went back left."

Conley summed it up neatly.

"Tony Allen saved us," he said.

Allen saved them from having to return to Memphis to play Game 6. He saved them from having to listen to the voices of doom.

"This is a different team," said Conley. "The heart of this team is amazing."

Conley couldn't stop smiling the whole time he talked. He was with the Grizzlies in the bad old days. He looked around the happy locker room.

There was the chunky younger brother, now the best center in the NBA. There was the power forward who was supposed to be a problem child, now nothing less than a civic treasure. There was the franchise that was an NBA laughingstock, now headed to a place few once dreamed it could go.

"I don't want to look back," said Conley. "I don't ever want to go back. This makes it all worthwhile, right here."

NO MORE PESSIMISM; THIS IS DEFINITELY A BLUE-LETTER DAY
MAY 25, 2013

Mayor A C Wharton, an Elvis impersonator and Grizz arrived by boat at the tip of Mud Island the other day.

"We're going to do something that's never been done before," said Wharton, who then hoisted Grizzlies flags up the Mud Island flagpoles.

It was a little ridiculous, honestly.

Why by boat? Why an Elvis impersonator?

"This is a great weekend in the great city of Memphis," said the mayor, which is certainly true.

Paul McCartney is playing FedExForum on Sunday. The Sunset Symphony will be held on the banks of the Mississippi on Saturday. Game 3 of the Western Conference finals tips off at FedExForum on Saturday night.

So if Memphis is acting a little nutty right now — and there's no question that Memphis is acting a little nutty right now — you have to cut the city some slack.

This is not life as usual in this place. This is not what we know.

Not so long ago, a big sports event in Memphis was some hot prospect showing up at Tim McCarver Stadium to play for the Double-A Chicks. Now Jim Rome is talking about the Grindhouse and there's a Budweiser Blimp circling over town.

There was a story about Memphis in *USA Today* on Friday (written by former Memphian Dan Wolken). There was a story about Memphis in *The New York Times* before that (written by former Memphian Scott Cacciola).

So, yes, the citizenry is swooning. It's a blue-letter day. And it's especially meaningful because a whole bunch of Memphians — I dare say the majority — never imagined a day like this would come.

Memphis was once a city of pessimists. Memphis was once a city that expected the worst.

Much of this is because of what happened on April 4, 1968. Walk over to the Lorraine Motel, stand before it, look on that wreath, and you can almost feel the sadness descend.

Memphis was a city of sadness, and of conflict and of flight.

Memphis was yellow fever and the sanitation workers' strike. Memphis was an unruly river and ungodly heat.

This spilled into everything, into politics, even into sports. Have you ever heard of a city trying to fight off the arrival of a major-league team? A whole bunch of Memphians fought against the Grizzlies because they said — this was the actual logic — that the team would inevitably fail and leave.

Now those same Memphians have painted their faces and their toenails and possibly even their houses blue.

They have turned growl towels into neckties and have worn them to church. They are naming their dogs Z-Bo and Big Spain.

Memphians are calling the Greenline the Grindline until future notice. They have stuck a headband on Le Bonheur's giant heart logo. Midtown Skate Shop can't keep enough "Grind City" T-shirts in stock. St. Jude Children's Research Hospital hung a giant growl towel that says, "St. Jude believes."

It is more authentic than any Elvis impersonator, and more organic, too. Not since the Showtime Lakers has an NBA team more accurately reflected a city's character. And the whole world knew Los Angeles was Showtime before that version of the Lakers. What did the world know about Memphis? Anything good?

Now the world knows Memphis grinds. It is what we do and who we are. When Lionel Hollins described Memphis as "the fat, grubby person" during his presser before Game 3, Memphians laughed and nodded and said, "Yep, that's us."

"Do we have a chip on our shoulders? Yes, we do," said Wharton. "I have a chip on my shoulder. Whenever I go into a room representing Memphis, I have a chip on my shoulder and I dare anyone to try and knock it off."

All that is what you'll hear and feel in the Grindhouse on Saturday night. It's not like anywhere else. The Memphis crowd is unruly, like that river. And now it is spilling over with real, hard-earned and heartfelt pride.

Memphis is no longer a city of pessimists. Memphis is a city of new-found faith.

"Why wouldn't I believe?" said Tony Allen. "It says it right on the towels."

GRIZZLIES-THUNDER KEEP ON DELIVERING THRILLS
MAY 1, 2014

Britton DeWeese was torn. On the one hand, the Grizzlies were playing Game 5, and the game was surging into overtime, and he could get updates just by looking at his phone. On the other hand, he was at Baptist Hospital for Women, and his wife, Kate, was in some distress.

"They were telling her to push," said Britton.

Yes, push. And you think you were in agony the other night?

Anyway, faced with this dilemma, this need to balance two of life's most pressing priorities, Britton did what any self-respecting Grizzlies fan would do.

"I looked at my phone," he said.

And?

"I kind of got in trouble."

Isn't four straight overtimes an acceptable excuse?

It should be. And I mean for all of us. For everyone caught up in this wild, exhausting and, yes, historic playoff series.

"Grizzlies," should be an acceptable reason for falling asleep during a work meeting.

"Tony Allen," should be deemed a correct answer for any question on the TCAP.

Mayor A C Wharton has already dubbed Thursday "Believe Memphis Day," so a happy Believe Memphis Day to you.

According to tradition, you celebrate Believe Memphis Day by waving a growl towel, telling your children the ancient story of the Zach Randolph trade ("and then they acquired him from the silly Los Angeles Clippers for Quentin Richardson") and bouncing the Oklahoma City Thunder from the playoffs for the second year in a row.

The Grizzlies are not taking that last part for granted, of course, and why would anyone? Yes, it's true that NBA teams that have taken a 3-2 series lead by winning Game 5 have gone on to win the series more than 80 percent of the time. Yes, it's true that the Grizzlies have held the Thunder to under 40-percent shooting for four straight games for the first time in franchise history. Yes, it's true there are already stories out there about who will replace Thunder coach Scott Brooks after his team gets eliminated. Yes, it's true that an Oklahoma City beat writer tweeted Wednesday that "the ship appears to be sinking" and "I have officially pushed the panic button."

But, c'mon. If you've watched this series, you know that none of that means anything. You know that it is impossible to predict what will happen in Game 6 or possibly beyond.

This is the series in which Oklahoma City has made three four-point plays, two in the final minute, and has lost all three of those games. This is the series in which the Grizzlies have blown a five-point lead with 18.1 seconds left (and won), a 17-point lead with 7:44 left (and won), a five-point lead with 1:20 left (and lost) and a 20-point lead with 15:43 left (and won).

This is the series in which Kendrick Perkins sent a game into overtime by hitting his only shot, and in which Mike Conley sent a game into overtime by losing his only turnover. This is the series in which Perkins sat on Mike Miller, and in which Beno Udrih emerged as a folk hero, and in which Joey Crawford froze Kevin Durant before a critical free throw, and in which Oklahoma City fans booed their own team.

This is the series in which Durant said he was happy to be a decoy, and in which Allen said the Grizzlies would have to keep milking that horse.

Wednesday, as it happens, Allen said the Grizzlies "just have to focus on each 48 minutes as they approach us," which would seem to be at least five minutes short.

Allen also said, "I tell you, man, it's definitely taking some miles off me," which is equally true for the fans.

It's been gut-wrenching and draining and riveting. It's been like nothing anyone has ever seen. So you can hardly blame Britton DeWeese for sneaking a peek at his phone Tuesday night, and never mind what else was happening in the room.

Britton is the guy who invented Grizzlies donuts at Gibson's, his family's donut shop. He wears a Grizzlies belt to work every day.

"The nurse said the doctor was watching the game in the lounge while we were waiting," said Britton, still trying to line up allies in his cause. "It was a really big game."

Sure enough, it came down to the final seconds. For both the delivery and the Griz. There was pain and joy and, finally, a new appreciation for life's sweetest miracles. The baby made it, too.

Naw. The infant was the best part, of course. His name is Dylan Edwin DeWeese.

"One of my brothers suggested Z-Bo," Britton said. "Another suggested Mike. My father said he beat the buzzer so he has been calling him Buzz."

And so there is your happy ending. There could be another one at FedExForum on Thursday night.

"We should be home in time to watch the Griz win," said Britton. Baby, wouldn't that be sweet?

CONLEY SHOWS TRUE GRIT
MAY 7, 2015

You know the hardest part of it for Mike Conley? It was Monday, after Game 1. The Grizzlies had been smashed by Golden State. It was clear they couldn't win without their starting point guard.

Conley heard from all kinds of people, dozens of people, telling him he had to play even though he'd just had surgery on his face. And he heard from other people, significant people, telling him to stay on the sidelines.

"My parents are telling me, 'Naw, you need to sit, you need to make sure you're healthy,'" said Conley. "I got all these people pulling me left and right and I don't know what to do."

So Conley did what he always does in this situation. He decided to do what was best for his teammates. He listened to his parents, and he listened to Grizzlies management, and he listened to the fans, and then he listened to his heart.

"I'm just like, 'I'm going to sacrifice and do what I can do for the team,'" Conley said.

Of such moments, Memphis legends are made.

That's not too much to say, is it? That Conley had a legendary Memphis night? That regardless of what happens in the rest of this series, Conley's performance in leading Memphis to a 97-90 win Tuesday night over the Golden State Warriors in Game 2 will be a story we tell ourselves again and again?

It's the story of a point guard with a heart as big as the Bass Pro Pyramid, with a will to win as unrelenting as the river that flows past the city he calls home.

It's the story of how Conley turned a night that was supposed to be about the wonder of one point guard into a night that was about the courage of another point guard instead.

That wasn't the goal, of course, because Conley is too classy to even think in those terms. He was just trying to compete.

That's it. That was the whole point. Let the Warriors celebrate Steph Curry, let them run a long tribute video before the tip, let them hand out posters and fill the arena with chants of MVP.

Conley just wanted to play. He wanted to do what he could. It was 10 days since he suffered multiple facial fractures, eight days since he had an operation that inserted a titanium plate into his face. He'd be lucky if he could get up and down the court.

Indeed, Conley and Grizzlies coach Dave Joerger didn't decide Conley would be healthy enough to play until just after the pregame warm-up, when they met on the court.

"I talked to coach and we both agreed I feel good enough to go," said Conley, before the game. "I expect to go out there and play to win."

Well, yeah. Of course that's what he would say. That he was going to play to win. But nobody else expected the Grizzlies to win this one. Shaquille O'Neal picked Golden State by 20. The Warriors were 42-2 at Oracle Arena this year. People in the Bay Area have already been discussing where to hold the championship parade, in San Francisco or Oakland. Nobody mentioned the possibility of Beale.

Then Conley went and flipped the whole night upside down. He dropped in his first 3-pointer, through that misting mask. Then he drove to the rim and scored on a layup. Then he hit a floater. It was like Willis Reed, except Reed only scored four points.

"He said he got good looks," said Gasol, deadpan. "Out of one eye."

Even Conley laughed at that.

But it was an astonishing thing to watch, especially in this place, especially on this night. The Most Valuable Player was outdone by the Masked Valuable Player.

"One-eyed Charlie," said Tony Allen. "The Masked Assassin."

Someone else suggested "The Phantom of the Grindhouse." It was that kind of multiple-nickname night.

But then came the moment of high peril, a moment that must have sent Conley's parents over the edge, not to mention every Grizzlies fan.

Conley drove and was knocked to the floor. He signaled to the ref to call timeout. After the whistle, Golden State's Draymond Green — there's no other way to say this — smashed him in the face.

Sure, Green was going for the ball. He wasn't necessarily targeting Conley's fractures. But the play was over. Conley had the ball on his chest. And, trying to rip it away, Green gave Conley a forearm to the mask.

Asked if he thought the play was clean, Conley said, "I wasn't able to see, I was on the ground and calling timeout."

Joerger said: "I'm not going to answer that."

This series didn't have a villain? It now has a villain. Nobody loves Draymond. Even Shea Flinn, the former city councilman, got into the act, with a highly official-sounding tweet.

"Whereas The Coward D. Green committed a scurrilous attack on M. Conley. Be it resolved that Hating GSW has been approved. Same-night minutes."

Do I have a second? Yes? All in favor?

I had a feeling that one would be unanimous.

Meanwhile, Conley got up and stayed in the game. Of course he did. He played 27 minutes and scored 22 points. His presence lifted the entire team.

How else do you explain holding Golden State to 39 points in the first half? That's only the second time that's been done all year. How else do you explain the defensive fury that limited Curry and Klay Thompson to a combined 13 of 34?

Allen, in particular, was maniacally brilliant. In Game 1, he walked through a junior dance team performance. Now he's walking through Thompson's terrifying dreams.

After every big moment, every critical steal, Allen hollered, "First-team all-defense! First-team all-defense!" We know this because television had Allen miked up.

"Oh, y'all heard that?" asked Allen. "I thought some of that stuff, they probably edited it out."

They left enough of the ferociously hilarious stuff in.

But then it was back to Conley, who by the end of the game was cramping on top of everything else. The Warriors cut a 16-point lead to seven with slightly more than three minutes to go. Seven points is nothing to Golden State.

So Conley struck a final blow. He lost Curry behind a Randolph screen, and hit a killer, pull-up, 25-foot jump shot to start Golden State fans heading toward the exits. It was the exact sort of play people have come to expect of Curry. But it was Conley dropping the shot on Curry instead.

"His face is caved in, and he comes out here and fights through it and plays lights out," said Allen. "That guy is a beast."

That guy changed clothes slowly after the game, like his whole body hurt, and who could doubt that it did?

There have been great games in the history of the Grizzlies, great individual performances but, given the context, given the stakes, have any been greater than this?

The man's foot still gives him trouble, among other things. That injury hasn't gone away. It's just, with multiple facial fractures and a titanium plate in your face, who can worry about a foot injury?

His parents didn't want him to play. His coach was iffy until Conley blurted out Monday that he expected to go. Then Conley went and lifted the Grizzlies to a win nobody expected with a performance that nobody can quite believe.

So, yes, it was the stuff of legend. It was the kind of game that can define a player and a team.

And as for Conley? How was he feeling after he could finally take off the mask for the night?

"I'm a little tired," he said. "I'm not going to lie."

A SEASON TO SAVOR
MAY 17, 2015

Like so much that is wonderful about the Memphis Grizzlies, the moment just happened, it was organic, totally unplanned. The Grizzlies had just beaten Portland in Game 2 of that playoff series. Happy fans spilled out on to the FedExForum plaza. The band started playing the "Cupid Shuffle," that cheesy tune you hear at a lot of wedding receptions these days. And all of a sudden, people started to dance.

At first, it was just a handful of people. Then a handful became dozens. Then dozens became hundreds. And suddenly it felt like half the population of Memphis was doing a line dance downtown.

Young people and old people were out there dancing. Black people and white people were out there dancing. Some of the dancers looked like they hadn't danced a day in their lives.

A video of the moment went viral. It could not have been more different from some other Memphis videos that have gone viral of late. But this video captured the best of Memphis. It captured much more typical Memphis. Just a bunch of people, good-hearted people, getting along and laughing at their missteps and celebrating their city and their lives.

So, lamentably, I'm going to have to disagree with all the Grizzlies players who said in the locker room Friday night that the 2014-15 season was a failure. If that was a failure, may we have another decade of joyous, rollicking failures like that.

I understand where the players are coming from, of course. The Grizzlies said before the season that their goal was to be playing in June. That didn't happen. They were eliminated by the Golden State Warriors in six games.

In the coming days and months, we will have plenty of time to discuss the ways in which this Grizzlies team came up short. Most of those conversations will revolve around shooting. The Grizzlies aren't very good at actually throwing the ball into the hoop.

It's astonishing, really, how they've remained so persistently bad at this seemingly essential skill. In the last six years, the Grizzlies have finished 29th, 30th, 30th, 27th, 30th and 30th in 3-pointers made.

In the Golden State series, the Grizzlies made 25 3-pointers in six games. Steph Curry made 26 himself.

So, yes, they need more shooting. For the umpteenth year in a row. But despite that flaw, the Grizzlies won 55 games and made it to the Western Conference semifinals. They are one of two Western Conference teams to have made the playoffs five straight years.

That's astonishing, when you think about it. It's just the Grizzlies and the Spurs. The Grizzlies were still playing when Kobe Bryant was sitting at home, and Kevin Durant was sitting at home, and Tim Duncan was sitting at home. They lasted longer than teams from Boston, Miami, Los Angeles, Dallas and New York.

Who knows what would have happened if not for the debilitating injuries at the end? The Grizzlies were able to go six games with the best team in the NBA even though Tony Allen had a bum hamstring and Mike Conley had a broken face.

But all that is just the competitive part. The tallying of W's and L's. The real success of these Grizzlies was captured in a phone call I got the other day on my radio show. It was from a man named Clay. He said he wanted to thank the Grizzlies because, over the last five years, they have "changed my quality of life." Clay wanted to thank the Grizzlies for all the moments of pleasure. He wanted to thank them for all the friends he has made.

It sounds preposterous, at some level. An NBA franchise changing the quality of a person's life? But that is exactly what a sports team can do at its very best.

Just look at the obituaries these days. Where people sum up the things that were most important to them. At least a couple times a week, an obit in this paper mentions the Grizzlies as something that sustained the deceased, or brought him or her joy.

Chris Herrington, of this paper, wrote a wonderful piece on the 82 best moments of the 2014-15 regular season. The last-second shot to beat Sacramento was one of them. The triple-overtime win over San Antonio was another. Now we can add a battered Conley appearing on the big screen during the Game 5 clincher over Portland, and Conley's selfless and triumphant return in Game 2 against Golden State, and Allen's "First-team all-defense" strip of Klay Thompson in that same game, and the raucous homecoming victory at FedExForum in Game 3.

But two more moments stand out to me, both of which happened off the court. There was the night that Jimmy Keep, the 89-year-old Iwo Jima vet, was honored by the Grizzlies. He hugged Zach Randolph, his favorite, because Z-Bo is "not afraid to bust your ass." Not long after that game, Keep returned to Iwo Jima, bearing a growl towel, the unofficial flag of the city he calls home.

And there was the story about Jade Rogers, a 24-year-old Grizzlies fan with cerebral palsy, who is wheelchair-bound and has endured more than eight surgeries. Rogers said she loves the Grizzlies because they "give me courage to go on, to persevere." When Rogers gets discouraged by the difficulty of her everyday life, she watches Grizzlies highlights on her laptop.

"I'll think how hard they work even if they're tired," she said. "I'll remind myself, 'If they can do it, I can do it, too.'"

So, no, this season was not anything resembling a failure. It was another year in an era that will be considered this franchise's Golden Age. It was the year the Bongo Lady made *The New York Times*. It was the year of Memphis vs. Errrbody. And it was the year a whole city danced to the "Cupid Shuffle," out of unselfconscious giddiness and joy.

None of this means the Grizzlies can solve the real and pressing problems of this city, mind you. An NBA team can't make crime or budget challenges go away. But the 2014-15 Grizzlies continued to move us in the right direction, one dance step at a time.

ACKNOWLEDGEMENTS

If it weren't for Mark McCarter and Joe Distelheim, I'd still be practicing law. They decided to take a chance on a Washington lawyer who wanted to be a sports writer, and gave me a job at *The Anniston Star* back in 1992.

The late Fred Turner then called me up to the big leagues, hiring me to cover the Florida Marlins for *The Ft. Lauderdale Sun-Sentinel*. I was utterly overmatched. He believed in me anyway. I wish I could tell him what that meant.

Gordon Edes showed me it was possible to be both a superb reporter and an elegant writer and became a true friend. John Stamm and Angus McEachran gave me my column gig. The late Ken Patterson, Geoff Grant, Gary Robinson and David Williams edited me with more patience than I deserved. And that doesn't include all the people on all the desks — too many of whom have had to find other work — who routinely saved me from myself.

I have been intending to put together a collection of columns for years. I want to thank Louis Graham and George Cogswell — the editor and the publisher of *The Commercial Appeal* — for allowing me to do that now. Neil White and his team at The Nautilus Publishing Company have been endlessly patient and helpful. John David Dowdle (art direction) and Chip Chockley (photography) are responsible for the handsome cover of the book. Dan Barron and Brad Carson have supported my radio career — and my ability to do things other than radio, as well.

I have the great fortune to have eight brothers and sisters and, at various times in my life, I have relied on each and every one of them. My ex-wife, Julia, is an excellent partner in child-raising. We also got vital help in that enterprise from Bettye Snipes and Lexie Johnston. Gary Parrish, John Martin and Scott Morris have buoyed me with their friendship and advice. My boys — Ben, Andrew and Peter — are the happiest part of my life.

Two people deserve special mention. Charles Fishman has been my best friend for nearly four decades. I would not have had the courage to leave the law without his encouragement. I will never be able to thank him enough. And Andria K. Brown has been with me throughout this project, sharing her wisdom, her words and her warmth. I am grateful to have her as my editor, and my companion, too.

Finally, I want to thank the people of Memphis for welcoming a Harvard lawyer into your midst. When I first moved to Memphis, I worried I'd have a hard time being accepted. I could not have been more wrong. I'm still not sure if my nearly 21 years in the city qualifies me as an official Memphian, but I am grateful to all y'all for making me feel at home.

ABOUT THE AUTHOR

Geoff Calkins is the lead sports columnist for *The Commercial Appeal* and the host of "The Geoff Calkins Show" on 92.9FM-ESPN. He has been named the best sports columnist in the country four times by the Associated Press Sports Editors and is a member of the Scripps-Howard Hall of Fame.

Calkins grew up as the eighth of nine children on a small farm outside Buffalo, New York. He graduated magna cum laude from Harvard College and Harvard Law School, and practiced law in Washington, D.C. for three years before deciding — at age 31 — that he'd have more fun, and have more of an impact, as a sports columnist. Calkins worked at *The Anniston* (AL) *Star* and *The Ft. Lauderdale Sun-Sentinel* before accepting the columnist job at *The Commercial Appeal* in 1996. He has three sons (Ben, Andrew and Peter), two amiable Bernese Mountain Dogs and an abiding faith that someday one of the teams of his youth — the Buffalo Bills or Buffalo Sabres — will win a championship.

INDEX

A

Adebayo, Sunday, 84
Adkins, W.A. "Bill", 82
Alamodome, 111, 115, 118, 305
Allen, Andre, 101, 110
Allen, Chad, 84-85, 102, 104
Allen Fieldhouse, 36
Allen, Tony, 305, 310, 316-317, 320-322, 325-327, 329-331, 333
American Athletic Conference, 201, 203-204, 209
American Basketball Association, 16
Anderson, Antonio, 100, 111-112, 114-115, 117
Anderson, Mike, 145
Anderson, Qadry, 177
Anglin, Travis, 181, 188
Anthony, Carmelo, 18
Archbishop of Canterbury, 71-72
Aresco, Mike, 204
Armstrong, B.J., 36
Armstong, Joan, 144
Armstong, Murray, 142-144, 146, 194
Armstrong, Sterritt, 143
Arthur, Darrell, 318
Askew, Vincent, 105-106
Atlanta, Georgia, 17, 165, 180, 243, 245, 291
Atlanta Braves, 17, 60
Atlanta Falcons, 163
Atlanta Hawks, 13, 18, 22
Auerbach, Red, 37
Augusta National Golf Club, 257
Augustin, D.J., 103
AutoZone Park, 48, 56-57, 163, 226, 228, 230

Avery, Maurice, 188
Azinger, Paul, 220

B

Bailey, Walter, 53
Baker, Bill, 250-251
Baker, Vin, 37
Ball, Richard, 235-236
Banks, Sean, 91, 110
Baptist Memorial Hospital, 289, 291, 325
Barbecue, 58, 280, 317
BarbecueFest, 30
Barclay, Arthur, 90
Barham, Drew, 129
Barnes, Rick, 103
Barone, Tony, 18-19
Barron, Doug, 98
Barron, Earl, 88
Barry, Dave, 235, 251
Bartlett, Tennessee, 112
Barton, Amelia, 69, 71-72
Barton, Derrick, 69-72
Barton, Margaret, 72
Barton, Will, 129
Bartow, Gene, 78, 94-95, 115, 158, 312
Baser, Kate, 262, 265
Baska, Amanda, 271
Bassett, Caude, 232
Batesville, Mississippi, 104
Battier, Shane, 5, 7, 8, 13, 22, 28-31, 304-306, 308, 313-315, 317
Baum, Ryan, 307, 309
The Beach Boys, 52
Beale Street, 119-120, 164, 304, 307, 315, 329
Becket, Ellerbe, 56
Bedford, William, 105, 107-108

Beijing, China, 273
Berry, Walter, 34
Bethea, Elvin, 165
Birmingham, Alabama, 46, 180
Blaylock, Mookie, 35
Blue Ribbon College Basketball Yearbook, 34
Blytheville, Arkansas, 268, 270
Boise State University, 202
Bonner, Matt, 305
Boozer, Carlos, 41
Boston, Massachusetts, 33, 36
Boston Celtics, 33, 36-37, 313, 321, 333
Boston Red Sox, 47, 154
Bowden, Bobby, 225
Bowen, Tom, 206, 209
Bowl Championship Series, 98, 202
Bowling Green State University, 209
Boyd, Dwight, 108
Brady, Tom, 203
Bramlett, John, 199, 209, 210
John 'Bull' Bramlett Lane, 209
Bramlett, Nancy, 209
Brigham Young University, 206-207, 209
Bronson, Stan, 134. 136
Brooks, Scott, 326
Brother Juniper's, 318
Brown, Brendan, 14, 17, 19-20
Brown, Charlie, 15, 27
Brown, Claire, 18
Brown, Hubie, 13-22, 30-31, 306
Brown, Kendrick, 37
Brown-Miller, Lisa, 254
Bruce, Randy, 138
Bryant, Bear, 159

Bryant, Kobe, 333
Buckhannon, West Virginia, 32, 34
Buck, Jack, 230-231
Buckles, Doug, 247
Buckner, Bill, 222
Budweiser Blimp, 323
Buford, Tommy, 70
Burk, Martha, 257-259
Burks, Antonio, 123
Burroughs, Derrick, 145
Bye, Karyn, 250-251
Byrne, Patrick, 188, 203

C

Cabin Creek, West Virginia, 9
Cacciola, Scott, 324
Calipari, Ellen, 87
Calipari, John, 3, 5, 85-87, 89-93, 96-102, 109-110, 112-122, 124, 128, 158, 193, 318-319
Calvary Episcopal Church, 71
Camden Yards, 56
Campbell, Chad, 64, 239-240
Canadian Football League, 6
Canadian Olympic Team, 251-253
Cannon, Alyce, 148-151
Cannon, Phil, 147-151
Cantler, Eddie, 136-137, 194
Caray, Harry, 49
Carney, Rodney, 91, 124
Carpenter Art Garden, 299-300
Carr, Chancy, 177
Carter, Donna, 259-260
Cates, Andy, 3, 306
Cates, Staley, 5, 7, 306
Chalmers, Mario, 120, 319-320
Chancey, Margaret, 71
Chaney, John, 88
Chatman, Shyrone, 87-88
Cheek, Joey, 275

The Cheering Elvi, 193-194
Cheylan, West Virginia, 9
Chicago, Illinois, 219, 251, 259-260, 266, 320
Chicago Bulls, 287
Chicago Cubs, 47
The Chicago Tribune, 18
China, 274-275
Chiu, Justine, 274-275
Christian Brothers High School, 238-239
Church Health Center, 319
Clapp, Stubby, 230
Clayton, Skyler, 63
Cleaborn Homes, 287-288
Cleland, Max, 156
Climer, David, 216
Clinton, Bill, 156
Cobb, Kevin, 176-177
Cohen, Steve, 84
Coleman, Will, 124
The Coliseum, 95, 104
College of William & Mary, 15
Collierville, Tennessee, 112, 181
Collins, Chris, 247
Collison, Darren, 114
Colonial Country Club, 239
The Commercial Appeal, 61, 72, 80, 122, 138, 272, 276, 333
Conference USA, 84, 90, 102, 112, 122, 127, 181
Conlee, Bubba, 169
  Bubba Conlee National Junior Golf Tournament, 170
Conlee, Chris, 168-171
Conlee, Janice, 169, 171
Conlee, Larry, 167-171
Conlee, Mark, 171
Conley, Mike, 304-305, 308-310, 313-314, 317, 321-323, 326-331, 333
Conrad, Kemp, 100, 151-153
Cooper, Kareem, 110
Cooper, Richard, 67
Cordova, Tennessee, 229, 255-256
Corky's, 262
Cornelsen, Brad, 203

Cosell, Howard, 159
Court Square, 38
Cousins, DeMarcus, 121
Covington, Tennessee, 168
Craig, Jim, 251-253
Craig, Joe, 202
Crawford, Joey, 327
Cross, Alan, 207, 209-211
Crossford, Tanya, 106
Crump Stadium, 190
Cuomo, Mario, 154-155
"Cupid Shuffle," 332, 334
Curry, Stephen, 328, 330-332
Cutchlow, Rohrk, 209
Cutcliffe, David, 244

D

Dalai Lama, 279-281
Dallas, Texas, 256
  Dallas Cowboys, 217
  Dallas Mavericks, 311, 333
Dalton, Andy, 202
Daly, John, 271-273
  "My Life In & Out of the Rough", 272-273
Daniel, Steve, 24
Daniels, Bill, 145
Dartmouth College, 251, 254
Davidson College, 70, 181
Davis, Al, 218
Davis, Bud, 199
Davis Cup, 69-70
Davis, Donte, 298-301
Day, Susan, 145
Dean, Taquan, 90
Delgado, Dimitri, 145
Denver, Colorado, 23
  Denver Nuggets, 23, 27, 35
DePaul University, 86
Derrick, Holly, 268-271
Derrick, Kenny, 268, 270
Derrick, Kimberly, 267-271
Derryberry, Kenny, 205
Derryberry, Tammy, 205
Detroit, Michigan, 101, 110, 115

K

Kaepernick, Colin, 203
Karam, Jacob, 202
Keep, Jimmy, 333
Kemp, Willie, 99
Kenon, Larry, 115
Kiley, John, 47-48
Killen, Amanda, 289-294
Killen, Jay, 288-294
King, B.B., 25, 118
King, Bernard, 16
King Jr., Martin Luther, 126
Kingsbury High School, 161
Kiper Jr., Mel, 196
Kirk, Dana, 82, 105-106, 108
Kirk, Milton, 232-234
Kiss, Richard, 58
Ku Klux Klan, 257-258
Knight, Billy, 29
Knox College, 68
Knoxville, Tennesse, 130,
    178, 218, 244
Koeneman, Bill, 83
Koeppel, Fredric, 272, 318
Koski, John, 216
Kraus, Bernard, 46

L

Lacy, Austin, 29
Ladyman, Libby, 198-201
Lake Placid, New York, 250,
    252, 254
Lamey, Bruce, 172-174
Lamey, Mary, 172, 174
Lamey, Nick, 173-174
Lang, Lynn, 232-234
Lapchick, Richard, 66-68
Lapides, Barbara, 160
Lapides, George, 157-160
LaRussa, Tony, 230
Lawler, Jerry, 307, 310, 315,
    319
Layton, Eddie, 46
Lea, Charlie, 46
Le Bonheur Children's Hos-
    pital, 65, 118, 324

Lee, Keith, 105, 108
Lee, Spike, 68
LeMoyne-Owen College, 68
Lenager, Mike, 39
Lester High School, 163-164
Lester Middle School, 301
Letterman, David, 74, 235
Lewis, Lennox, 236-238
Liberty Bowl, 145, 176, 198,
    204-205, 215, 218
Lilly, Hannah, 10-13
Littler Mendelson, 154
Little Rock, Arkansas, 223,
    318
Longoria, Eva, 307
Looney, Carson, 58
Looney Ricks Kiss, 56
Lorraine Motel, 126, 324
Los Angeles, California, 74,
    113, 217, 224, 251, 324
    Los Angeles Clippers,
    326
    Los Angeles Dodgers,
    15, 47
    Los Angeles Lakers, 28,
    30, 113, 324, 333
    The Los Angeles Times,
    111, 116, 222
Louisiana State University,
    243, 245-247
Love, Kevin, 111, 113-114,
    117
Lowe, Sidney, 9, 30
Lowenstein's, 61
Lowery, Myron, 279-280
Lucchesi, Joey, 79
Lynch, Paxton, 201-203, 205-
    208, 210-211
Lynn, Mike, 5

M

Mabone, Ules, 61
Macatee, Bill, 241
Mack, Doneal, 93
Madden, John, 17
Malmo, John, 216
Malone, Karl, 170
Malone, Keiwone, 205, 207

Manassas High School, 163
Mangum, Gary, 75
Manna House, 276-278
Manning, Archie, 159,
    241-247
    *"The Ballad of Archie
    Who,"* 241
Manning, Eli, 241-248
Manning, Olivia, 243
Manning, Peyton, 177, 218-
    219, 242, 244
Marrero, Eli, 231
Martin, Tee, 225
Massimino, Rollie, 106
Matheny, Mike, 231
Matthews, Joan, 63
Matthews, Steve, 183
Mautz, Alex, 292-293
Maynard the Goat, 191
Mayo Clinic, 139
Mayo, O.J., 308, 310, 313
McCain, Bobby, 206
McCarver, Tim, 17
    *Tim McCarver Stadi-
    um, 5, 323*
McCormack, Tim, 145
McCullough, David, 33
McDowell, Hank, 21, 126,
    178
McDyess, Antonio, 309-310
McFadgon, Scooter, 88
McGrady, Tracy, 31
McGwire, Mark, 46, 230-231
McKee, Joyce, 288
McLain, Denny, 47
McMahon, Eric, 40-43
McMahon, Mary, 42-43
McMillin, Zack, 74
Means, Albert, 232-233
The Med, 94, 260-262
Megar, James, 70
Melrose High School, 66-69,
    81, 126, 232
Memphis Blues, 46
Memphis Chicks, 5, 46, 159,
    161-162, 227, 323
The Memphis Flyer, 49
Memphis in May Triathlon,
    260, 266
Memphis Mad Dogs, 215
Memphis Madness, 93, 123,
    318
Memphis Maniax, 6

P

Packer, Billy, 117
Page, Jim, 292
Paine, David, 67
Painter, Rob, 229-230
Palacios, Juan, 91
Palmer, Arnold, 237
Palmer, Vicki, 287
Parker, Howard, 27-28
Parker, Tony, 37, 307, 310
Pastner, Josh, 124-125, 128-129, 131, 312, 319
Patterson, Brett, 140
Patterson, Eddie, 167, 170, 172
Patterson, Emma, 140, 142
Patterson, Joshua, 140, 142
Patterson, Samantha, 140, 142
Patterson, Scott, 137-140, 142
Patterson, Tracy, 137-142
Patton, Ricardo, 86
The Peabody Hotel, 4-5, 230
Peay, Austin, 205
Pebble Beach, California, 256
Pera, Robert, 316
Perkins, Kendrick, 326
Perl, Arnold, 306
Perry, Elliot, 80, 124, 320
Peterson, Charlotte, 145
Philadelphia, Mississippi, 151
Philadelphia, Pennsylvania, 74
The Philadelphia Daily News, 68
Philadelphia Eagles, 164
Phillips, Bob, 60, 62
Phoenix, Arizona, 43
Phoenix Suns, 41, 313
Pickler, David, 315
Pine Hill, 63
Pinehurst, North Carolina, 256
Pitino, Rick, 33, 36, 78, 90-92
Pittsburgh Steelers, 217
Ploehn, Decker, 63

Poier, Barb, 24
Poier, Don, 23-25, 304, 306
Pondexter, Quincy, 322
Poplar Avenue, 171, 317
Popovich, Gregg, 310
Porter, David, 312
Porter, Joe, 69, 71
Portland Trail Blazers, 34-35, 331, 333
Posey, James, 13, 22
Potter, Harry, 293
Powers, Chris, 17
Pranica, Pete, 23
Prescott, Allie, 160-163, 227, 228
Prescott, Barbara, 160, 162
Presley, Elvis, 125, 312, 316, 323-324
The Press-Scimitar, 68, 158
Price, Aaron, 107
Price, Nick, 220
Price, Peerless, 225
Price, Tic, 86
Proctor, Roderick, 208
Professional Golfers' Association, 64
   B.C. Open, 239
   Championship, 238
   Masters, 64, 237, 257-258
   Open, 255, 256
   Tour, 239
Pro Football Hall of Fame, 163-164
Providence College, 92
Pugliese, John, 41
The Pursuit Team, 5, 163, 312, 316
The Pyramid, 2, 6, 8, 57, 79, 84-85, 87-88, 113, 229, 237, 328

Q

Quail Ridge Golf Course, 167
Quitman County Elementary School, 104

R

Rabishaw, Dan, 262
Ramsey, David, 46-49
Randolph, Zach, 304, 306-311, 313, 316, 320-322, 326, 331, 333
   Z-Bo or Zeebo, 307, 315, 317-318, 324, 327, 334
Rapp, Jim, 145
Rawlins, V. Lane, 84, 135, 161, 176, 178
Reed, Billy, 292-293
Reed, Randy, 242, 244-245
Reed, Willis, 329
Reeve, Christopher, 138
Reilly, Rick, 310, 311
The Rendezvous, 65
Rendtorff, Linda, 53
Republic Coffee, 318
Rhodes College, 47, 70-71, 137-139, 153, 156, 158
   Rhodes Lynx, 154
Rice, Anthony, 90
Richards, Keith, 210
Richardson, Jason, 29
Richardson, Quentin, 326
Ricks, Frank, 55-59, 318
Ripken, Jr., Cal, 64
Ripley, Tennessee, 37
Robbins, Lenn, 219
Roberts, Chuck, 95
Roberts, Judy, 110
Roberts, Laura, 110
Roberts, Loren, 63-66
Robinson Jr., Archie, 166
Robinson, Cliff, 8
Robinson, Eddie, 164
Robinson, Jeff, 93
Robinson, Joyce, 205
Robinson, Paul, 205-206
Robinson, Ronnie, 67, 126
Robinson, Steve, 86
Robison, R.M., 198
Rockne, Knute, 185
Rodgers, Pepper, 214-215
Rogers, Jade, 334
Rogers, Langston, 241, 243
Rome, Jim, 323

West, Jerry, 9-12, 14, 18, 29, 31, 36-37, 306
West Memphis, Arkansas, 107
West, Patricia, 12
West, Tommy, 135, 184, 188, 190, 192, 194-195, 197, 199
West Virginia, 11
West Virginia Wesleyan College, 34
Wharton, AC, 323, 325-326
White House, 27
White, Reggie, 158
White Station High School, 148, 160
Whitmore, Darrell, 231
Whyte, Sandra, 251-252, 254
Wilco, 289, 294
Wiley, Dorothy, 68
Wiley, Ralph, 66-69
  "Why Black People Tend to Shout," 68
Wilfong, John, 82, 105, 107-108
Wilfong, Win, 108, 124
Williams, Burnetta, 286-288
Williams, DeAngelo, 138, 145, 191, 194-197, 201
Williams, Jason, 7, 19-20, 23
Willingham, John, 53
Wilson Air Center, 316
Wimbledon, 69-72
Wimprine, Barbara, 183-186, 189
Wimprine, Danny, 182-189, 193
Winbigler, Gretchen, 292
Winn, Bob, 179
Wise, Kelly, 88
Wolken, Dan, 324
Woloshin, Dave, 60
Womack, Ann Fisher, 295-297
Womack, Camille, 295-297
Womack, Joseph, 296
Womack, Nell, 295-298
Womack, Rob, 295-297
Woods, Andre, 177
Woods, Tiger, 64, 255, 257, 259
Woodson, Charles, 218-219

World Series, 47
World War II, 11, 15, 69-70
Wortham, Amber, 9
Wortham, Larry, 9
Wright, Carlos, 97
Wright, Lorenzen, 7, 9, 19, 78, 80, 306
Wrigley Field, 230

Y

YMCA, 226, 229
Yoda, 14
Youngblood, Jack, 165
Young, Sam, 318

Z

Zimmerman, Janet, 291-293

Made in the USA
San Bernardino, CA
08 December 2016